PRINCIPLES AND PRACTICE IN RECORDS MANAGEMENT AND ARCHIVES

Series Editor: Geoffrey Yeo

D0998962

Preserving Archives

Second Edition

Other titles in the Principles and Practice in Records Management and Archives series

[Series Editor: Geoffrey Yeo]

Archives: principles and practices, by Laura A. Millar
ISBN 978-185604-673-2

Community Archives: the shaping of memory, by Jeannette A. Bastian and Ben Alexander (eds)
ISBN 978-1-85604-639-8

Management Skills for Archivists and Records Managers, by Louise Ray (ed.)
ISBN 978-1-85604-584-1

Managing Records in Global Financial Markets: ensuring compliance and mitigating risk, by Lynn Coleman, Victoria L. Lemieux, Rod Stone and Geoffrey Yeo (eds)
ISBN 978-1-85604-663-3

PRINCIPLES AND PRACTICE IN RECORDS
MANAGEMENT AND ARCHIVES

Series Editor: Geoffrey Yeo

Preserving Archives

Second Edition

Helen Forde and Jonathan Rhys-Lewis

facet publishing

Published by Facet Publishing
7 Ridgmount Street, London WC1E 7AE
www.facetpublishing.co.uk

Facet Publishing is wholly owned by CILIP: the Chartered Institute of
Library and Information Professionals.

British Library Cataloguing in Publication Data
A catalogue record for this book is available from the British Library.

ISBN 978-1-85604-823-1

First published 2007
This second edition 2013

Text printed on FSC accredited material.

Typeset in 10.5/13 pt Bergamo and Microsquare by Flagholme Publishing
Services. Printed and made in Great Britain by MPG Books Group, UK.

Contents

Introduction to the series

Records and archives are important resources for individuals, organizations and the wider community. Records are created in the course of the functions and activities of organizations and the personal lives of individuals, and are preserved and maintained to support business and accountability and for cultural use. They provide evidence of, and information about, the actions of their creators and the environment in which those actions occurred. They extend and corroborate human and corporate memory and play a critical role in maintaining awareness of how the present is shaped by the past. Records are kept by almost everyone, but their management (and especially their medium-term and long-term management) is a professional discipline with its own distinctive body of knowledge. Within the discipline, 'records' and 'archives' are sometimes used as synonyms, but in English-speaking countries 'archives' usually denotes records which have been recognized as having long-term value. The term 'archives' can also be used more widely, to refer to collections of historical materials maintained by organizations, individuals, families or community groups, or to the locations where such materials are held.

The series Principles and Practice in Records Management and Archives aims both to disseminate and to add to the body of professional knowledge and understanding. Each text in the series is intended to offer a detailed overview of one or more key topics. The archives and records management discipline is experiencing rapid changes – not least as a result of the digital revolution – and the series will fully reflect the new technological context as well as the societal changes and governmental initiatives in many countries that are placing new emphases on compliance, accountability, access to information and community relations. Some volumes in the series will address theoretical and strategic issues relating to the creation, management and interpretation of records and archives or their role in society; others will give practical guidance for those seeking successful and effective ways of managing them and presenting them to users. The authors come from many countries worldwide and are recognized experts in the field.

Preserving Archives

This volume provides a practical introduction to the preservation of archives. Effective methods of preservation are essential if archives are to be accessible to future generations of users, and *Preserving Archives* offers an overview of operational and strategic solutions applicable both to traditional paper and parchment archives and to digital formats. Written for non-specialists as well as professional archivists, it is a source of expert advice on archive buildings, equipment, storage conditions, security control and disaster planning; on the moving, handling and exhibiting of documents, and the use of surrogates; on establishing a conservation workshop; and on many other aspects of archive preservation.

The first edition of *Preserving Archives*, published in 2007, was the first comprehensive text on archive preservation to be published in the UK. It was written by Helen Forde, who is a former Head of Preservation Services at the Public Record Office (now The National Archives) in London. For this revised and updated edition, she has collaborated with Jonathan Rhys-Lewis, who is an experienced preservation and collections management consultant. Both authors are regular speakers on preservation topics at training events and conferences in Europe and internationally. The book builds primarily on the authors' experience in the UK, but the issues which it addresses are of concern to archivists worldwide and it will also be of value to those facing similar challenges in other countries.

Geoffrey Yeo, Series Editor

Preface to the Second Edition

Preserving Archives is a guide for all those with a responsibility for archival or special collections on the issues to be dealt with in developing successful preservation policies and strategies. While the chapters build up to implementation, they can also be read individually if required. Some archives will need advice on specific problems, others will require assistance with developing more general programmes. The reader can pick and choose as necessary; the notes and references, example boxes in the text and bibliography present further guidance for those who require more specific details.

The text is based on lectures given to successive cohorts of postgraduate archive students in the UK, from those who have recently taken their first degree to those who are acquiring a professional qualification at a later stage in their careers. *Preserving Archives* is intended to act as an aide-mémoire for them and their successors as students, as well as others who may need assistance in a particular situation. The book can be used as an overall guide or as a reference source for a particular area of practice. And it is not only for archivists: librarians and museum curators are also often faced with difficult decisions to make on preservation and much of what is included applies to paper-based materials held in other organizations. National and international examples are given and referred to, making comparisons possible and introducing the reader to a wider picture than just the UK. While there will clearly be national differences, many of the baseline and guiding principles will be evident in all forms of collection management and it is for the individual users to refer to their own national standards where appropriate.

The importance of understanding more traditional archival materials is underlined by its prime place at the beginning of the book, followed by the equally important topic of preserving digital material. The crucial role played by archival buildings, the security within them and the importance of good storage conditions for the archival materials are central to the text, followed by an emphasis on developing strategies to mitigate disasters. Clear guidance is given on how to manage and develop policies for the use of surrogates in both analogue and digital formats. Moving archives is a hazardous business, as is holding exhibitions or lending material to other organizations. There is further information on how to prevent damage by pests without resorting to toxic chemicals. Training is central to many of the topics described and the importance of training staff and users in good handling practice is covered; additionally, the use of volunteers for preservation programmes is covered in detail with examples of good practice. The final chapter suggests ways to identify priorities, planning issues and strategies to ensure that the actions taken are consistent with available resources and overall plans for the archive and also build up sustainable preservation strategies.

By following the text, noting the case studies, using the suggested aids to developing high standards and exploiting the wealth of references and suggested publications, an archive can be confident that the material it holds will be in good condition both for those who want to use it now and in the future.

Helen Forde and Jonathan Rhys-Lewis

Acknowledgements

This book could not have been written without the help over many years of colleagues in the Public Record Office, now The National Archives, friends and colleagues in archives and libraries all over the world and successive archive students at the Department of Information Studies at University College London. We are particularly grateful to all those who answered our queries and shared their knowledge so generously, to those who checked parts of the text and to all those who gave permission for the reproduction of texts or pictures.

The second edition has been no less supported by the generous input of professional colleagues, and associations, present and past, both in the UK and abroad; with particular thanks due to the Preservation Advisory Centre, University College London Special Collections and Preservation staff and freelance consultants Helen Lindsay and Caroline Bendix.

1

Introducing archive preservation

Introduction

Preservation of archives is the means by which the survival of selected material is ensured for enduring access. Perceptions that archivists preserved materials just for the sake of it are out of date and incorrect, if indeed they were ever correct; preservation and access are two parts of the same mission. Without sustained preservation activity it would not be possible to satisfy the myriad of users worldwide who beat a path to the door of archives and record offices, or who search for information on the web. Using archives has become a popular pastime for young and old, whether they are researching family history, requesting information under Freedom of Information Acts or pursuing historical facts. This increasing trend is unlikely to reverse and more than ever organizations must ensure that the material will be available, not only to the current generation but also to those of the future. Organizations must, as a matter of policy, look beyond their immediate requirements and utilize strategies and techniques to ensure that the originals, or if that is impossible the information contained in them, will be available for as long as needed. This book is designed to give readers the tools to manage preservation issues; it is not a manual on how to cope with every eventuality as these differ widely and advice for one archive might be quite inappropriate for another. Alongside this is the key intention; to act as a lead and guide for the varying needs, questions and research of fellow professionals charged with the responsibility of preservation.

How has the relationship between conservation and preservation developed?

Once, looking after documents was within the remit of all curatorial members of staff, many of whom no doubt undertook basic repairs to the best of their rather limited ability. In the 1950s and 1960s archive conservation began to develop as a distinct skill – one which, given their increasing responsibilities in other directions, curators were happy to cede to conservators. At that time *conservation*[1] was a wide-reaching term embracing many aspects of what is now included under the umbrella of *preservation*. Since then, those employed as archive conservators have become specialists in the intervention techniques required to stabilize badly damaged material. Their work has become grounded in science, they have adopted techniques to achieve economies of scale in some applications and they have become fully qualified professionals with rigorous programmes of accreditation[2] and continuous professional development. Their status has changed from that of pure craftsmen, although a strong element of dexterity remains in their training. They often remain the best qualified staff to carry out training in document handling or measuring and monitoring environmental conditions, but others can be trained to take these tasks on; actual conservation work remains their specialist preserve.

Definitions

In subsequent years the management of preservation became a concern as resources and targets got tighter; lack of understanding between archivists and conservators also caused difficulties in some places, not least because it was rare for conservators to be involved with management issues. Nevertheless, the relationship between and responsibilities of the two activities gradually clarified. *Preservation*, led by one or more specialists who may or may not be conservators, became a holistic activity in concerns such as environmental conditions or pest management. *Conservation* became defined very clearly as an intervention activity to stabilize the condition of a document, requiring the skills of a trained conservator while remaining part of the spectrum of preservation activity; it was, and is, definitely at the more expensive and individual end.

Slowly, the perception that preservation is the responsibility of all those who work in or use an archive has became more widespread and at much the same time moves have been made to identify common ground in preservation activities between archives, libraries and museums. Care of the materials entrusted to cultural heritage organizations is one of the easiest and best possible partnerships. This led to a search for more common vocabulary – hence the use of terms such as *stewardship* and *collections care*, each with a slightly different emphasis but essentially covering the requirement to ensure enduring access.

Preservation is used in the following text as the overall term; it has the advantage of being widely understood, although *collections care* may be a more current term for the holistic activity.

Any text which refers to *archives* has a difficulty with the fact that in English the term is used to describe both documents and the organization which looks after them and makes them accessible. In the following chapters the term *record office* is used to describe the building or organization if the meaning is ambiguous; otherwise the context should make the distinction clear.

Summary

This chapter has introduced the reader to what constitutes archive preservation, or whatever term is used to indicate the need for care and protection of archival material to ensure continuous access. It has emphasized the importance of archival material for establishing the right to information and the consequent role of preservation activities within access programmes. Understanding the terminology used, and the way in which it has developed, is important in leading to understanding about how to care for archival materials and archive buildings. The following chapter continues the explanatory theme, indicating the importance of background understanding about archival materials before undertaking any kind of remedial activity.

Notes

1   Immediately after World War 2 some junior staff were employed at the then Public Record Office (now The National Archives) in a triple capacity. Their duties included carrying the coal for the fire in the reading rooms, acting as messengers and 'mending documents' – which they had to do upside down in case they were tempted to read them.

2   These accreditation programmes are now managed by the Institute of Conservation (ICON). The Professional Accreditation of Conservator-Restorers (PACR) scheme implements standards for the care of the cultural heritage across a range of disciplines. Conservator-restorers accredited by PACR have demonstrated to assessors that they have the appropriate knowledge, practical skills and sound professional judgement.

2

Understanding archival materials and their characteristics

Introduction

Archival materials are complex in their manufacture and use, and some understanding of their history and different characteristics is important for successful preservation. The chemistry involved is largely the preserve of conservators undertaking pure and applied research, but some basic knowledge, particularly of modern materials, is necessary. Paper and parchment constitute the vast majority of carriers – excluding magnetic materials and electronic media – in most archives in the UK and many other countries. Other materials, such as palm leaves or bark, are found elsewhere in the world, but are rare in Europe and are not covered here. Understanding the problems of different materials is one thing; finding the solutions is quite another and these will depend upon the circumstances in each archive. There are, however, two exceptions; these relate to nitrate-based and cellulose acetate-based film, both of which may deteriorate quickly, or in the worst case, self-combust or explode, if action is not taken upon discovery of degradation.

This chapter looks at the structure and manufacture of the materials most commonly found in UK and many other archives throughout the world, including:

- paper
- parchment
- inks
- photographic materials
- audiovisual materials
- optical materials
- tapes
- discs
- digital storage media.

Paper

Paper is the material most widely used for archives and therefore merits particular attention. The materials from which it is made have varied over time, resulting in more or less stability; this reflects the common perception of paper as a disposable product, but in practice it is a remarkably resilient writing medium.

The development of paper

The Chinese invention of paper in AD105, as an alternative writing medium to silk or cloth, has traditionally been associated with T'sai Lun, of Hunan province, although some recent discoveries suggest that it was being used at least a century earlier. Wadding has also been discovered in a tomb in Shanxi province but the structure provides no evidence of fibre beating, an essential operation which forms the hydrogen bondings which distinguish sheet paper from wadding.

In the Western world paper began to rival papyrus in the late eighth century AD, although Chinese paper makers are known to have been in Turkey as early as 648 and had passed on the art to the Arabs by the middle of the eighth century. They, in turn, introduced paper to Spain (paper mills are thought to have existed in Xativa by 1056), and subsequently to Italy. By the early 13th century paper was being imported into France from Syria for important documents, and around 1326 an indigenous French paper industry had been established (Peraudeau and Maget, 1973, 5). Paper at this time was probably of poor quality, used largely for ephemeral purposes such as wrapping; the more durable parchment was still being widely made and used. It was not until better-quality paper was required in larger quantities for printing, after the introduction of the Gutenberg mechanical press in 1446, that the industry began to grow substantially.

Paper can be found in England from the 14th century, imported through the Netherlands or from France. There are references to its use in the 13th century, for example in a 1384 Common Plea roll,[1] but it was a further century before John Tate established a mill in Hertfordshire, where the first paper was produced in 1495. The complexity of the manufacturing operation, the training required and the organization necessary to collect the raw materials and sell the final product all suggest that planning must have taken place for several years before. As elsewhere, the impetus to the establishment of the mill is likely to have been rapid developments in printing.

When paper was introduced on a larger scale in the 16th century it was initially used for the documents associated with the new Tudor system of local administration. Thereafter the increasing complexities of government, as well

John Tate's first order

One of the first orders Tate received for paper was for an edition of *De Proprietatibus Rerum* by Bartholomaeus Anglicus in which the following poem, found in the colophon, refers to the paper maker:

And John Tate the yonger, Joye mote he broke
Whiche late hathe in England doo make this paper thynne
That now in our Englysth this boke is prynted inne.

[Hills, 1988, 6]

as an enormous growth in commerce and communications, stimulated the industry, resulting in the spread of paper mills wherever the terrain was suitable. Increasing literacy and the expansion of the printing industry meant that paper was commonly used, and not only for communications; it began to be graded by quality, the poorer types being used for wrapping paper, and the best for fine editions of books or for documents of special note, and subsequently for banknotes.

Consumption of paper

Coleman (1958, 11) reckoned that the annual consumption of white paper per head rose from ¼ lb at the beginning of the 16th century to 2½ lbs at the end of the 18th century, and to nearly 130 lbs by the middle of the 20th century (1950s). This last figure includes all the paper used in many different spheres and reflects the substantial developments in education, communication and commerce in the 19th century.

In spite of the major problems threatening paper demand in the industrialized world and the slowdown of the demand growth rate in the group of emerging economies, the world paper and paperboard deliveries may still exceed 400 million tons for the first time in 2012 (www.pulpapernews.com/2012/01/outlook-2012-global-paper-consumption-to-fluctuate).

What is paper made of?

Paper consists of wood and plant fibres in which are found cellulose, hemicellulose and lignin. Despite some differences in the methods used in making oriental and occidental paper, both types rely on a supply of raw or recycled (i.e. rag) plant fibre for cellulose, and on a supply of clean water.

In the East the fibres most commonly used were mulberry, Kozo, Mitsumata and Gampi (China and Japan) or jute (India). These long, strong and flexible plant fibres create a strongly bonded paper which is especially prized. In the West, recycled cellulose materials were predominantly used, although the addition of rags to raw cellulose (China) or recycled paper (Rajasthan) was not unknown.

The reason was simply that the West lacked the appropriate quantities of plant material to support a rapidly growing paper industry and, as a consequence, relied on linen made from flax (*Linum usitatissimum*) or hemp (*Cannabis sativa*). Both plant materials were in use very early in the textile industry, and later formed the raw materials for paper makers.

How was paper made?

In the East the fibrous stems were stripped of bark and then soaked to produce a cellulose pulp. In the West rags and used clothing formed the basis for the pulp, but they had to be processed first. The textiles were sorted by fibre type, colour, weight, degree of soiling and type of weave and then washed thoroughly before being cut into strips and mixed with potash (K_2CO_3; *potassium carbonate*) or lime (CaO; *calcium oxide*). This mixture was then left to ferment, or ret, for several days before being battered with wooden stamping hammers in troughs of flowing water. All the non-cellulose residue was washed away and the resulting pulp was then mixed with water in a ratio of 2:100 and formed into sheets on flat moulds made from close-meshed wire;[2] the process was very similar in the East, although the moulds were made from bamboo strips.

In Europe the traditional method of forming the paper sheet was carried out by two men. The vatman formed the sheet by dipping the mould into the vat full of pulp before the coucher tipped the resulting sheet of fibres, which adhered to the mesh, on to drying felts. Several layers were heaped up before the pile was pressed to get rid of excess water. The felts were then removed and the sheets hung out to dry for some months in a drying house or shed. The Oriental practice was to paste the sheets up to dry on a wall, which was sometimes heated. In both cases the resulting sheets of paper were very absorbent and required sizing with a gelatine coating before use. The strength of the size, made from boiled parchment, hooves or bone in an aqueous solution, was determined by the use to which the paper was to be put; paper intended for manuscript purposes required less absorbency than that used for printing. The final finish, or glazing, was traditionally done by hand with burnishing stones although the pressing and glazing hammer introduced in the West in the 16th century gradually superseded the hand techniques.

Further industrialization followed the increased European demand for paper, stimulated by growing literacy and more widespread book production. The Hollander beater with rotating horizontal knives replaced the stamping hammers in the 18th century and speeded up the preparation of rags by cutting out the need to rot the material. By the 19th century experiments were under way in using alternative substances such as jute (*Corchorus capsularis*) and cotton waste, associated with the growing cotton trade. This was the direct result of a serious decline in the availability of rags. Alternative grasses, such as esparto (*Stipa tenacissima*), alfa, rye, wheat and barley stems were tried, though esparto was the only material to show much success. Manila hemp (*Mussa textilis*) produced a stronger paper.

From the 1850s wood pulp has been used as the basis for paper, although the effect of resin and lignin (both of which can cause deterioration in paper, especially when exposed to light) continued to give cause for concern, leading to many experiments with other components. Today the paper industry uses sulphate of soda to break down wood chips to produce the raw pulp for high-quality paper, while untreated wood pulp, often known as mechanical, or ground, wood, continues to form the basis of cheap papers such as wrappers or newspapers.

Some common issues with bound papers

Paper archives were frequently bound together as a means of keeping them together and secure; as an early method of preservation it has often worked well. However, there are associated problems. If the sewing gives way, as is often the case with large and heavy volumes, loss of, or damage to, the papers may occur; alternatively the leather may deteriorate, producing a fine red dust known as red rot. This degradation is the result of vegetable-tanned leather being exposed to high temperatures and humidity levels, and atmospheric pollutants. This results in serious deterioration of the leather and causes structural weaknesses to the bound items.

Scrap books, commonly found amongst personal archives, can suffer from all these problems and in addition the variety of materials pasted in – let alone the paste itself – can result in degradation from different chemical reactions, between, for example, different textiles or photographs. A conservator should be consulted for appropriate advice.

What are the problems with modern papers?

Many of the difficulties encountered in the preservation of more modern papers result from the additives used in the manufacturing process. Alum (*potassium aluminium sulphate*, $KAl(SO4)2$) hardens the size and reduces the drying time but leads to a more acidic paper. Acid attacks the plant fibres and this action is accelerated by exposure to sunlight and oxygen or pollution from the environment. From the early 19th century alum-rosin (pine resin without the turpentine) was added to the pulp, reducing the need for repeat dipping and drying operations. More recent and cheaper forms of alum (bauxite treated with sulphuric acid) have resulted in very acidic papers. By contrast, chlorine, widely used as a bleaching agent from the mid–18th century, led to highly alkaline papers due to inadequate rinsing. In both cases, damage to the fibres results in weakened paper.

The role of lignin as a natural constituent in paper has also generated controversy; some claim that it is detrimental to paper permanence. To date, experiments in various parts of the world have not clarified the situation. Other types of paper pulp also include additives; specialist papers used for high-quality photographic reproductions in books often contain china clay, barium sulphate or titanium dioxide. Coated papers have also been developed for specific purposes, usually copying ; these include varieties well known in the 20th century such as carbon paper, onion skin paper or Thermofax. Carbon paper is coated on one side with carbon and was interposed between the top copy and another blank sheet in a typewriter on to which carbon print was transferred by the action of the keys; onion skin paper is a thin light translucent paper used with carbon paper for transferring text and Thermofax is a heat-coated paper used in copying machines from the 1950s; it is less permanent, as the text fades in time and can only be preserved by re-copying with a more reliable method and onto a more stable paper base. While few might want to preserve used carbon paper, it has its place in forensic studies and consequently might need consideration, not least because this type of paper is unlikely to be durable.

Which papers are genuinely permanent?

In the latter part of the 20th century efforts were made to check the use of acidic paper for documents or printed materials with lasting value. Some countries have introduced legislation to ensure appropriate survival; others have relied on national and international standards. Most experts agree that the alkaline/acid content of paper together with the presence of an alkaline buffer, to counteract any future contact with acidity, determines whether or not a paper can be classed as permanent. The issues are complicated by the lobbying of paper manufacturers, who see the issue of permanence as applying only to a very small section of the market.

From the 1980s onwards a substantial campaign in the UK and the USA to improve the quality of paper used for certain types of printed material, and for the production of good-quality paper generally, has resulted in the adoption of new processes. These cause less degradation for certain materials and enable, where appropriate, the use of the permanent paper symbol (Figure 2.1), the international standard ISO 9706; 1994 (E). This standard was developed to specify and identify 'paper which will undergo little or no change in the properties that affect its use when stored in a controlled environment for long periods' (National

Figure 2.1 Permanent paper symbol

Preservation Office and Library Association, 1995, 2). The crucial point is that it must be manufactured from virgin pulp, not from recycled materials. It is based on the American National Standard for Information Sciences – *Permanence of Paper for Printed Library Materials* (ANSI Z39.48:1984). Additionally, see BS ISO 11108:1996; *Information and documentation. Archival paper. Requirements for permanence and durability*. Advocacy for the use of recycled paper has blurred the issue of paper permanence, confusing the public about what the former can, and cannot, be used for. More publicity is needed to clarify the different and appropriate uses of varying grades of paper.

Parchment

Parchment was the writing medium most frequently used in medieval Europe until the development of printing stimulated demand for a cheaper, more easily handled alternative. Once paper was being produced in bulk it quickly eclipsed parchment owing to its versatility.

The development of parchment for archival use

Parchment was developed as an alternative to papyrus, although its use was complementary rather than competitive. Accounts as early as the IVth Dynasty in Egypt (c. 2700–2500 BC) refer to the use of 'leather' as the preferred medium for sacred documents. The format was frequently a roll of skins stitched together, end to end, a style which persisted for some centuries in England, despite the inconvenience in use. Parchment was employed as a writing medium all through the classical period and gradually superseded the Roman use of wax tablets for note-taking or ephemeral matter. By the second century AD it was used increasingly for important documents, illuminated manuscripts and books. The main factors contributing to its predominance over other media included the durability of the material, its availability and the ease with which it could be made up into book form. It was stable if stored in dry conditions, making it suitable for archival purposes, and the codex (book) format, which may have developed from the Roman habit of joining wax tablets together, proved ultimately to be the most convenient method of accessing information.

The use of parchment in the British Isles owed much to the spread of Christianity and the need for texts, both ordinary and illuminated. Not surprisingly, more of the latter have survived, including such prime examples as the late seventh-century Lindisfarne Gospels[3] and the slightly later Book of Kells.[4] However, the developing complexities of administration before the Conquest in 1066 had already stimulated the widespread use of parchment for Anglo-Saxon charters and one of the most notable early Norman documents, the Domesday Survey,[5] was recorded on parchment. From the 11th to the end of the 15th century parchment was the accepted medium for most written communications and important documents, stimulating a considerable industry. Even after printed book production brought about a switch to the widespread use of paper, parchment continued to be used for legal purposes; many archives contain examples of 18th- and 19th-century settlements and deeds written on parchment. The decline in the use of parchment for printed material was at least partly due to the sheer quantity of animals required; it has been calculated that each copy of the 42-line Gutenberg Bible required at least 170 calf skins in its manufacture (Reed, 1972, 167), an impossible resource to maintain.

What is it made of?

The word 'parchment' describes a product, rather than a particular type of skin. It refers to a sheet of writing material produced by subjecting an animal skin to a series of processes including defleshing and de-hairing before drying under tension. The word 'vellum', frequently used as an alternative, historically referred to such a sheet made from calfskin, sometimes foetal, and therefore scarce and costly. The word is now used to imply a high-quality product rather than the origin of the skin.

The same process can be applied to a wide variety of mammalian skins, but in practice was usually restricted to sheep and occasionally calves, goats or even deer. The geographical area from which the animal originated, and its species, diet and age, dictated the quality of the finished product (Haines, 1994, 15). Manufacturing processes were refined over the centuries, culminating in great technical expertise in the Middle Ages. These skills have largely died out and only a few manufacturers now produce parchment for very specific purposes.

How is it made?

The skin of the animal, in its unprocessed form, consists of several layers which have to be stripped down before it is possible to create parchment. The epidermis, the outer layer of skin, retains the hair follicles, and is not required for the parchment product. The dermis, the layer beneath, is the area from which parchment, and other leathers, is mainly derived. It consists largely of collagen fibres, bundled together to form a three-dimensional network, easily identifiable under a microscope. The species, age, health and eating habits of the animal affect these fibres, which alter in character accordingly. Thus the hides of older animals are tougher and less fine than those of younger ones. Fat cells, found largely in sheep, are also present but must be removed to ensure a good writing surface for parchment.

Processing the skins and producing usable parchment at the end involves a complex series of manual, rather than mechanical, operations and depends on slow changes to the material. This is not surprising, given that the use of parchment had dwindled by the time of the Industrial Revolution, giving little cause to develop new mechanical processes. This has also been a factor in the relative costs of paper and parchment, contributing to the comparative rarity of contemporary parchment manufacturers.

Initially the skin was flayed to remove hair and wool before being air-dried or salted, to ensure that it was workable when the procedure began. This was essential, since it was not possible to process all skins as soon as they became available; neither was it possible otherwise to prevent putrefaction and damage to the dermis. Once a number of skins had been collected, they were rehydrated by soaking for up to 48 hours, and were then ready for unhairing. This process achieved the removal of fat and the cleansing and loosening of the fibrous network. Historically the skins were soaked in straight lime liquor in wooden or stone tubs, although a lime and sodium treatment is more common today in order to speed up the process. The former, less aggressive liquor, used over a longer period of time, had benefits for the ultimate quality of the parchment. Careful monitoring was important to ensure that the depilatory action of the lime was not detrimental.

Next the skin was scraped on both sides over a curved wooden board known as a beam, though more recently this has been achieved with the use of a de-fleshing machine. The medieval texts[6] that describe the next stage – stretching and drying – are all clear that the process must be carried out with great care, as it is crucial for the quality of the finished product. A rectangular or sometimes circular frame was prepared in advance and the skin was stretched across it and held in place either by wooden clips or by pebbles round which were twisted cords which could be adjusted gradually to increase the tension. It was extremely important that the skin was tensioned as fully as possible to achieve the characteristics of a good writing material with a uniform colour; less tension was required for the tougher translucent parchment used as window coverings or on drums. Further scraping with a lunar-shaped knife was then followed by drying the skin at a slow, even rate, which resulted in a much better parchment than one dried rapidly in the sun; the former increased the flexibility and even opacity of the finished product. The final stages included rubbing the skin with pumice stone and finally dusting very lightly with fine powdered chalk. Too much chalk caused subsequent inks to lie on the surface without penetrating the fibres of the skin.

Inks: from carbon ink to laser printing

Care in the manufacture of a writing surface is negated if the ink used is not durable. Until the 19th century most European ink was made domestically, following basic recipes which were widely available. In consequence the many variations resulted in widely differing standards of density, solubility, colour, resistance to fading and adhesion to the paper or parchment.

What are inks made of and how?

Carbon inks were simple to make, consisting of lamp black (the burnt residue from oil, resin or tar) suspended in a vegetable gum (obtained from the acacia tree) or animal size (water in which parchment or bones had been boiled) in an aqueous solution. They were blue–black in appearance and were quite widely used, but suffered from the defect that they were soluble in water, and smudged on the paper in high humidity.

Iron gall ink, also known as gallotannic ink, was much more stable and was in common use by the end of the 15th century. Demand for a better quality ink, which did not clog the pen and was ineradicable, was growing with increasing literacy. The combination of tannin and vitriol (iron sulphate), suspended in gum arabic and water to create a coloured liquid, had been used since antiquity, although domestic production and the varied quantities and ingredients used resulted in widely differing colours and strengths. Reed (1972, 155) quotes a 15th-century recipe based on an eighth-century text; it suggests powdered gall nuts boiled in water to which is added gum arabic and vinegar before further reduction and a final addition of copperas (*ferrous sulphate*) and lamp black. Such inks were very stable and lasted almost indefinitely, particularly when they fused with the collagen fibres in the surface of the parchment. Although it can be a light brown, the colour was usually dark, making the distinction between a carbon and iron gall ink difficult.

Accurate identification is important, as the corrosive action of the latter is a very distinct threat to the paper or parchment on which it was used. Concern at the deterioration of some music manuscripts and art work has led to research projects[7] to investigate the reactions between the inks and the carrier materials and the destructive qualities of the iron or other transition metal ions, frequently copper, in the ink. The aim of the research is to investigate the corrosion in order to understand the causes fully and to develop processes to stabilize the ink and prevent further damage.

Modern writing inks are the result of the need for more fluid inks that do not clog the nib of the pen. The development of the steel nib for a dip pen in England in the early 19th century was followed by the invention of the fountain pen with its reservoir for ink. Gallotannic inks proved corrosive and the sediment blocked the channel in the pen, but the development of inks using vegetable dyes led to much greater fluidity. The major disadvantage of this type was the solubility of such ink, but the requirements of writing instruments increasingly drove research into developing new varieties. Chemicals were introduced in the mid-20th century to enhance the drying capabilities of the liquid, and solvents were developed to clean the channels in the pen as it was used; still later, complex aniline dyes were introduced. At the same time research into making pens with more rounded writing ends (ballpoints) was finally having some success once the issue of controlling the ink had been solved by using capillary action, rather than gravity. The point of the pen itself is a tiny metal ball, which rotates in a cavity filled with ink. Fibre-tip pens work on the same principle. Recent developments in the manufacture of ink include instant drying, and a reduction in the fading, smudging and leaking which characterized many of the early products.

Inks used in typewriters, copying machines and computers

Typewriting ribbon consists of fabric impregnated with either ink or carbon, the former being reusable multiple times. The image is formed by the impact of the typewriter keys which transfer the ink or carbon to the paper. The dot matrix printer, common in some early computer applications, uses impact technology in the same way. The print is usually stable but is subject to fading, particularly if the ribbon is used multiple times.

Electrostatic toners are used in copying machines including fax machines and laser printers, and documents created using these materials are frequently found in archives. Static electricity is used in both copying machines and bubble-jet printers to create an image on a sensitized surface, before it is transferred to paper. This is achieved in laser printers by the use of a beam to draw the image onto the sensitized surface. The toner is then drawn to this sensitized area of the paper. Dry toners are composed mainly of heat-sensitive polymers, carbon or colouring pigments, and a carrier to generate the electrostatic charge. Liquid toners consist of suspended pigment or dyed acrylic resin particles in an insulating liquid which is sprayed on the electrostatic image. The result is more permanent than that created by dry toners since the image penetrates the paper fibres, whereas the dry toner merely forms the image on the surface. Colour toners are composed of organic dyes, often subject to fading and colour change.

All toners are vulnerable to:

- heat
- oxidation
- pollution

- separation of components
- environmental condition change.

Using appropriate papers and maintaining the machine may well have a major impact on the quality of the final copy, since this influences the success of the fusion of the toner with the paper.

Ink-jet or bubble-jet printing is a non-impact technology which uses tiny droplets of ink blown on to a surface to create an image. The ink, which is comprised of water, glycol and dye, is vaporized by tiny heat resistors and forms a bubble, part of which is then converted into droplets which adhere to the paper. Various processes are used, depending on the required outcome, but the technology is mostly used in office printers. The chemical stability of this printing is uncertain and appears to be subject to light fading. It is also soluble in water and the quality of the paper and external factors, such as heat, humidity and pollution, influence its permanence. The technology is increasingly used for printing digital photographs.

Photographic materials

Photographic negatives and prints are commonly found in archives, museums and libraries, frequently attached – by one means or another – to paper records, stored in unsuitable enclosures at the back of files, rolled in drawers, stored in packets, hung in pockets designed for slides or stuck on to paper or thin board in photograph albums. There is a wide variety of types of photographic materials (and the processes that created them) and identification of these is a specialized skill; suggestions for further reading and research can be found in the Bibliography.

The first descriptions of photographic processes by Talbot and Daguerre in 1839 were the culmination of many years of experiments with the light sensitivity of various chemicals. Daguerre conceived of the print as an extension of an artistic process, but Talbot realized the value of being able to print multiple copies and his direction was the one followed by subsequent photographers.

What materials are used?

Early photographic printing processes, which resulted in images known as photogenic drawings, cyanotype prints, salted paper or platinum prints, suspended the silver or iron salts within the fibres of the paper used as the base for the print. Within a few years however, glass plates (used for negatives or positives) were developed as a base, coated with a sensitized emulsion; this two-layer process preceded the 20th-century three-layer process for both negatives and prints which is comprised of a base, a binder and the final image material. The names of the binders used in the process, including albumen (egg white), collodion and gelatin, are used to distinguish the different processes developed in the 19th century. Other descriptions include references to the base, such as glass plate negatives. As the process of taking photographs became quicker and cameras became smaller, glass plates, which were both heavy and fragile, were no longer convenient.

Cellulose nitrate was used as a base for negatives until the middle of the 20th century, when it was replaced by cellulose acetate. This in turn has been superseded by inert polyester as a base material (see the section below on film materials for more details). The base for photographic prints is usually resin-coated paper. The major component in forming the image is silver suspended in the binder, although iron, platinum and tin have also been used – hence the descriptions such as ferrotype. In colour photography silver is not present in the final image but is used to start the process of the formation of dyes. Deterioration of the image, whether on the negative or the print, is usually due to reaction with light (particularly with daguerreotypes) or pollution, or as a result of failure to wash out the chemicals used when fixing the image.

Digital photographs are rapidly becoming the most common method of taking pictures, obviating the need to process film. Prints from digital pictures can be made on ordinary paper or coated paper according to preference and the permanence of the print will depend on the quality of the materials used and the adequate fusion of the printing ink with the paper.

Analogue audiovisual materials: wax cylinders, shellac and vinyl discs and film

Materials used for all types of audiovisual recording, and frequently found in libraries and archives, differ radically from the materials used for writing, being multi-layered and complex in their construction. They are also machine-dependent, making the decisions about permanent preservation more difficult; is the information or the medium on which it is carried the more important?

> The balance between the significance of the artefact and the significance of its information content effectively determines whether the preservation activity is to focus on the former or the latter. If the content is deemed to be the principal point of interest then it may be appropriate – and perhaps even necessary – to transfer it into some other format or medium to ensure its continued survival and accessibility.
>
> (Feather, 2004, 5)

These issues for analogue audiovisual materials have been faced by archivists for many years; those concerned with digital materials are beginning to face very similar problems.

What forms do analogue audiovisual archives take and what are they made of?

One of the earliest recording mechanisms used in the world was the wax cylinder; the information was recorded in vertically modulated grooves along the cylinder's surface. Pure wax cylinders are known as self-recorded; they are unique cylinders about 4½ in. high. Replicated cylinders are wax/celluloid tubes over a plaster core and, as the name suggests, the recordings are copies. They were used for music and ethnographic recordings from 1896–7 until the late 1920s, although by then they had been superseded by discs. As with many early analogue recordings it is very unwise to handle or play these without professional assistance; damage caused can result in partial or complete loss of the recording.

Shellac discs (78 rpms), often referred to as 78s, were widely used in the 20th century for recorded music and speech. They were played initially on wind-up, though more latterly on electric, gramophones. The discs, or records, are made of mineral substances, frequently shellac, held together by organic binders and coloured with lamp black; the signal is recorded in laterally modulated grooves. Chemically these are fairly stable unless they are stored in high relative humidity. However, they are very fragile, and require storing, handling and playing with great care.

Instantaneous discs were used in the broadcasting industry, being replayable immediately after recording, unlike the shellac discs which required processing. They consist of a cellulose nitrate coating on aluminium plate, and as such are highly vulnerable. Expert advice should always be sought in order to transfer the information urgently to another medium.

Microgroove discs (33 or 45 rpm), often referred to as 33s, 45s, singles or vinyls, replaced shellac discs in the second half of the 20th century, being much less fragile and having a longer playing time. The 45s were developed specifically for the music industry, since the playing time is convenient for single tracks of popular music. They are made from polyvinyl chloride–polyvinyl acetate (PVC–PVA) copolymers, which are usually quite stable. The grooves are cut laterally, or at 45° for stereo discs. The greatest weakness of these discs is vulnerability to mechanical damage due to improper handling or poor quality replay equipment.

Moving film is frequently found in archives, even in those not specifically devoted to film. Like photographic material, it was often additional recorded information stored with paper records. The late 19th century saw considerable development of photographic processes, leading to the first photographic negatives being printed on a flexible film support, at Eastman Kodak in 1889.

The base was normally cellulose nitrate, which was still in use until the early 1950s despite the unstable nature of the material. (Manufacture stopped rather earlier, but batches of film were stored and used gradually.) Not only is it highly flammable but it also releases toxic gases (nitric oxide, nitrous oxide and nitrous dioxide) as it deteriorates. If water is present the gases will combine to form nitric acid, which can degrade the film further, as well as the containers in which the material is stored. This autocatalytic process can completely destroy the film. Moving the film or keeping it close to a source of heat can result in self-combustion. Fires which are the result of nitrate combustion flare up very fast and are notoriously difficult to extinguish, as they do not require oxygen.

Early example of filming

Queen Victoria recorded an early instance of filming in her journals:

3 October 1896
At twelve went down to below the terrace, near the ballroom, and we were all photographed by Downey by the new cinematograph process, which makes moving pictures by winding off a reel of film. We were walking up and down.

Some weeks later she saw what may have been the result:

23 November 1896
After ten went to the Red Drawing Room where so called 'animated pictures' were shown off, including the group taken in September at Balmoral. It is a very wonderful process, representing people, their movements and actions as if they were alive.

(Hibbert, 1984, 334)

How is nitrate-based film identified?

Nitrate may be used in the main body of the film, or sometimes just on the headers and footers; it may also form the base of still photographic negatives. Some nitrate film made for professional use can be identified by the name of the manufacturer and the type of film by a stamp along the edge. Amateur roll films were not marked but their tendency to roll very tightly should raise suspicion. Kodak sheet film has a V notch on the edge.[8]

The characteristic smell resulting from the formation of the acid is one way of identifying deteriorating film; at this stage it may still be possible for experts to copy the photographic image but, as the film deteriorates further, the image begins to fade. Other signs include:

- discolouration of the film to amber, brown or yellow
- film appearing sticky
- blistering or bubbling of the surface of the film
- brown powder covering the film as a result of chemical reaction in storage in metal film cans.

What should be done?

The local fire brigade must be alerted immediately if cellulose nitrate film is suspected in the collection. Do not try to move or otherwise dispose of it, as there is a danger of spontaneous combustion. The British Film Institute,[9] among other specialist organizations, can be contacted for advice. Further suggestions about storage of film can be found in Chapter 6.

Identifying cellulose acetate-based film

Cellulose acetate film, alternatively known as safety film, superseded cellulose nitrate as a more stable base in the early 1950s. It was used for a wide variety of films and tapes, including microfilm. However, it is not as stable as originally thought and its deterioration, like that of cellulose nitrate film, is autocatalytic. The plastic support of the film becomes acidic and shrinks, affecting the image. Organizations and countries that have investigated the scope of the problem have reported substantial quantities of such film stored in archives, libraries and museums, much of it in less than optimal conditions.[10]

The standard method of identifying degrading cellulose acetate film is by the smell; the deterioration of the film causes chemical reactions within the plastic support to form acetic acid, or vinegar. The additional danger is that the presence of acetic acid puts otherwise stable materials at risk.

Signs include:

- a smell of vinegar
- negatives curling
- base shrinking and becoming brittle
- formation of bubbles and crystals in the film
- formation of channelling in the film.

What should be done?

Isolate any material from other film and contact a specialist film archive for advice. Further suggestions about storage of film can be found in Chapter 6.

Identifying polyester-based film

Polyester-based film, which dates from the mid-1970s, is inert and few problems have been encountered. The coatings adhering to it may vary but essentially they provide a means of fixing the image to the film, as well as protecting it and making it function more easily. The base is generally regarded as stable and not subject to deterioration, although one study in the USA has found evidence of deterioration of the gelatine emulsion layer on the polyester base (Szczepanowska and Wilson, 2000). Characteristics include:

* ink smudges
* image transfer to adjacent materials
* discolouration
* blistering
* separation of the emulsion
* 'soapy' odours
* some illegible images.

Any film dating from the mid-1970s is highly likely to be polyester-based, and therefore, provided it is stored correctly (see Chapter 6), should remain reasonably stable.

The use of video formats has been widespread and all collections will have examples of the many and varied systems that were developed in a rapidly changing commercial market. The conservation and preservation of these formats is complex and requires very specialized knowledge; however, there are numerous resources on the internet to provide guidance and local film archives or specialist repositories will be able to provide advice.[11]

Optical materials: CDs and DVDs

Optical media differ from other machine-readable materials as they are read by laser from the protected lower surface of the disc. They are therefore less susceptible to surface damage, but are very vulnerable to manufacturing defects; one flaw in the multi-layered format can wipe out all the stored information. Manufacturers vary in their estimates of how long optical materials will last but the discs should have a reliable lifespan of at least ten years. In practice, the operating systems are likely to become obsolete more quickly than the discs.

What are they made of?

CD-ROMs (compact discs, read only), often referred to just as CDs, consist of a polycarbonate body pressed from a master mould which holds the digital information as a series of tiny pits; this in turn is covered by a reflective layer of metal, generally aluminium, and the whole is protected by a layer of clear varnish, the most vulnerable part. The information is read by laser.

CD-Rs (recordable CDs) record the information on a layer of organic dye which can be very unstable due to light exposure. However, those which use a gold reflective layer and phthalocyanine-based dyes are considered stable and are used for preservation purposes. The industry regularly claims to have made a breakthrough over the expected lifespan of optical materials, but this type is generally regarded as the best to date.

CD-RWs (rewriteable CDs) are manufactured differently, using phase-change and magneto-optical technology, and are not used for preservation purposes.

DVDs (digital versatile discs) are constructed in the same way as CDs and come in a number of formats – DVD-ROM read-only, DVD-R and DVD+R recordable, and DVD-RAM, DVD-RW and DVD+RW which are rewriteable. As with CDs, the most stable is the DVD-R if manufactured to a high standard, but they are all more vulnerable than CDs due to the increased amount of information held on them. DVD-RW and DVD+RW discs use phase-change and magneto-optical technology and are not suitable for preservation purposes.

Magnetic materials: tape, hard disks and floppy disks

Magnetic materials are widely used for recording sound and pictures, as well as computer software. As with other machine-readable materials they require dedicated hardware for access and are widely used for domestic and office purposes. In consequence, they are familiar objects to many who nevertheless are unaware of their vulnerability. The same reservations about their likely survival rate apply as to optical materials above, namely that the data on such materials should be migrated on to more reliable formats as soon as possible.

What are they made of?

Magnetic tape is used for analogue and all digital video formats, and consists of a polyester support film coated with a matrix, a magnetic layer of fairly stable iron-oxide particles – or a chromium substitute (video consumer formats), which is less stable. The matrix also contains a resin or plastic binder and sometimes includes lubricants and fungicides. Metal particle tape is very vulnerable due to:

- the potential corrosion of metal particles
- the use of modern pigment-binding materials (polyesterpolyurethane),

where hydrolysis (enhanced by atmospheric humidity) weakens the binder and leads to a smear-off of pigment particles or mould growth
- external stray magnetic fields, generated by other magnetic items or machines with electric motors
- the tape carrier becoming brittle and easily broken
- fluctuations in temperature and humidity and/or high levels of both
- print-through originating from direct layer-to-layer contact in the wound-up tape.

Magnetic disks or diskettes, used in computers, are frequently known as 'floppies', since the plastic disks are flexible, though housed within a rigid protective casing. The magnetic matrix is on one side, or sometimes both sides, of the disk and the information is read through a slot in the casing by the read and write head of the computer. They are less vulnerable to damage than tape, being less exposed.

Minidiscs

Minidiscs are a digital replacement for analogue audio cassettes. Software digitally compresses analogue-recorded sound data, making it an access medium, not a preservation medium.

Portable digital storage

As the quantity of information produced by both individuals and organizations continues to grow rapidly, and file sizes increase hugely, the options for storing data have continued to develop. The storage capacity of portable hard drives has increased dramatically to meet this need – at this time up to 3TB of storage with USB flash drives or 'sticks' up to 1TB. Both devices are susceptible to faults, electro-magnetic pulse, fire and physical damage.

The developing use of 'Cloud' storage is discussed in the next chapter.

Summary

This chapter has reviewed the properties and characteristics of archival materials found in most European and many other countries. Knowing the vulnerability of such materials and understanding the best strategies for mitigating risk forms the basis of the following chapters, starting with the issues encountered in the preservation of digital materials.

Notes and references

1   The National Archives, TNA:PRO 40/498.

2   The construction of the moulds was similar in both East and West, with 'laid' lines forming the closer-set mesh supported by 'chain' lines, which were at right angles and much further apart.

3   British Library Cotton MS Nero D.IV.

4   Trinity College Dublin Library MS 58.

5   The National Archives, TNA:PRO E 31/1, 2.

6   See, for example, Lucca MSS, Codex 490 (Bib.Cap.Lucca) ff. 21–25; Theophilus Presbyter, *Schedula Diversarium Artium* (BL MSS Harley 3915, f.128r).

7   From 2011 a website devoted to the study of Iron Gall Ink Corrosion has been hosted by the Cultural Heritage Agency of the Netherlands: www.ink-corrosion.org/prognosis/.

8   There are many useful references to Kodak date symbols accessible via the internet.

9   British Film Institute, 21 Stephen Street, London W1T 1LN, www.bfi.org.uk.

10 See, for example, the Australian National Strategy for Cellulose Acetate Collections. In 2008, the British Library proposed to de-accession its Cellulose Acetate microfilms: www.bl.uk/aboutus/stratpolprog/ccare/introduction/preservation/policy&position/Position%20Paper-%20de-accession%20cellulose.pdf. See also the Image Permanence Institute's Guide for Acetate film: https://www.imagepermanenceinstitute.org/webfm_send/299.

11 http://videopreservation.conservation-us.org.

3

Managing digital preservation

Introduction

To the archivist the need to preserve selected digital information of long-term value is fairly self-evident, but to many of those involved in the creation of data the importance of strategies for preservation is not so obvious. Assumptions are made about the longevity of digital information which are quite unfounded, even when the evidence of the potential fragility of the medium is there for all to see. Archivists and records managers have to develop new approaches and engage earlier to ensure that serious loss of information does not take place in the context of rapidly rising use of the technology. Digital preservation is a much more stable technique than it was even ten years ago, but the discussions and debates surrounding it need to be translated into active strategies, adopted by all organizations with a concern for the future of their documentation.

This chapter looks at:

- why digital preservation is important
- why it is perceived as difficult
- what decisions are needed to ensure that the appropriate digital material is preserved over time
- who should be involved
- how to start and maintain the process.

This chapter does not deal with the technical aspects of digital preservation; advice on this is best sought from the national archives of the relevant country, such as The National Archives (TNA)[1] or organizations such as Digital Preservation Coalition (DPC) in the UK,[2] and in the USA, the National Digital Stewardship Alliance or the impressive guidance and developmental work carried out by the Library of Congress.[3] The DPC is a consortium of library, archive and research organizations, brought together to pool ideas, promote best practice and publish research on digital preservation issues.

Why is digital preservation management important?

Digital preservation (the act of ensuring enduring access to electronic material) is rarely undertaken by the same person who deals with the more traditional forms of archive preservation. Increasingly, however, it is essential for all archivists to understand some of the management principles and strategies adopted to achieve it and the contribution that different professions can make to this. The most important point is that building preservation into any digital project at the outset is much easier, more efficient and vastly cheaper than attempting to preserve, or re-create the material at a later stage. It is technically possible to do the latter but at very considerable cost and trouble. Better not to have to try.

Deterioration of early space exploration records

The 1975 Viking Lander tapes, which recorded data collected on the first visit to Mars, have deteriorated to such an extent that they are no longer readable despite attempts at storing them in appropriate conditions. Scientists in the United States have had to reconstruct the information from paper documents.

It differs from traditional preservation management for several reasons:

- Preservation of the medium/carrier of the information is not sufficient.
- Digital information is in a technical format which may not survive more than a few years, creating an urgency for decision and action at the point of creation.
- The data can deteriorate or vanish without warning, especially if no management techniques are in place.
- The data can only be read through the medium of technology which also becomes obsolete.
- Issues of authenticity and authorship are more complex than for traditional materials, as the text can be changed and widely copied.
- The surrounding metadata[4] is needed for the data to be fully functional, adding an extra dimension to preservation management.
- Digital materials can be used in different ways, particularly for research purposes, but only if proper preservation techniques have been employed.

Most organizations, and many individuals, now create much of their documentation digitally, in many cases in even greater quantity than before;

versions of documents passed electronically from person to person, for correction and addition before the final format is agreed, result in substantial series of files. This is no better illustrated than by the proliferation of social media, primarily Facebook and Twitter; the archival challenges are huge – recognizing the records, establishing their quality and confirming the custody issues – but the digital preservation issues are no different. These need management to prevent the individual being swamped with unnecessary versions or any uncertainty about the final agreed text. If the versions are to be retained – and traditionally many historians have been grateful for rough drafts of final documents which indicate thought processes and development – they need to be catalogued and indexed in an electronic document and records management scheme (EDRMS),[5] which streamlines access and ensures an audited process of decision-making. The importance of this cannot be overestimated. In the medical world, for example, the value of keeping, managing, auditing and verifying data on new drugs could hardly be more important. Similarly, ensuring the survival of electronic information on the location of toxic landfill sites is essential for responsible stewardship of the landscape of the future. What is frequently underestimated is that the preservation of such digital materials is a continuous management process which must be maintained and developed as the technology advances, or as organizations change and responsibilities alter.

Legal requirements to retain certain information now cover material held digitally as well as in traditional formats. Increasingly, retention is required by statute. Failure to preserve such information for appropriate periods – e.g. as required in the UK by the Data Protection Act 1998 or the Freedom of Information Act 2000 – could have very serious consequences, raising the status of good digital record management and preservation. The European Union's Markets in Financial Instruments Directive (MiFID) has clear requirements for the preservation of digital materials in order to prove transparency and probity in financial organizations. Similarly, in the USA, issues of corporate responsibility have led to legislation,[6] resulting in a more methodical and structured approach to record-keeping. Few want to follow the fate of the investment bank Morgan Stanley (in 2005), which suffered high penalties in the US courts due to its inability to access information. That case highlighted the need to manage and retain all types of electronic documents, including e-mails.

Why is digital preservation difficult?

The digital world has not yet been accepted universally. The concepts are different and difficult for many, especially those not privy to the long-standing debates and discussions of record managers, IT specialists, archivists and librarians. Archives are in a transitional state; it is often necessary to run two systems in tandem, a position which is changing for some but for others will last for some time. Even when the digital revolution is complete archives will still need to preserve paper documents in their strongrooms, since digitization of complete holdings is highly unlikely, let alone almost impossible if predictions about the costs involved are correct. And if archives are finding this transition difficult, with the dual responsibilities involved and the additional costs and changes in practice, the creators of digital materials are finding the rapid variations required in attitudes and practices even more difficult.

Traditional archive materials are tangible, accessible with the naked eye and have often been around in different formats for centuries. Digital materials, on the other hand, are:

- only accessible through machines
- stored on tapes or discs which are short-lived if inappropriately managed
- prone to sudden oblivion due to faulty materials or keyboard operator error
- frequently overtaken by new versions of both hardware and software often managed only poorly, if at all.

In addition, a whole new vocabulary has been created around electronic materials which must be learnt and understood – and in some cases adopted – by archivists more accustomed to their own terminology. Digital preservation requires a mix of IT and archival skills and collaboration between the different professions.

A further difference involves the time-scale. Paper deteriorates, but only slowly, and, unless by deliberate destruction or as result of a major disaster, is unlikely to disappear completely. By contrast, the maximum lifespan of any electronic media is assumed to be no more than ten years (Brown, 2008). It can be lost permanently, and instantaneously. The contrast between the two could hardly be starker and goes some way towards explaining why digital preservation is perceived to be difficult.

Changes are taking place, too, in the types of records selected for permanent preservation. Those traditionally regarded as appropriate for permanent preservation tend to be predictable; they document an administration, providing evidence of development, such as decisions to expand a business, or a record of events – such as births, deaths and marriages. With electronic records additional categories are being considered for permanent preservation, including research data and information captured through new technologies like geographical information systems (GIS), creating a responsibility to document such information adequately in order that it can be understood and interpreted by later generations. This has not always happened and it is not unknown for such data to be inexplicable until a better-organized paper copy is found and used for the interpretation of symbols or the explanation of columns of figures. Historians and archivists have serious concerns that many of the electronic sources for the history of the last 30 years will be lost through failure to manage the preservation issues.

Mind the Gap

Mind the Gap (Waller and Sharpe, 2006), a study commissioned by the Digital Preservation Coalition, concluded that many organizations, from a wide range surveyed, did not know the full content of their electronic holdings, did not know how long they needed to preserve information for and did not have the necessary preservation strategies in place. Of the respondents to the questionnaire, 70% were aware that they had lost information already, 87% admitted that this might include key information about their organizations and only 18% had worked out a preservation strategy, despite a management commitment to digital preservation in over half those surveyed. And this is even when 64% of the respondents admitted to having digital data to support intellectual property rights, and 22% having it to support patent applications. These organizations clearly regard electronic documentation as a valuable investment, but fail to progress to the logical next step of proper preservation management. The conclusions in the report point to a need for:

- more proactive lobbying for implementation
- assistance in developing robust strategies which give confidence that the right information is being captured and retained
- funding of projects on digital materials with long-term value to include an element for sustainability.

The authors recommend that organizations work together and with commercial developers of software and hardware to ensure that open file formats are used which favour appropriate preservation periods of retention. This could hardly be a more ringing endorsement of the need for preservation management of digital assets to become a priority.

Costs of digital preservation

The cost of managing digital preservation is potentially high and frequently under-calculated for the long term. The difficulty is partly due to inexperience and lack of working examples; this is a new venture and the usual guidelines are wanting.

The UK Digital Preservation Needs Assessment (UKNA) surveys which contributed data to *Mind the Gap* (Waller and Sharpe, 2006) revealed a widespread concern that digital preservation was an additional cost to organizations still saddled for the foreseeable future with the costs of traditional preservation; few had assigned a special budget to meet their long-term needs for the management and preservation of digital materials. This is hardly surprising, not least because preservation costs are hard to isolate from other costs relating to the creation of and access to digital materials. An earlier cost model developed by Cimtech suggests a schematic method for assessing the relative costs in seven key areas based on the lifecycle of digital materials (Hendley, 1998). Prediction of costs relies much on the anticipated period of access, a prediction that few organizations find easy to make. Experienced staff are currently few and far between and are consequently often expensive, particularly for local authorities or those without commercial backing.

A recent study (Kejser, Nielsen and Thirifays, 2011) carried out by the Royal Library and the National Archives in Denmark assessed the Cost Model for Digital Preservation (specifically the costs of Digital Migration) and concluded that 'One of the main problems of cost models is that they are inaccurate per se. It is, therefore, important to define the degree of accuracy and precision of CMDP.' Clearly there is still much work to be done.

Another approach by The National Archives in the UK (Gollins, 2009) 'Parsimonious Preservation', has drawn attention to the fact that 'many institutional IT systems (and their support teams) provide as a part of normal business the capability to address many of the challenges of capture, custody and integrity facing the new digital curator' and that the 'more imminent threat is poor capture and storage of the original material in a safe and secure way' – an interesting twist to encourage archive professionals to review the positive impacts that already exist rather than panic about the complexities of the digital record.

These factors, together with lack of practical experience in the field, lead to nervousness about potentially open-ended commitments to which it is very difficult to attach a realistic budget; many organizations are wary of venturing into such unknown territory. This is further underlined by the difficulty of assessing the cost/benefit of digital preservation in a meaningful way. Equally, doing nothing about digital preservation is a difficult option, and one which will become increasingly hard to maintain. One of the key recommendations made by the authors of *Mind the Gap* is: 'Funding bodies should support research into the long-term value of digital information and models of how that value may change with time' (Waller and Sharpe, 2006, 7).

What should be preserved?

In many ways the process of creating, selecting and preserving 'born digital' material (that which is created in digital format without any analogue equivalent) has re-emphasized the importance of the records management principle of the lifecycle of documents.

To ensure appropriate survival, consideration must be given to the relative importance of the content and to appropriate preservation tactics even before the material is created. In other words, content creators are being forced to do what has long been the desired goal of those charged with ensuring the preservation of traditional materials: they have to match appropriate materials and methods to the perceived importance of the documentation created. In terms of traditionally produced material this can mean using recycled paper for economy where long-term survival is unnecessary, or ink, rather than ballpoint pen, for important items. For digital material a similar decision is needed about the length of time a document is deemed likely to be required, but dictated by the likely life expectancy of the technology rather than the medium; the definitions of these timespans can be defined roughly as:

- short term: access for a predicted length of time but with no intent to preserve the material beyond that or beyond the point at which the technology has changed
- medium term: access beyond the lifetime of the technology with which it was created but not for permanent access
- long term: indefinite access to the information even if not in its original format.

The decision made about the longevity required for the information will influence the nature of the metadata (information describing the electronic documentation accurately) needed to enable continued access.

These time-span considerations also apply to any decision to preserve analogue archival materials which have been digitized (converted into digital format) – commonly, archival data such as parish registers, census enumerator returns or service records, all of which are heavily used. Such digitization projects are popular with the public, offering remote access and manoeuvrability of data, and they enable archives to provide access for a much wider audience. They also offer major benefits in terms of the ability to link databases and to discover hitherto unknown connections between disparate pieces of information. Investment in such projects has been widely promoted, but not all those involved have understood the importance of ensuring the preservation of both the digital image and the original analogue version.

Moving Here guidelines for preservation

The *Moving Here* project on immigrants to the UK has fully understood the importance of preserving both the digital image and its original analogue version. Initiated in 2002 with a substantial grant from the Big Lottery Fund, this project continues with assistance from the Heritage Lottery Fund. *Moving Here* explores, records and illustrates why people came to the country over the last 200 years and what their continued experiences were and continue to be. It offers free access, for personal and educational use, to an online catalogue of versions of original material related to migration history from local, regional and national archives, libraries and museums. Now encompassing 50 partners, the organization has had to issue guidelines on, among other things, the preservation of images in different ways. The project received further funding from the Heritage Lottery Fund over the period 2005–7 to develop links with regional partners and The National Archives. See www.movinghere.org.uk/help/.

Who should be involved?

Archives have a choice over who is involved in the preservation of digital materials, as they do for traditional preservation. The organization's preservation policy must also include and fully integrate digital preservation. The commitment to the preservation of digital records is fundamental to an organization's key aims. The National Library of Australia (2008) expresses this perspective very well in their Digital Preservation Policy: 'The Library has a business interest in and commitment to preservation and has been active in developing infrastructure to collect, manage, preserve and keep our digital collections available. This is recognized as ongoing core business for the Library and critical to its future relevance.'

It amounts to little more than deciding whether to use in-house expertise or to pay for external assistance, although this is not necessarily an easy decision. The advantages and disadvantages of both are very similar to those for any expert role, but the budgetary considerations for both are considerable. For either solution a skills audit is clearly a first priority to understand the level of current expertise and identify the gaps.

In-house solutions

In-house solutions require flexible arrangements, new lines of communication and a clear understanding of the importance of co-operation across the whole organization, both at strategic and operational levels. New technologies lead to the development of specialists whose role may not fit into the traditional roles found in an archive. Equally, organizations may well lack staff who can act as digital preservation project managers and co-ordinate the skills found among other different groups such as:

- information technologists whose skills lie largely in managing the current data rather than considering its long-term future
- creators of the material who are the appropriate authorities for deciding on retention periods but who are unlikely to have technical expertise
- archivists who will have the ability to manage the holdings for access and understand the strategic need for digital preservation, but may not be backed up by a strong corporate vision at senior management level for the preservation of digital material.

Faced with this diversity of skills and personnel it is important to establish new working relationships between the various stakeholders, which may cut across traditional boundaries within organizations and require new methods of working. Additional training will be needed, and further expertise may have to be brought into the organization.

Adopting an in-house solution can provide valuable experience and the development of specialist skills which will stand the archive in good stead in the future; it can also be very expensive, and being at the cutting edge is not always a worthwhile or comfortable investment. However, it provides a means of raising awareness across an organization together with a sense of ownership, both of which are valuable outcomes.

Contracting-out solutions

Contracting out the work requires sufficient knowledge of the requirements to be able to communicate successfully with the organization undertaking the work. This in itself may dictate the employment of specialists to scope the project and assist. Issues that must be raised, and which must be clearly understood, will include:

- national and international standards
- confidentiality
- quality assurance
- access arrangements.

Using outside contractors has drawbacks, which may include:

- lack of control over the work unless the contract has been drawn up very tightly

- high costs
- over-dependence on one contractor (relatively few exist to choose from, as it is a new business)
- the risk of being involved in business failure.

Against that, using outside experts to provide the service may provide a breathing space for an organization during which the necessary skills can be developed to bring the operation back in-house. Also, contracting-out costs may be lower than the significant expense of building an in-house infrastructure to support the activity; without the additional work existing staff may be released to concentrate on other services, and economies of scale may be achieved by combining with others for a shared service between small- or medium-sized organizations. Either solution has its merits and its drawbacks.

A new development is Cloud Storage. This is primarily (for the user) a virtual store for digital files and data. Hosting companies provide large, secure data centres with vast storage capacity. The customer then uses the facility to store files and/or data, with access managed through a web-based interface. While this development potentially suggests the end of the hard drive and other portable storage devices, there are significant concerns regarding both access to and the security of personal information.

What is the starting point?

It must be clear that, while one person has to lead on digital preservation, it is an organization-wide responsibility, cutting across traditional boundaries and engaging a spectrum of stakeholders. All staff must be engaged, since they contribute to the electronic archive in whatever role they play. A regime of best practice in terms of

- regular back-up of all files
- rigorous management control over the software used in the organization or the bodies which will be transferring material to the archive
- regular transfer of current, backed-up material to another site

must be the scenario for successful digital preservation. It involves responsible creators who think through the long-term implications for their documentation, together with retention and review management practices to ensure that material is retained, is in the correct place and is reviewed to timetable. Access issues will have been considered, which may result in the creation of two copies of the information – one for immediate access and the other for longer-term preservation to ensure continued access. Access issues will also have implications for the type of file format chosen. The National Archives in the UK has identified two types of files: those which do not contain embedded logic (Word files without macros, ASCII text files or HTML files) and files which do contain macros, Flash or embedded links. Choosing the right file format is important for subsequent ease of both access and preservation; organizations should identify the simplest format to suit their requirements and those of their depositors. Decisions should take into account that some formats are more suitable for longer-term storage than others that are largely used for distribution and access.[7] For more guidance on file formats see DPC Technology Watch Series Report 09-02 October 2009.[8]

Much of this activity should be routine and will not be within the remit of the person responsible for digital preservation, hence the need from the outset for communication and co-operation between all staff involved. These sentiments are crucial to the concept of 'Parsimonious Preservation' (Gollins, 2009) mentioned earlier in the chapter.

The first decision to be made relates to whether the preservation activity is to take place in-house or not; budgetary issues are likely to loom large in these discussions, together with a review of in-house expertise and resources (see above).

The next decision required relates to the strategies to be adopted for transferring the media if it is to be preserved long-term. Throughout, the importance of adhering to national and international standards[9] is crucial, though in a rapidly moving field it has to be recognized that they may become obsolete before they are accepted internationally.[10] Ensuring that they are adopted throughout the processes of creation, retention, accession and preservation involves co-ordination and acceptance by all stakeholders. If achieved this will make the final preservation strategy easier and possibly cheaper.

Thereafter, several electronic options for digital preservation are currently available: these must be discussed with those expert in evaluating and monitoring them. It is a rapidly changing scene but the following are current options which have stood the test of some time and are in use in many organizations. They can be adopted in combination as required; all have their pros and cons.

File format migration:

- Re-formatting electronic files to open-format software ensures that the data is not lost if the proprietary software provider fails or is taken over.
- Using emulation software will imitate the properties of outdated hardware so that material created with it can still be accessed. The drawback to this is that it is essentially a static process which does not

add any value to the material being preserved; further developments in manoeuvrability or analysis of the information are not incorporated.

Media migration:

- Electronic material can be migrated from one carrier to another for continued access when technological change has rendered the first obsolete. The more complicated the migration process, the less easy it is to make an exact copy with the original functionality.
- Hardware and software can be retained for use with outdated types of materials. This is hardly viable in the long term, since technical knowledge and support will only be available for a certain length of time.
- Digital archaeology can rescue otherwise inaccessible data; this is a last-hope measure when other solutions have failed, requires specialist input and can be very costly.[11]
- Data can be printed out in analogue form, or copied to microfilm; this is a solution adopted by some organizations as an interim safeguard, especially if digital preservation policies and strategies are not in place. Although the raw information may be preserved it reduces the functionality of the original, particularly if the data is complex and dependent on electronic manoeuvrability. It adds to the quantitative storage problems of analogue material and the costs of conversion are considerable and quite complicated; it is not recommended as a solution.

Salvage of 1986 BBC Domesday Project files

The most-quoted example in the UK of the need to recreate data is that of the British Broadcasting Corporation's 1986 Domesday Project laser files. These were salvaged in 2003 as a result of a combination of expertise from some of the original team on the Domesday Project, the re-creation of the technical documentation and the use of a retained laserdisc player at The National Archives (Darlington, Finney and Pearce, 2003). This, however, is not the only example, and it did not have financial implications other than the waste of the original project resources. Many organizations have suffered from data loss with far greater consequences in the form of lost business when it has not been financially feasible to excavate deleted or outdated files and file formats.

What happens next?

Once a preservation strategy has been decided upon, the data must be prepared. Many of the useful suggestions made by Jones and Beagrie (2001, 89) will be applicable for either in-house or third-party storage and preservation; in the case of the latter they act as reminders for preparation work and issues to be included in the specification, and in the case of the former they map out the necessary actions to be taken by staff. Most should become standard practice once an organization becomes accustomed to managing digital materials as a matter of course. They include:

- assigning unique numbering to identify the resource and provide a location marker, with which all associated material is also marked
- developing handling guidelines which give best practice
- validating materials to check for viruses, legibility, accuracy, description, intellectual content, structure, formatting and associated procedures
- refreshing and reformatting where necessary for long-term preservation; a regular routine, at specified intervals, which must be introduced to avoid media degradation
- copying as a safeguard for access and preservation purposes and for off-site storage
- writing to different software from different suppliers to protect data against malfunction, corruption or embedded viruses
- embedding quality control procedures to ensure that data has not become corrupt due to storage or after media refreshing (checksum[12] comparisons)
- checking that readability has not been compromised (incorporating random checks every six months if automated processes are not available)
- making security checks to ensure that all procedures are carried out
- ensuring that access to storage areas is controlled
- ensuring that all legal requirements are complied with
- ensuring that all passwords, identity security procedures and security checks are both used and changed regularly
- developing a disaster plan to cope with natural or man-made emergencies, together with strategies for recovering corrupt files and media or unreadable files
- providing the appropriate environmental conditions (see Chapter 6) in the storage area for electronic media
- developing strategies to ensure that material stored online is migrated to a larger file server before reaching a critical capacity.

Once a system is in place it will require monitoring to ensure that it produces the necessary solutions for the organization, and that it is running smoothly and efficiently. The manager of the process will require regular training in a field which is developing very fast and, if relevant, in-house staff on the project will also need training. While digital preservation is a relatively new preoccupation for archivists and records managers, confidence has developed comparatively fast that the international efforts to find answers that, at the least, do not compromise the validity of the information have arrived at workable solutions. The challenge is now to embed recommended practice into everyday operations and promote the digital record as integral to all archive collections.

Summary

Managing digital preservation is a challenge that most archivists will face, and the adoption of the correct strategies – while understanding the pitfalls – is crucial. This chapter has outlined the importance of managing digital information and indicated some of the difficulties as well as the practical steps required for success. The following chapter looks at the physical characteristics of archival buildings and the importance of an appropriate envelope for the survival of all types of archives.

Notes and references

1   See www.nationalarchives.gov.uk/information-management/projects-and-work/digital-preservation.htm.

2   See www.dpconline.org/advice.

3   www.digitalpreservation.gov/ndsa, hosted by the Library of Congress and including Digital Preservation Outreach and Education and the National Digital Information infrastructure and Preservation Programme.

4   'Information which describes significant aspects of a resource . . . will assist in ensuring essential contextual, historical and technical information are preserved along with the digital object.' (Jones and Beagrie, 2001).

5   Electronic Document and Records Management System. The National Archives, *Migrating Information Between EDRMS*, www.nationalarchives.gov.uk/documents/information-management/edrms.pdf.

6   The Sarbanes-Oxley Act 2002 introduced major changes to the regulation of financial practice and corporate governance after a series of high-profile scandals.

7   www.dpconline.org/component/finder/search?q=file+format+migration.

8   www.dpconline.org/publications/technology-watch-reports.

9   For example, BS 4783.

10   The aims of the Document Lifecycle Management (DLM) Forum (www.dlmforum.eu) include monitoring and disseminating standards and good practice, and should be consulted for up-to-date information.

11 The IT History Society's Hardware Database,
    www.ithistory.org/hardware/hardware-name.php.
12 'A computed value that is dependent upon the contents of a packet. Sent along with
    the packet when it is transmitted. The receiving system computes a new checksum
    based on data received, compares this value with the one sent with the packet. If the
    two values are the same, the receiver has a high degree of confidence that the data
    was received correctly.' http://archives.govt.nz/advice/continuum-resource-
    kit/glossary/definitions-full-list.

4

Archive buildings and their characteristics

Introduction

Archive buildings are the first stage of protection for the materials kept within them and, as such, are crucial in ensuring survival. Archive buildings, of greater and lesser complexity, have been developed from this basic premise all over the world, adapted to differing climates and the needs of the archives themselves. The importance of understanding the need to build them in the right place, of constructing them in an appropriate way, and of employing experienced practitioners to minimize the threats posed to fragile materials, cannot be overestimated. Likewise, the issues surrounding the adaptation of buildings for use as archives must be appreciated and considered.

This chapter looks at:

- the ways in which archive buildings have developed internationally and in the UK in particular
- issues to consider before constructing an archive or adapting an old building
- how to get ideas over to an architect
- exterior and interior layouts and specifications.

How has the concept of archive buildings developed?

Continuity of custody in secure ownership constitutes the fundamental guarantee of archival authenticity. Hence, security has always been at the forefront of all decisions on the storage of archival material. This is obvious from the choice of storage places over time – for example, the Qumran caves in which the Dead Sea Scrolls (from 200 BC) were hidden, the massive bronze chests in the Forbidden Palace in Beijing in which documents of the Chinese dynasties were stored from the 15th century, and the construction of the

Lyndon B. Johnson Museum and Library to house presidential papers of the 20th century. The concept that a building must also be attractive to users and staff is of more recent origin, and has been achievable partly as a result of applying modern technology, including electronic security. This change also mirrors the recognition that public archives are the documents of the people, who have a right to access information and to consult both historic and contemporary documents.

How did archive buildings develop in the UK?

Keeping the documents of the Crown, and subsequently of central government, safe was a major concern in the UK from the time of the Norman Conquest in 1066. Medieval kings carried their valuable items with them on their itineraries but by the beginning of the 13th century the need for stability resulted in Westminster becoming the permanent centre for the departments of state, with the records housed in adjacent locations. The number of buildings used for storage grew during the succeeding centuries until by the early 19th century there were over 60, scattered throughout London. The fire at the Houses of Parliament (1834),[1] which destroyed many parliamentary records, highlighted the need for sound construction and fireproof storage but issues to do with location and design delayed the start of building on the Rolls Estate in Chancery Lane until 1851. At the same time the Victoria Tower at Westminster was constructed to house the records of Parliament (1860). Contemporary debates about the value of installing heating, the need for adequate fire prevention and security issues mirror those of the present day, with an emphasis on the value of cool storage and self-contained strongrooms. Despite 19th century additions to the building at Chancery Lane, not least to accommodate readers, further development for the ever-increasing volume of records was impossible by the middle of the 20th century and the present site at Kew was selected,[2] offering the opportunity to incorporate new thinking in the construction of a national archive. The design of the first building on that site was influenced by a few new archives built in other parts of the country after World War 2[3] – e.g. Lancashire County Record Office – but also crucially, by international contact and discussion.

The opening of the first building at Kew in 1977 gave impetus to the development of other new record offices in the UK, such as the J. Paul Getty Jr. Conservation Centre at Berkhamstead for the National Film Archive (1986–7), the Northamptonshire Record Office (1991) and the Modern Records Centre at Warwick University (1993). Elsewhere, warehouses, schools and redundant churches offered space for conversion. St George's

Church in Edinburgh was developed as the West Register House of the Scottish Record Office (now the National Archives of Scotland), North Yorkshire County Record Office made use of a converted furniture warehouse, and Suffolk Record Office utilized a Victorian board school. However by the end of the century purpose-built facilities were being favoured over adapted buildings, partly on the basis of cost; refurbishment frequently required major rewiring, re-plumbing and floor-strengthening to bring the facilities up to the standards required. The requirements of access legislation has also had a significant impact on the move to improve facilities for those wishing to use archival material but that, in turn, is increasingly being provided by online access. However, no archive will ever be able to digitize its entire holdings and so suitable physical access remains the goal for many.

Building of the Public Record Office, now The National Archives, at Kew

The move to Kew took place in two phases; the first, in 1976, removed the modern records from central London and the second, nearly 20 years later, the remaining medieval and early modern records. To accommodate the entire archive a second building had to be erected on the site in the 1990s, enabling the project to benefit from earlier experiences.

In the 1970s modern technology was hailed as a solution to the problems of automated retrieval systems and controlled environmental conditions, although the ultimate impact of electronic record-keeping was only dimly foreseen. Storage capacity in Kew 1 was calculated on the basis of provision to the end of the century, based on the then current rates of accrual of paper records. Much attention was given to movement within the new building, minimizing the distance large documents had to travel to reduce wear and tear. Purpose-built conservation and reprographic areas were also specified, having been housed in adapted accommodation on the Chancery Lane site.

Experience of the way in which the first building operated informed the design and fitting out of the subsequent building, Kew 2. Vast storage areas, extending over whole floors, had proved difficult to maintain at the appropriate environmental levels; greater flexibility in use of space was required, necessitating mobile shelving; and specialized storage areas were required for photographic materials. Developments in HVAC (heating, ventilation and air-conditioning systems) and electronic security systems were incorporated, together with up-to-date fire protection.

What other ideas have developed for archive buildings?

Although the 1976 building on the Public Record Office site at Kew was hailed as innovatory, in practice other ideas were being developed elsewhere, such as the use of high thermal inertia building techniques[4] in the Deutsches Bundesarchiv in Germany to avoid expensive and often unreliable air-conditioning systems. High thermal inertia has attraction as a method of naturally insulating a building, although doubts remain about its total efficiency. At best it can probably reduce reliance on air conditioning considerably, but experiences in the last 30 years have demonstrated that it is still necessary to monitor and adjust supplementary heating and cooling systems in response to external weather conditions and diurnal (seasonal) changes and effects.

In France Michel Duchein, Inspecteur Général in the Archives de France, wrote a definitive text on archive buildings (Duchein, 1966), outlining French thinking on storage and buildings. The volume became a landmark in the theory and practical execution of building new archives and the ensuing international discussions prompted the establishment of the Buildings Committee of the International Council on Archives (ICA),[5] which has published papers on modern archive buildings[6] and undertaken case studies.

The National Archives of the United States came into existence in 1934 after the construction of a repository in Washington and following prolonged lobbying. Since then the College Park, Maryland repository has opened and presidential libraries have been added to the responsibilities of the archive staff.

In Canada the design of the National Archives Gatineau constitutes a building within a building since the extreme weather conditions in Ottawa make it impossible to guarantee stability of temperature and relative humidity within a single outer wall.

Since these beginnings, research into conventional methods of stabilizing temperature and relative humidity with insulation and careful management has demonstrated how to avoid breakdown of complicated mechanical installations and spiralling fuel costs. Some countries with very hot climates have reverted successfully to traditional building techniques to protect the holdings of libraries and archives, maximizing the natural protection offered by the use of local building materials and styles; archives and libraries are frequently built with minimal external windows, and sections of the building are often centred round an internal courtyard with more shade. Other countries, with different temperature extremes, have excavated storage areas, notably in Scandinavia,[7] or used natural rock resources with very stable environments,[8] though both of these bring their own problems in terms of dependence on electrical resources for access and the risk of flooding for some.

In the UK, Dr Chris Kitching has published two studies of new buildings (covering the period 1977–2005) which have provided a significant analysis of practice and developments in the building (and adaptation) of archives. Alongside this valuable coverage, is the Major Archives Projects Learning Exchange (MAPLE), which was set up in autumn 2007 to support organizations currently planning or managing large archive projects to provide a forum to share experiences, knowledge and plans via an e-mail list and through sharing documentation.[9]

Green building and the sustainability agenda

Both of the initiatives outlined in the previous section are underpinned by a growing pressure to produce buildings that not only have a low impact on their immediate local environment but are also constructed of materials, and use systems to manage the use of the building, that can be sustained into the future. The economic environment in the 21st century can no longer sustain any practices that overuse or waste resources and local government services especially are subject to environmental audits and have to calculate their 'carbon footprint'. Consequently, new archive buildings that are under construction have either incorporated, or considered and rejected for good reason, a range of 'green' alternatives to reduce consumption and safeguard the environment. These include:

- solar panels for hot water
- photovoltaic cells for electricity
- wind turbines for generating electricity
- ground source heat pumps for heating
- rainwater harvesting for toilets
- high levels of insulation
- sun-pipes for corridors
- sedum roofs.

Much research is needed to ascertain the full impact of these alternative sources of generating or conserving energy and their appropriateness for use in archive buildings. However, there has been significant research within the building establishment [10] and some useful strategies are becoming established amongst a growing number of archive services, including:

- reviewing all energy use – carry out an energy audit
- collecting data about energy use
- turning off HVAC plant to the storage areas at the weekends
- reducing the number of daily air changes
- changing all bulbs to energy efficient versions.

Time and the economic pressures will show if the archive world has moved to address these issues soon enough.

What should be considered before building or adapting an existing building to house an archive?

Any decision about moving to a new building, or an adapted one, will depend very largely on factors outside the direct control of the archivist. These are, in almost all cases, to do with funding and also the appropriate political moment at which to invest in such a project. Lobbying for new premises is a crucial part of any attempt to move, but the ultimate decision will be made by the controlling authority, whether government, local politicians or the board of a business or charity. It may be that the archive is in a shared building and this will present a range of preservation risks to the collections; however, this should not be an impediment to improving standards of storage or collection care. The need to liaise and interact with other departments and staff, and to promote the particular needs of the archive collections, is a vital part of developing a sound and holistic approach. The issues outlined in this section will not differ for those in shared accommodation from those fortunate enough to be re-housed in a new building. Other considerations than the needs of the archive will have to be taken into account and priorities financed. However, the volume of new buildings erected in the last 25 years in the UK suggests that archivists have been quite successful in overcoming these obstacles. The same is true in other countries where, despite the low profile of archives in many cases, resources have been forthcoming, although frequently without the publicity – and sometimes controversy – surrounding the construction of major libraries or galleries.

Preparation for a bid to construct a new archive should start well before any realistic prospect of funding is in sight. It should include:

- visits to and discussions with other archivists and architects who have successfully commissioned and constructed new premises
- learning to emulate success in different circumstances
- understanding how to avoid mistakes.

The key document for study in the UK is British Standard PD 5454: 2012, *Guide for the storage of archival documents*. Other countries have similar standards, or sometimes the national archive supports an advisory design team to ensure consistency and standards for the regions (see 'British and international standards relating to archive preservation', page 257).

At all costs the archive must have such outline plans ready for development at the moment, often unexpected, when authority is given to proceed. Forethought will be well rewarded, since demands for detailed information – often about parts of the building which may not be constructed first but for which components require ordering and manufacture – will be made almost at once. It is not too much to suggest that all archives ought to keep on hand a plan prepared in outline, with supportive arguments marshalled, since on occasion moves are forced rather than sought and the timing may be quite different to what has been anticipated.

What needs to be explained?

It is essential to work out with whom, how and when to communicate at the outset. All the stakeholders, who should have already been identified, will need information about decisions and progress. Many of the issues about archives, their needs and those of their users taken for granted by professional archivists will have to be explained to all those involved, who may include, among others, any or all of the following:

- senior staff
- the architect
- contractors
- other staff who may be involved, e.g. in making financial arrangements or agreeing contracts
- non-professional staff and volunteers
- users and user groups
- local authority planners
- historic building specialists.

For those who are not regular members of the archive staff it will be necessary to start with a definition of what an archive is, what it does and what makes it successful. The English use of the word 'archive' includes both the concept of the body of records held and the building itself, which is also sometimes referred to as a record office. This may need pointing out. In the context of this chapter 'archive' refers to the building.

Definition and purpose of the archive

An archive is the secure repository for information, held in varying formats, that has been selected by the parent organization for permanent preservation, and where users can access this information. A successful archive building is one that:

- protects the materials within it from excessive heat or cold, fire, water, theft and pollution (in many cases the material is the official record of an organization, and as such requires all appropriate safeguards for its survival)
- provides appropriate, comfortable and secure[11] access for those who wish to use the facility or work there.

Location

Few locations are ideal and compromise is nearly always essential. Nevertheless it is important to identify the criteria for the selection of a site. These should include the following:

Security of the site

It should be away from:

- military installations
- hazardous plant such as munitions or chemical factories
- airports
- rivers
- floodplains
- sea defences
- pollutants.

Flooding is becoming an increasing concern in the UK and elsewhere and advice will be required from the appropriate government department. Land heavily polluted by previous users should be avoided.

Access to the site

It should be easily reached by public transport for staff and readers; suppliers and contractors should be able to reach it easily by road. In the past it has been regarded as important that an archive should be close to the administration for which it works but that is a decision for each organization to make in the light of its requirements. Proximity to other resources of a similar nature – libraries or museums – can be an advantage for the user, though the ubiquity of online resources may make this less necessary in the future.

Size of the site

It should be adequate for current and future storage needs. The latter is a policy matter for the organization, requiring debate and decision. Projected storage requirements should be the subject of annual review so that information on likely future needs is easily available. Some of the major questions to be answered are:

- Does the archive propose storing rarely accessed material off-site in addition to the new facility?
- How is it proposed that such material will be accessed if required, physically or digitally?

- Is it anticipated that a reduction in storage space will be required when accruing electronic records outnumber those preserved on paper? If so, what are the implications for space requirements and when?
- Is it anticipated that the use of the building by the public will increase substantially during its lifetime, or is it more likely that digitization programmes will enable adequate off-site visits?
- Does the archive anticipate expansion or taking over additional functions – e.g. a local history library – necessitating not only more storage space but more room for staff and users as well?
- Will the site under consideration allow future building upwards, below ground or on the ground? Is the spare capacity to be used before it is needed for the archive? Is it feasible or desirable to leave it untenanted before the archive requires it?

Site considerations

The site should preferably be flat, empty and sufficiently sound geologically to withstand the construction of a building with considerable demands in terms of weight load. Prevailing wind direction should be taken into account. In the UK any opportunity to locate the storage areas on the north side of the facility to minimize heat gain should be seized; in the southern hemisphere the preferred location will be the south side. If the archive is to be constructed in a residential area additional reassurance may be needed by those living in adjacent properties about:

- the building construction methods
- working hours, including any projected weekend working
- noise
- possible local disruption to roads or traffic
- site access
- possible pollution or use of noxious chemicals (especially if conservation or copying processes are to be included).

Local planning rules may well limit the height or appearance of the building.

Whatever final decision is made about the location, it is highly likely that some flexibility will be needed. To prevent this from compromising the final success of the archive, drawing up a risk register and working out the best ways to minimize any dangers is good practice. This is part of project management in any case, and should be undertaken at all stages and for all aspects of the project.

How should the architect be briefed?

Project management is a very specific skill, and not one which archivists are usually taught. Before embarking on any sizable building scheme it is highly recommended that some training on how to approach the many complex issues is undertaken, both by the project leader and the team selected to see the project through.

Drawing up specifications for a new building is not easy but textbooks and standards are available to provide help. It is essential that the preservation details are developed by archive staff, who are aware of the needs of the collections, rather than the architect, who will need assistance on the purpose and layout of the building and the location of the various functions. A project team will be required and at the very beginning the roles of its various members must be defined; this is the time to reach an agreement with the architectural team about responsibilities, timetables and project management.

Some building layout questions to consider

- Has a flow chart of the various functions of the archive been drawn up to demonstrate the relationships of one part to another?
- Has every member of staff considered his or her needs in relation to a new building? How are functions/operations going to change as a result of a new building?
- Has the project team established regular staff meetings with specialist input? This will be vital throughout the project.
- Is the storage area to be surrounded by other functions of the archive, or will it be a separate section?
- How can the public areas be separated from the staff and storage areas, given the configuration of the site?
- How is it best to route the services so that no pipes go through the storage areas?
- Can the public areas be sited sufficiently closely to the storage areas to avoid too much fetching and carrying?
- How can any necessary vertical movement to and from the storage areas be achieved? How to avoid the use of stairs?
- Is a kitchen to be installed, and if so, can it be kept well away from any storage or reading areas?
- Are washrooms to be installed and, if so, can plumbing for toilets, washbasins and showers be kept well away from any storage or reading areas?
- How is the security to be managed – traditionally with keys or electronically?

Building with preservation in mind is going to produce a much better result than if various safeguards have to be added later. A good building will be achieved where the whole is better than the sum of the parts – in other words, the various parts should work together to provide a well co-ordinated building affording the maximum protection to its contents while allowing access to staff and users. The following relates to some of the issues the archive and its staff must consider and decide; more will undoubtedly occur to each organization.

- External walls should be constructed from non-combustible, waterproof materials which offer high insulation. Four-hour fire resistance should be the norm for all parts of the construction.[12]
- Internal walls of the storage areas should conform to the same specification but should be left bare or finished with a microporous paint which allows the surface to breathe; oil-based paints are discouraged, owing to the danger of off-gassing, and a non-porous surface risks creating condensation if the temperature varies. Office accommodation and public areas will need to conform to the appropriate standards. Any conservation or reprographic functions will need to be housed within walls suitably constructed for the type of activity carried out.
- Roofs must be insulated to prevent heat gain, and be watertight with a minimum of openings; smoke outlets are probably the only opening required (see Chapter 5 for security issues). The pitch of the roof must enable the rapid removal of storm water; flat roofs have proved to be hazardous even in countries where there is little rain.
- Doors should be self-closing in the event of fire, have the same four-hour fire resistance as surrounding walls and fit sufficiently tightly to act as smoke stoppers. They should not have grilles or panes to allow the passage of air (see Chapter 5 for security issues).
- Stairways and lift shafts should be enclosed by walls, dampers or doors that have four-hour fire protection. Vertical shafts can act as flues for smoke, fire or toxic gases and must therefore be capable of being isolated.
- Repository or storage area floors should be appropriately load-bearing, as calculated by a structural engineer, bearing in mind that in the event of any flood or water ingress paper documents become much heavier. The floors should be level, enabling the use of trolleys for horizontal movement. This is also essential for any installation of mobile shelving, where the floor surface must be hard – preferably sealed concrete. Sealing is necessary for all floor surfaces to avoid dust, pollution or off-gassing; carpet is unsuitable for floors due to its potential for dust collection (which in turn encourages insects), and the movement of trolleys would quickly wear it out. Quarry tiles or non-slip, sealed, inert, hardwearing plastic tiles should be specified to enable thorough and easy cleaning. The floors in conservation or reprographic areas will need to be proofed against chemical or water spillage and be tanked.

- Drainage points must be installed within the building, especially on the repository floors, in any toilets or kitchens and in conservation and reprographic areas where water is used regularly. In vertical shafts they must enable water to escape in an emergency. These should be fitted with valves to prevent backup from floods elsewhere.
- Windows will be necessary in the public and office parts of the building, but not necessarily in the repository area, where control of natural light is important. However, PD 5454: 2012 concedes the need for staff to be able to see outside, particularly if they are working in the same enclosed place all day. In this case it suggests small, non–opening windows, barred and glazed with strengthened glass, treated to prevent UV gain.

Perimeter design should not be ignored in the preservation strategy connected with the new building. Security lighting will be necessary at night, or infrared lights to detect unauthorized movement. Appropriate planting might involve low-level thorny bushes close to the building to deter thieves, or, depending on the design, the area might be left clear to avoid the provision of hiding places. A boundary wall or fence may be deemed necessary, depending on the location of the building; defining the boundary is valuable but a balance has to be struck between security and access. Local authority crime prevention officers will be able to offer advice according to the location.

What about the interior layout of the archive?

The relationships between the various parts of the building is a matter for the individual archive; it will be necessary to conduct a rigorous risk assessment to ensure that functions do not clash, leading to possible damage to the records. All facilities should also comply with local legislation on, for instance, disabled access.[13]

Storage area

Some archives have adopted a layout which involves the storage area being surrounded by administrative offices, thus inhibiting unauthorized access. This has security advantages but creates difficulties when additional storage is needed. A more practical layout locates the storage area behind the public areas, with controlled access for nominated staff only. The size and vulnerability of the holdings of the archive must be taken into account when deciding on the proximity of the storage area to the reading rooms. It is worth considering easy communication between the two, at least for documents which are difficult to handle, such as maps or outsize volumes. A storage area which is at some distance from the administrative offices and the reading rooms is difficult to manage and increases the risk to documents being taken between locations; they may get wet, get lost or be stolen. Any lengthy journey encourages temporary storage in unsuitable places for the sake of convenience – e.g. unsecured office cupboards.

Accommodation for staff fetching and carrying documents within the storage area must be provided, especially if they are there for most of the working day. They are likely to require computer access to catalogues and location indexes and comfortable seating, given the physical nature of their job. Desks and chairs for professional staff are frequently found in storage areas but it is not best practice; all but the shortest piece of work should be done in staff offices with the appropriate equipment and tables.

Public areas

These should be located so that visitors can access all facilities freely without entering staff or storage areas. Although they are usually designed with access issues to the fore, good facilities for the public will create the right environment to demonstrate the commitment of the archive to its primary purposes of preservation and access. These include:

- an entrance hall, which may include a new readers' point, a staff desk to direct readers, register them or assist in some other way: it may be tempting to put exhibitions in this area but the security risks must be evaluated; such areas have proved vulnerable in the past
- reading rooms, including enquiry points, document or surrogate ordering areas, catalogues and indexes, and microform and computer access points; reading rooms should be laid out with clear sightlines for supervising staff, avoiding blocked corners or areas where readers cannot be seen; sufficient space should be provided to move trolleys about within the area
- toilets (and washing facilities to encourage regular hand washing), cloakrooms and lockers: it is important to provide facilities for the safe deposit of personal belongings in order to prevent too much being taken into the reading rooms
- a restaurant or café
- rest areas with comfortable chairs for those who bring their own food and drink; vending machines are frequently provided where there is no on-site restaurant or café.

Readers should have no need to go anywhere else in the building.

Conservation workshops (see Appendix 2)

These should be located where appropriate drainage and dedicated electrical wiring can be supplied. Access for easy delivery of conservation material – such as rolls of leather or polythene sheeting – is helpful and the requirement for waterproof flooring indicates that this area is most sensibly located on the ground floor. The weight of some of the equipment also suggests that a solid floor is preferable. Venting may be required if fume cupboards are installed. If chemicals are used they should be stored in a specially constructed cupboard away from the main building. Public interest in conservation is such that a central location within the building, easily accessible to visitors, may be appropriate. It is also helpful to have close access to the storage areas for conservation staff, who may have to spend considerable time there, monitoring environmental conditions or undertaking preservation assessments.

Reprographic workshops

These will have many of the same requirements as conservation workshops, depending on the size and complexity of the operation. Most equipment will be large and heavy and any processing equipment will need specialized drainage facilities for chemical or silver retrieval. Racking in a secure part of the workshop will be required for any material which has to remain in the area overnight, and a chemical store will be needed, away from the main building for safety reasons. It may be sensible to locate reprographic functions close to the reading area so that readers and staff can easily communicate over orders for copies.

Staff working areas

These will vary from those requiring standard office-type accommodation to those requiring greater table space to catalogue documents. Space calculations for the latter function must be considerably greater than for standard operations. Staff areas should be easily accessible for trolleys for moving documents about.

Provision of facilities in which staff can eat and drink – as opposed to using their desks – is common; many archives find it easier to keep such areas clean and vermin-free than if food and drink are consumed all over the building. Health and safety regulations may also suggest that providing a central water boiler is preferable to the use of individual kettles.

What are the problems with adapted buildings or historic buildings?

The overriding problem with adapted buildings or parts thereof, is that they were intended for purposes other than those for which they are now used and they may not meet the required standards for archive preservation.[14] If additional space in the current building becomes available for the use of the archive it will be important to consider many of the issues outlined in the previous sections. Pressure to use redundant buildings or areas within buildings for archives is common; archivists must be able to produce specifications and detailed arguments for the quality of facilities needed to ensure that preservation requirements are met. In many cases where conversions are the only solution, additional precautions are advocated to minimize risk. Common problems include:

- inadequate structural stability or floor-loadings for the weight of materials to be stored; calculations must include the possibility of using mobile shelving and the increased weight which this will entail; reinforcing the floors for conversion may be extremely expensive
- poor or flat roofing and leaking gutters or drains
- water or drainage pipes running through storage areas without adequate protection
- inadequate building materials and insulation, resulting in difficulty in maintaining appropriate environmental conditions; the expense of installing and running air-conditioning under these circumstances must be factored into estimates for conversion and running costs
- inappropriate ventilation and air circulation: too many ill-fitting windows and doors admit dust, dirt and pests; conversely, too little air circulation encourages mould growth
- inadequate security for an archive – a building with many doors, windows or roof lights may require extensive remodelling to conform to appropriate standards; shared buildings are particularly vulnerable and explanations about requirements must be outlined to any new neighbours
- inadequate fire resistance which will have to be remedied with the installation of appropriate fire detection, alarms and suppression systems
- inappropriate configuration of the rooms to suit the needs of users and staff; this involves, in particular, the need to keep the public and private areas of the building separate.

Despite the above list of potential problems some buildings in the UK and elsewhere have been adapted very successfully; sometimes, part of a building is used as a public function and adjacent storage built for the archives. These include Suffolk Record Office in Ipswich, where the search room is in a converted school building with a 1990 purpose-built repository and office block on the playground. Other conversions have included a car showroom in Sheffield, part of a gaol in Ruthin for Denbighshire Archives and St Luke's Church for the Oxfordshire Record Office.

Historic buildings suffer from many of the above defects, although they may have been used to house archival and library material for many years. A survey (Hughes, 2002) undertaken between 1999 and 2001 revealed that 40% of the curators contacted regarded the condition of their holdings as poor or very poor. Common problems include:

- listed or historic status – Grade I or 2* in England, Grade A or B in Scotland – limiting the options for changing the structure or introducing measures to improve environmental conditions
- extensive use of wood as a building material or as panelling, reducing the options for changing the environmental conditions; under most circumstances in historic buildings any such permissible changes must be undertaken slowly to allow the collections to adapt
- historic interest which reduces the flexibility of the use of the rooms; research has also shown that visitors to such properties bring with them a significant amount of dirt and dust, most of which is shed in the earlier parts of their tour; if the library or unprotected archive is at the beginning of the visit, it will suffer accordingly
- use of a library or archive for commercial purposes such as entertaining, holding concerts or filming by television or film companies
- large windows traditionally installed for maximum light gain; much damage has been caused as a result of uncontrolled light to archival and library materials as well as textiles.

The National Trust[15] has experienced many of these problems in its properties and uses conservation heating as a solution, together with carefully controlled visitor levels. Humidistats measure the relative humidity of each room, maintaining it at 50–60%, and the temperature of each is kept at no more than about 5°C above the outside level. This approach is non-invasive, largely invisible and is sensitive to the needs of each room and its contents.

Summary

Buildings are the first line of defence to ensure the survival of archival materials, and this chapter has outlined some of the theory and techniques that need to be applied. It has underlined the need for understanding and communication, especially in relation to different professional terminology and definitions, as well as appropriate standards and guidelines. It has also discussed the advantages and disadvantages of adapted buildings and the importance of taking these fully into account before deciding whether to build a new facility or adapt an existing one. Having considered the external shell of a building in this chapter, the following chapter surveys the means to secure it.

Notes and references

1   Domesday Book narrowly escaped being destroyed in the fire when permission to move it to a safer location was refused until the Prime Minister had agreed (Hallam Smith, 1986, 151).

2   This 'suitability' unfortunately included a tendency of the site to flood, being next to the river Thames. However, extensive flood protection was installed, the storage areas are above ground level and the construction of the Thames Barrier in 1982 has reduced the risk. Ironically the first edition of British Standard 5454: 1977 (*Recommendations for the storage and display of archival materials*), advocating the avoidance of any site susceptible to flooding, was published the year after the building was opened.

3   Elizabeth Ralph regarded the post-war crop of new buildings as an improvement on those constructed earlier: 'In all these varying schemes much preliminary thought was shown and the results, compared with the Kent repository of the thirties, showed far greater simplicity, a use of larger units of area, less window space and much improved fire precautions' (in Hollaender, 1962, 64).

4   High thermal inertia is achieved by a technique using double cavity walls, forced air insulation and materials which provide very effective insulation, construction and lining.

5   See www.ica.org.

6   See *Archivum* (1986) and more recently building case studies on the ICA website (www.ica.org/11076/studies-and-case-studies/building-case-studies.html). ICA Bibliography on Archival Buildings, www.ica.org/10826/studies-and-case-studies/ica-study-n2-bibliography-on-archival-buildings.html.

7   For example, the Riksarkivet in Stockholm completed a 100 km storage facility in 1968.

8   An example of this is the Church of Jesus Christ of Latter-day Saints in Utah.

9   www.nationalarchives.gov.uk/information-management/projects-and-work/major-archives-projects-learning-exchange.htm.

10 In the UK; The Building Research Establishment, www.bre.co.uk. Internationally; BREEAM is the world's foremost environmental assessment method and rating system for buildings, www.breeam.org/index.jsp.

11 Ted Ling (1998, 19) makes the point that explicit issues to do with the occupational health of staff are regarded as more important now than in previous periods and that

the environment in which staff work must be taken into account.

12   Four-hour fire resistance is interpreted as incorporating construction elements
which are designed to prevent fire from breaching the walls, doors, openings, etc. for
a minimum of four hours and to maintain structural integrity so that the interior of
the protected area does not reach temperatures that will damage the assets stored
within during that period of time. Some authorities also cite a maximum
temperature threshold within the four-hour limit, meaning that beyond that
temperature the contents will be damaged. This is important in the case of a steel
safe, where the contents can vaporize from the outside heat, although the walls of
the safe remain standing.

13   From 1 October 2010, the Equality Act replaced most of the Disability
Discrimination Act (DDA).

14   See Preservation Advisory Centre leaflet *Managing the Preservation of Library and
Archive Collections in Historic Buildings*, November 2002,
www.bl.uk/blpac/pdf/historic.pdf.

15   See Sarah Staniforth (2007) on conservation heating, www.getty.edu/conservation/
our_projects/science/climate/paper_staniforth.pdf.
Smiths Gore, *Energy Conservation in Historic Houses: a guide for historic house owners*, May
2009, www.smithsgore.co.uk/assets/x/145854.

5

Safeguarding the building and its contents

Introduction

All archives need to install certain safeguards against threats, both to the records themselves and to the people working in the building, both public and staff. This chapter looks at the main threats and ways of mitigating them; they include:

- security provision
- fire prevention, detection and suppression
- water detection.

Security

Security is 'the very essence of a repository' (Kitching, 1993, 33) and must be taken very seriously. Breaches of security are potential threats to the validity of the documents stored in an archive, since loss of custody could jeopardize authenticity. But physical security installations are not enough. They must go hand in hand with good security procedures to ensure the maximum protection possible, always bearing in mind the need for access to the building by the public. A balance must be struck between fortress–like security and permitting rights of access to information. Not all security precautions need apply to the whole building and where archives form only a section of a building this must be recognized. Selecting the appropriate level of security for each part is important, as overprovision results in irritation and delay, as well as possible reliance on installations where better or tighter procedures might provide a preferable solution. To ensure that the measures are appropriate a risk assessment must be carried out; no two archives will face exactly the same problems. A major issue, common to all archives, libraries and museums, is that staff are a greater risk to the organization and its holdings than members of the public. This is an uncomfortable truth, but one which must be taken into account when considering appropriate security measures and procedures.

Questions for security risk assessment[1]

The following questions might form the basis for a risk assessment but will be supplemented by others relating to particular circumstances.

- Are any roof lights or basement openings planned?
- What kind of external lighting/security lighting is planned?
- What kind of planting is planned round the building?
- Will internal CCTV be installed?
- Will intruder alarms be installed?
- Will a special store/cage for very important material be installed?
- How is staff access to the repositories to be controlled?
- Are cloakrooms for coats and bags of users included in the plans?
- Will security barriers be installed at the entrance to the reading rooms?

Have a security supremo!

Every archive should nominate one member of staff to be in charge of security. Some parent organizations will have security personnel on the staff, but they may be employed for general security rather than for the more specialized needs of an archive. The archive must be able to liaise with them and put forward its requirements. In an emergency it is also important that one person can take responsibility for security arrangements from a position of knowledge. Additionally, having one person in control reduces the risk of broadcasting the details of any security systems too widely.

External security is only as good as the construction of the building. Door and window frames should be strongly constructed with locks that conform to national standards;[2] alternatively, an electronic locking system must meet the same specifications. To minimize risk the building should have as few doors as possible to the outside. Any which are not regularly guarded, such as those giving access to a loading dock, should have steel shutters for security when not in use. Opening windows within easy reach of the ground, basement lights and any skylights or roof openings should have grilles or bars fitted to prevent access. Non-opening windows which are vulnerable should be glazed with toughened glass. Drainpipes can be fitted with spikes or treated with non-congealing paint if they appear to offer a means of access to upper floors. Where buildings adjoin the archive it is important to review possible security threats, such as the roof and any fire escapes.

What systems can be installed to assist security?

Consider any or all of the following security installations:

- Intruder alarms – these should be connected to an alarm monitoring centre or the local police station for rapid response. In Europe they must be installed according to BS EN 50131-1, and the procedures should be agreed with the police, who will need information about the archive to facilitate appropriate reaction in an emergency. Advice from the local crime prevention officer will ensure that the system installed is appropriate for the building and its location.
- Internal key-operated locks – these should also conform to national standards.[2] The disadvantage of this type of security system is that the keys themselves must be kept securely and rigorous procedures have to be in place to ensure that they are only taken out according to a schedule of need. The return of the keys also needs to be monitored and noted. In a small archive run by a handful of people this may be manageable, but safeguards and procedures still need to be in place. In a larger organization other options should be considered.
- Electronic locking system – this will be more satisfactory when the multiplicity of keys required is too large to manage. In such a system access permission can be changed easily, cards can be replaced without compromising the entire system and different degrees of security can be introduced within the building according to need. Against that, emergency methods of opening doors in the case of electronic failure or other emergency, such as fire, must be safeguarded. It will be important to ensure that the security system does not clash with fire regulations, which may require some doors to be open, or vice versa. In the archive disaster plan (see Chapter 7) it is worth considering the possible security risks if repository doors are opened automatically as a result of a fire alarm. Discussion of these issues with the local crime prevention and fire advisory staff is essential.
- CCTV – this is widely used in the search rooms of larger archives and libraries, where it provides valuable additional security, but resources are required for scrutinizing the monitors and ensuring the maintenance of the tapes and equipment. Recordings can be used in court as evidence if necessary. Each organization will need to decide how wide the coverage needs to be.
- Panic buttons – these can be installed in areas where there is any likelihood of staff working with or invigilating the public on their own. These are a last resort, a better solution being the presence of additional

members of staff, but buttons act as reassurance for staff in the case of an emergency.

What procedures need to be in place to maximize security?

Procedures to ensure that security issues are routinely observed are important. They should be immediately obvious to the public, reinforcing the image of the archive as an organization that takes security seriously.

Searches of bags and briefcases on entry and/or departure are carried out by many organizations; these must be carried out uniformly and consistently, irrespective of the status of the users. A search on entry is a routine physical measure to detect any weapons, sharp instruments such as knives or scissors, or explosives being carried into the building. Archives may appear to be fairly low on the list for this type of crime but they contain many documents which some might regard as prejudicial to a particular cause. Thieves intent on stealing documents have brought scissors and razor blades into archives and libraries undetected in the past, and incidents of paint throwing are not unknown. As public places, archives have a responsibility both to the safety of the documents and to their staff and visitors. Searches of bags on departure are carried out, sometimes randomly, in some archives, although stricter rules about how many papers and books can be taken into the reading rooms (see below) reduce the need for routine searches.

One measure rarely enforced is a strict search of all staff bags and briefcases on departure; this is short-sighted since, regrettably, staff present one of the more vulnerable parts of any security system. The vast majority participate willingly and with understanding but occasionally a problem arises. Random searches might be a solution to avoid the cost and irritation of daily searches. The introduction of any such measures must be undertaken with sensitivity.

Some archives and libraries restrict the numbers of papers and books that can be taken into the reading rooms and ban any bags, including handbags. The need for bag searches is greatly reduced if readers are required to show their papers on leaving the reading rooms; the inconvenience can be reduced by the provision of transparent carrier bags into which to put personal possessions, including laptops.

Lockers and secure coat hangers for readers are essential if they are required to leave bags, briefcases and outer garments behind when entering the reading room. A suitable location for the cloakroom will be near the entrance but within sight of staff or security personnel, who can keep an eye on it. The archive should require all readers to make use of the facility without exception; coats or jackets have been commonly used to conceal items being removed illegally.

Registration of readers is an essential security procedure, as well as providing evidence of reader usage, gender, distance travelled to the archive, etc. From the preservation point of view it offers a means of contacting readers if a query arises about material they have been looking at. Collaborative schemes with agreed security checks for identifying readers can reduce the need for separate identification at each archive.[3] Others require additional proofs or letters to identify readers from bona fide sources, and issue cards with a signature and sometimes a photograph of the reader. Very few allow readers in without some form of identity check, and those without systems that automatically record visits – in practice most archives – require a reader to sign in on each visit. This has the additional advantage of registering readers' presence in the building in case of an emergency evacuation.

Visitors badges should be issued to those who come to the archive but are not readers. They should be escorted through the building to their destination and accompanied when they leave. This identifies all those who may be in staff areas. Contractors should also wear identifying badges and should be invigilated if they are working anywhere within the storage areas or where documents are usually found. This can be difficult to resource but the consequences of failing to provide supervision can be disastrous. Film or radio crews should also be identified as visitors, and certainly need supervision. Security procedures will have to be outlined to both media crews and contractors to ensure they are aware of the nature of the building and its contents.

Whether staff wear an identification badge depends on the organization and its general procedures; it can be helpful to know who is staff and who is not, especially in a large organization, where staff turnover may be quite high.

Almost all archives require readers to order the documents they want to see by using duplicated slips or online ordering. This is a basic safeguard, both to record the movement of the documents from storage to the reading room and back and to record the frequency with which certain items are required. (This information can be used to decide on priorities for a surrogate programme, a further preservation measure; see Chapter 8.) Using either method, a duplicate slip is created to leave in the place of the document in the storage area, to be matched up when the document is returned bearing the original slip. This creates a procedure which should ensure that documents are returned to the correct location after use.

Invigilation, or supervision issues are high priority as a method of ensuring security in the reading room. This is resource-intensive, as it is not acceptable practice to have one member of staff invigilating while also trying to answer readers' enquiries and fetch and issue documents. It can be difficult for small archives struggling to provide a service for the public, but the risks must be recognized and managed. Too many lapses in invigilation have led to the theft of documents, even where security appears to be adequate. To aid invigilation, several options are available:

- Move the furniture so that sight lines throughout the room are clear for the supervisor.
- Raise the desk so that he or she can see over the whole area.
- Block off corners into which it is not possible to see.
- Install convex mirrors to see round corners.
- Install CCTV above the readers' desks.
- Limit the opening hours to times when sufficient staff are free to invigilate.

A location index is an essential tool for security, as is an up-to-date catalogue. Without this information an archive has no method of knowing what documents it holds or where they are. Relying on human memory for the latter is mistaken; at some point members of staff will retire or move elsewhere, changes will be required in the configuration of the storage area or additional storage will be required on an alternative site, changing the original layout. New accessions have to be fitted in and shelves changed. The corollary to having a location index is that all the shelves and bays must be identified in sequence. Many archives maintain an index on cards or lists; others are moving to an automated index, which is clearly easier to update. Clear responsibility for the index and ensuring changes are registered regularly is important.

A catalogue of all documents held in the archive is a basic access tool but is also essential for preservation; if the archive does not know what it holds it has no proof of custody. In addition, detailed information which enables readers to select the documents they require accurately reduces the movement of documents to the reading room and back, and avoids the necessity of handling multiple items in pursuit of one in particular. Both contribute to the long-term survival of the archives.

Accurate information about holdings is important in the event of a disaster: the catalogue should, ideally, be duplicated elsewhere for safety, but if not should be a priority for salvage. Quite apart from the value of a catalogue for identification purposes in such circumstances, the mere recording of a document or series in the custody of the archive can offer crucial information, such as ownership of land, pension rights or even identity to those who need it, even if the physical documents have disappeared.

Fire prevention, detection and suppression

The installation of systems and equipment to raise an alarm and initiate mechanical extinction of any fire is a policy matter for all archives. The degree of protection required will vary according to circumstances and budget; these are some of the options for prevention:

- suitable choice of non-combustible building materials
- suitable locations for any electrical equipment, plant or services
- attention to good procedures and maintenance of any equipment which might cause fire
- no-smoking rules within the building
- storing any chemicals or combustible material away from the archive building; these might include chemicals used in conservation or reprographic processes[4]
- isolating electrical equipment when the building is not in use
- removing any nitrate-based film to specialist storage.

What kind of detection systems are available?

Fire detection can be achieved with the installation of suitable equipment, again matched appropriately to the needs of the archive. Options vary:

- basic smoke detectors
- complex air aspirating systems using sampling pipes and automatic fire alarms
- early warning air sampling systems (which can detect invisible pre-combustion particles in the air using laser technology before a fire actually ignites)
- digital linear heat detection cable (similar to older methods using line-type detectors to detect thermal rise) installed in the building.

The advice of the local fire protection service will be important,[5] as will adhering to appropriate standards.[6] Additionally smoke control and heat system standards[7] must be incorporated into the brief for the architect, as well as the installation of a fire control panel to identify the seat of any problem. The location and type will need discussion with the fire protection service, the architect and the installation engineers.

All fire detection systems emit a warning alarm, which must be audible throughout the building. Installations must be checked rigorously before the building is commissioned and staff must be trained to use fire equipment situated throughout the building.

What extinguishers are available?

Systems to extinguish fires automatically have become increasingly sophisticated, and ever more expensive. Early opposition to sprinkler systems due to unreliability has to some extent reduced, although even some modern installations have their detractors. The ability to pinpoint the exact location of a fire as it ignites and to prevent it spreading is recognized as invaluable; it is merely a question of how it is best achieved with a minimum of risk.

Technological developments will extend the options; as in many other aspects of equipping archives, project managers need to be aware of what is being developed in other areas of industry to ensure that they are benefiting from research and innovation. It is also a question of resources, since the installation of such systems is not cheap. It is worth remembering that the incidence of fire in archives is relatively low and the risks need to be evaluated before opting for an extremely expensive system. Those fires which have occurred, barring the Norwich fire of 1994 (Kennedy, 1995, 3–6), have mostly been small and easily extinguished. Reliance on manual fire suppression, however, is dependent on vigilance and adequate training, together with proximity to the local fire station and expert help. Not all archives, and particularly those owned privately or part of a much larger organization, have these advantages.

So what are the options? There are two main options: gaseous systems and water-based systems.

Gaseous systems

These have been popular over the past 25 years but environmental issues have reduced their availability and popularity. They include the following:

- Halon, which disrupts combustion chemically, was installed by many archives hoping to avoid the hazards of unreliable water-based systems; however, the use of Halon has been phased out due to the presence in it of chlorofluorocarbons (Montreal Protocol, 1987).[8] The choice is now either adaptation of an existing system using an alternative gas or a complete replacement.
- Carbon dioxide has been used in the past. It works by replacing oxygen in the endangered area and consequently extinguishing the fire. However, the concentration required is much higher than the safety limits for the health of staff and for that reason it is not recommended.
- Argonite is sometimes used as an environmentally friendly replacement for Halon, being a mixture of 50% nitrogen and 50% argon; it reduces the oxygen concentration to 12.5%, a level acceptable to human

exposure over short periods but too low to maintain a fire.
- Inergen and other gaseous systems all suffer from the same problem: how best to store the gas, since substantial storage space is required for the canisters either in or close to the storage rooms. In addition the efficacy of any application is limited in large areas; each works best in air-tight compartments and needs efficient and safe methods of extraction.

Dorset Record Office decision about fire suppression

Dorset Record Office considered the options for replacement of its Halon fire-extinguishing system in 2001. The cost would have been £90–150,000. Options included:

- a water misting system – this would have been effective but disruptive to install in the existing premises
- a halocarbon agent gas system – this needs a high concentration of gas in the affected area, it can damage organic materials, it is hazardous to health and it requires cylinders to be stored in close proximity to seat of fire
- an inert agent gas system – this is safe, fast and cheap to replace; the major drawbacks are high pressure release and the large number of canisters required.

As a result a low-pressure Inergen (nitrogen, argon and carbon dioxide) system was chosen as a replacement to utilize existing pipework and ensure safety (Woods, 2002).

Low oxygen level system at Boston Spa

Low oxygen levels are being used at the British Library's new facility at Boston Spa in the UK, which provides additional storage capacity (260km) for 7 million items from the UK national collection. OxyReduct® creates an environment where fires cannot start, by continuously reducing the oxygen level in a closed area and by adding nitrogen to the air. The 21 metre high racking uses a fully-automated storage and retrieval system, thus reducing the need for people to access the storage area.

Water-based systems

These have become much more sophisticated in recent years, offering the options of directed flow wet or dry pipe systems, or misting. All are predicated on the requirement to create as little collateral damage as possible. Water is the greatest threat to traditional archival material, and severe damage and expensive salvage operations result from even moderate soaking. Wet and dry pipe systems have been installed successfully in several major archives internationally. Modern technology enables the seat of the fire to be pinpointed accurately and the nearest sprinkler(s) only to be activated.

Dry pipe systems have some disadvantages, which include:

- increased complexity due to the need for additional control equipment and air pressure supply components; proper maintenance is essential for reliability
- higher installation and maintenance costs
- lower design flexibility; strict requirements govern the maximum permitted size (typically 750 gallons) of individual dry-pipe systems
- increased fire response time; it can be up to 60 seconds before discharge
- increased corrosion potential; residual water may cause pipe corrosion and premature failure (this is not a problem with wet pipe systems where water is maintained constantly in piping).

Misting systems operate by producing a fine mist of water droplets of 5–40 microns which turn to steam and dilute the oxygen feeding the fire. This produces minimum damage to other material unaffected by the fire, especially if it is boxed.

Some archives will want to install different systems in different parts of their buildings. A tiered approach is likely to concentrate the most sophisticated system in the storage areas, with hand-held extinguishers in corridors and public areas. Training for staff in the use of these, together with alarm and evacuation procedures, is essential.

Water detection

If storage areas are near water supplies of any sort, the installation of detectors will provide early warning of slow leaks or build-up of moisture. Detectors can be placed on the floor adjacent to the area where the water source is located and will emit an alarm if the battery becomes wet; this relies on staff being present to react to the alarm. They can also be placed strategically under roofs, especially where there is a void which might not otherwise be checked frequently. Alternatively, alarm systems can be installed throughout the building and can cut off water supplies automatically. The choice is largely dictated by the cost and ease of installation.

Environmental issues

Environmental control is a major concern in all archive buildings and must be taken very seriously when new facilities are being planned or concern has been raised about current conditions; Chapter 6 deals with the issues and the best means of monitoring and controlling environmental conditions in storage areas. Chapter 10 covers the issues of environmental control in exhibitions. Elsewhere in the archive building temperature, relative humidity and light should be controlled as far as possible wherever original documents are being used or are out of their protective coverings.

Summary

This chapter has covered the essential issues of making the building and the operations within it secure, of ensuring fire protection and detection and preventing water ingress. These are crucial elements of a good preservation strategy for the archives stored within a building. Storage is the subject of the next chapter, outlining best practice and weighing up the advantages and disadvantages of different methods.

Notes and references

1   The UK Collections Link provides a wide range of advisory material on security for heritage organizations: www.collectionslink.org.uk/discover/security.
2   For example BS 3621 in the UK.
3   Some county record offices in the UK collaborate to register readers on the County Archive Research Network (CARN) system, guaranteeing entry to participating offices on the basis of a registered proof of identity at one. CARN is owned and administered by the Archives and Records Association (UK and Ireland).
4   In the UK this should be in conformity with the Control of Substances Hazardous to Health regulations, 2002 (COSHH).
5   Under the Regulatory Reform (Fire Safety) Order 2005 in the UK, the responsible person must carry out a fire safety risk assessment and implement and maintain a fire management plan.
6   For example BS 5839-9: 2011 in the UK.
7   For example BS EN 12101-6: 2005 in the UK.
8   The Montreal Protocol stipulated that the production and consumption of compounds that deplete ozone in the stratosphere – chlorofluorocarbons (CFCs), halons, carbon tetrachloride and methyl chloroform – were to be phased out by 2000 (2005 for methyl chloroform). See country-specific regulation.

6

Managing archival storage

Introduction

The building itself may be the most important safeguard for the archives it holds but that alone is insufficient; they require additional care within this envelope. Even if the building itself is not perfect, good storage space, well maintained and managed, will make a big difference to survival. Many archives face the fact that their holdings include different media which, according to many national standards should be stored in differing temperatures and environmental conditions. For many it is impractical or impossible to comply with the requirements; compromises have to be made. In all circumstances, the types of materials stored and any external or internal factors which may affect them need to be considered, the risks need to be assessed and the best solution in the circumstances adopted.

This chapter looks in more detail at:

- why environmental conditions matter
- what needs to be controlled
- mould and how to prevent it
- measuring and monitoring conditions
- special arrangements
- costs
- shelving, racking and plan chest specifications
- boxes and enclosure specifications for different archival materials
- equipment needed
- possible future storage developments.

Why do environmental conditions matter?

Control of the environmental conditions within any archive, library or museum is crucial to the survival of the material stored within it.[1] If the conditions are inimical the material will disintegrate even more quickly than as the result of inevitable natural decay. The purpose of controlling the temperature, relative humidity, ambient light, ultraviolet light and air quality is to ensure that such deterioration is retarded to a point at which the material is as stable as possible. It is a preventative measure which, if successful, will largely avoid the need for active intervention by conservators. Failure to maintain appropriate storage conditions may lead, among other things, to brittle paper, outbreaks of mould, fading of photographic prints or damage by particulate deposits.

There is general agreement that the more stable the conditions, the better the material will survive. Evidence suggests that even where the temperature and relative humidity levels are less than ideal, stability has been a major factor in survival. The appropriate storage levels for mixed media objects present wider challenges. Fluctuations put stress on the fibres of paper and parchment and on photographic and film emulsions, not to mention the leather or cloth used in bookbinding. Achieving such stability, particularly for a range of archival materials, requires constant monitoring and vigilance.

What needs to be controlled?

A recent report by the Preservation Advisory Centre (2013) identified weakness in the provision of environmental monitoring and control as one of the major areas of risk to affect the survival and future potential use of archival and library materials in the UK. The elements to be monitored and controlled fall into several categories: relative humidity, temperature, light and pollution.

Relative humidity

The moisture content of the air is expressed in relation to 100% saturation. Thus 75% relative humidity (rh) is three-quarters of the potential saturation that the air can hold. Materials such as paper, parchment, textiles, photographs and film all absorb water and are affected by the ambient relative humidity. The main objective of any system to control it must be to maintain a stable percentage level inside the storage areas, irrespective of exterior fluctuations.

Recommendations in national standards for the optimum relative humidity in archive storage vary slightly according to country and regions of the world. For material rarely accessed a period of acclimatization is recommended before use. All stress the importance of maintaining stability.

Main storage conditions should be achieved either by appropriate construction design (see Chapter 4) or by air conditioning (see below); many repositories will use a combination of the two, relying on the air-conditioning system to fine-tune the temperature and relative humidity and to provide additional air filtering and circulation.[2]

A major threat posed by relative humidity above 65% within a storage area is mould growth (discussed below).

Temperature

This is expressed in degrees Celsius (°C) or Fahrenheit (°F). The main objective in archive storage areas is to maintain a stable temperature consistent with the level of access to the materials. Cycling temperatures cause stress to the materials being stored and over time will contribute to deterioration.

PAS 198: 2012, Specification for managing environmental conditions for cultural collections

The rates of many deterioration mechanisms (chemical, biological and physical) increase as temperature increases. Changes in temperature within a collection space can also cause deterioration. Given the different dependencies on temperature of these mechanisms, and their differing impact on collection items, a universal temperature range and permissible fluctuations for collections cannot be specified. Attempts to establish a universal safe zone for all collection items by providing conditions required only by sensitive collection items can result in unsafe conditions for atypical collections, as well as leading to unjustifiably increased use of energy.

Light

The amount of visible light received per unit of surface area is measured in lux (1 lux = 1 lumen/square metre). One lux is equal to approximately 0.09290 candle power, and exposure is measured in lux hours. Light damage is cumulative, depending on paper quality, the ambient temperature and the intensity of the light. Ultraviolet light (UV) has shorter wavelengths than visible light and the effect of UV is more damaging to paper and other archival materials than visible light. Sunlight may contain as much as 25% UV light, while fluorescent bulbs may emit 3–7% UV.

Exhibitions, by their nature, require greater exposure to light: this is frequently interpreted as permitting a maximum of 18,000 lux/hours (360 hours at 50 lux) for sensitive materials such as inks and dyes.

Pollution

Pollution is measured by particle deposit. Achieving good air quality, particularly in built-up areas, may necessitate the installation of full or partial air conditioning. PAS 198: 2012 advises that an organization puts in place a clear process to evaluate, monitor and subsequently mitigate the negative impacts of pollutants to the collection materials.

Mould: why is it such a threat?

An outbreak of mould seriously stains and weakens the structure of paper, parchment, audiovisual material or magnetic tapes, and obliterates text. Although not toxic in itself the mould can cause hazardous health conditions for staff with chest problems, asthma or other respiratory conditions. Within a storage area it can spread very quickly, particularly in conditions which favour its growth. There is no known way of eliminating such an outbreak; the spores are airborne and ever present, and will flourish and multiply if the conditions are favourable. Chemicals are not effective as a deterrent or a cure, and the damage to the paper is irreversible.

Mould consists of fungal spores (*mycelia*) which take thousands of different forms. It appears as a growth forming on vegetable or animal matter, commonly as a downy or furry coating, associated with decay or dampness. Viewed under a microscope it appears in a complex web formation. It spreads by releasing spores into air currents or by adherence to other objects. Much of the damage caused is due to the digestive enzymes excreted by the fungi. To grow, mould requires a level of 65% relative humidity or more; temperature is less crucial as some moulds will flourish at low temperatures, although freezing will cause them to become dormant. Poor air circulation encourages mould owing to the consequent rise in moisture levels; less evaporation takes place if air is stagnant. Mildew, often used incorrectly as an alternative term, is a distinct form of mould. Poor standards of cleaning, resulting in dirt, dust and debris build-ups will present a further attraction for many moulds.

What can be done about mould in the storage area?

If an outbreak of mould does occur, take the following steps immediately it is detected:

- Insist that all staff wear masks (to the appropriate FFP rating)[3] and protective clothing while in contact with mould.
- Remove all affected material to alternative, well ventilated,

temperature- and humidity-controlled storage; at the very least, remove to different racking where the environmental conditions are known to be stable and the relative humidity is below 65%.

- Determine, and put right, the cause of the outbreak; it may be the result of a damp exterior wall, a leaking pipe or radiator, a hole in the ceiling or even condensation from uninsulated walls. Dehumidifiers may reduce the amount of moisture in a small confined space but are not a long-term solution. They need to be emptied regularly; this is a problem overnight or at the weekend unless they are plumbed into a drain. Cold-air fans will help air circulation.
- Spread the affected material out to dry, turning leaves of books frequently or standing volumes upright and fanning out the pages to improve air circulation; cold-air fans will help.
- When dry, use a soft brush or a low-suction vacuum cleaner to remove the dry mould, brushing it away from the centre of books and away from the body. Cleaning must be carried out in a well ventilated area, away from other collection material and any staff. Alternatively an archival cleaning machine can be used (see Figure 6.1 for an example; Bassaire Trolley), although this is an expensive piece of equipment for a small archive.[4] It provides a flat surface surrounded by air extraction gullies that blow all harmful spores away from the staff doing the cleaning.

- Ensure that the original area affected has dried out and that the environmental conditions are stable – it may take time for an equilibrium to be established.
- Wash down all affected shelves; any fungicide must conform with national regulations.
- Return the archival material to its original storage area, re-boxing it if necessary.

Figure 6.1 Bassaire trolley ([© Bassaire Limited)

Measuring and monitoring temperature and humidity

Good building maintenance is the most important first step towards maintaining appropriate environmental conditions. Perimeter walls, the roof and any drainage pipes, gullies, gutters and roof ventilators must be inspected regularly and repairs made promptly. Daily monitoring of the relative humidity and temperature of the storage area (at regular times) will build up a picture of seasonal variations in conditions. This is most effective when the data is compared with external, ambient conditions that will reflect seasonal variations; this information will then enable the calculation of the building's insulating efficiency and capacity. In any large building, or building shared with others, maintenance staff will be responsible for the environmental conditions; these are key staff with whom archive staff responsible for preservation must have regular contact. It is unlikely that they will have received much, if any, training in the importance of stability of conditions in archival storage areas, but their co-operation is essential if the archive is to achieve national standards. Single-building archives may have their own maintenance staff, who should be included in all discussions about environmental standards and how to maintain them. Communication is essential to foster understanding and support.

A modern air-conditioned building should incorporate a building maintenance system (BMS) to monitor many aspects of the condition of the interior of the building and control them at levels to which the system has been set. It downloads information electronically at a set point in time for monitoring by the maintenance staff. Control of ordinary office conditions may be easier to achieve in this way than control of conditions required for specialized storage. Purpose-built archives with air conditioning should have separate mechanical systems for their storage areas, set to the standards and parameters required. However, it is essential that independent monitoring is also carried out to ensure that the BMS, or any other system, is working properly. It is advised that the person with responsibility for preservation invests in a standalone monitoring system, which will enable them to collect and interpret environmental data in addition to readings from the BMS and allow an independent view.

Knowledge of the equipment needed to undertake this − whirling hygrometers, thermohygrographs and radio-telemetric measuring instruments or digital loggers − forms part of the training of conservators, and monitoring of conditions is therefore often regarded as their responsibility. It may be equally sensible for those in charge of the storage to take responsibility, since they are regularly in the area and can recognize problems more quickly as they arise. Irrespective of who takes responsibility for it, a range of equipment is required; more or less may be needed, depending on the size of the institution, the expertise of the operators and the budget available. In general terms, the customer will find that the more expensive the equipment, the more accurate the data. It is important that static measuring equipment is not moved, as readings from the same place will be necessary for comparison year on year.

Radio-telemetry systems (see Figure 6.2 for an example of a radio receiver as part of a radio-telemetry system) are used by some organizations, principally museums and galleries, to monitor environmental conditions in a number of buildings (and in multiple locations); the information is downloaded in real time and displayed at one central control point or accessed via a web browser. These systems have not always proved adaptable to archives and libraries, where the building mass and the use of metal shelving sometimes interfere with the radio signals. However, there have been significant improvements, especially for a multi-site facility where it is important to keep a constant watch on environmental conditions in different locations.

Simple data loggers (see Figure 6.3 for an example) are an alternative solution which can be placed around a building in agreed locations, the information they collect can be downloaded regularly on to a computer. They require little maintenance except calibration, but some of the cheaper models do not last for more than about two years before needing replacement. Some display the current conditions on an LED screen so can be spot checked by staff – while this is a useful function it does not compare with the immediate impact of a chart showing the fluctuations over a number of days. For this, the information has to be downloaded very frequently; charts and/or graphs can then be compiled in other proprietary software. It is vital to ensure that an annual budget is in place to calibrate all of the units.

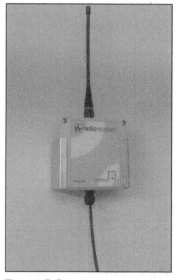

Figure 6.2 Radio telemetric system

Figure 6.3 A data logger (Available from www.pel.eu)

Thermohygrographs are less commonly used to monitor environmental conditions as new technologies become established (see Figure 6.4 over the page). These measure and record conditions on a renewable weekly or monthly graph, rolled around a drum. The latter is driven by a battery, or electronically, and revolves to enable a 24-hour record to be taken. It has to be calibrated regularly and the graph paper must be replaced at the appropriate intervals. Placed and kept in agreed locations, these are a valuable method of recording environmental conditions on a regular basis with the additional advantage that they can be monitored by anyone who has been given basic instruction.

Figure 6.4 A thermohygrograph

Properly maintained and calibrated they should last for many years.

For more constrained budgets, simpler equipment includes hair hygrometers for reading the current relative humidity and thermometers for reading the temperature. An electronic hand-held reader (see Figure 6.5), will give a reading of both temperature and relative humidity. The latter, however, have to be used with care as they take time to adjust as they are moved from location to location. While they require calibrating regularly the disadvantage of all three is the time needed to take readings on a regular basis, since none are automatic and different staff may interpret the readings with variable accuracy. Staff time will be needed to log conditions individually at a set moment each day in order to record the daily and seasonal fluctuations which occur in most environmental systems. This is time-consuming and difficult to sustain, and if more sophisticated equipment can be afforded it is worth the investment.

The whirling hygrometer (see Figure 6.5) has traditionally been used to establish the base against which any of the other instruments for measuring relative humidity are calibrated. This hygrometer consists of two bulbs, one wet and the other dry, with calibrated tubes; the former is enclosed in fine mesh which is itself kept wet from the reserve of distilled water poured into the container at the bottom. The hygrometer is whirled round in the area to be monitored and the resultant readings on the wet and dry tubes read off

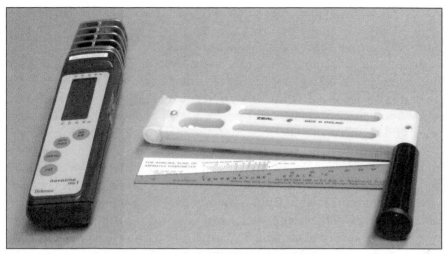

Figure 6.5 Electronic hand-held reader and whirling hygrometer

against a hygrometric table supplied by the manufacturer. This establishes the actual relative humidity and all other instruments should be calibrated to the same norm. However, the use of data loggers and calibration kits has enabled most institutions to establish accurate and consistent data.

Measuring and monitoring light levels

Light causes damage to paper, bindings, plastics and many archival inks, emulsions and pigments. It causes photochemical deterioration, due to the reactions of molecules to light energy, resulting in weakening of fibres, fading and change of colour. Light levels in any one area are measured by battery or digital lux meters.

How can light levels be reduced?

These can be regulated in storage areas by:

- designing the rooms without windows
- covering existing windows with dense material to exclude daylight
- installing treated window glass or covering glass with special film to cut out UV light
- installing filters on fluorescent tube light fittings to cut out UV light
- installing infrared sensors in storage areas to turn off lights after movement has ceased

• boxing and wrapping all material so that it is not exposed to light.

Any or all solutions are possible. When archival materials are necessarily out in the light, in the reading rooms or at staff desks where the visible light levels may be in excess of 300 lux, they should only be removed from their boxes or protective wrapping when they are required, and they should never be allowed to lie out in sunlight. Strong light from photographers' cameras or television cameras should be kept to a minimum. Parchment and photographic materials, in particular, are very prone to react to the heat generated by such cameras and can be seen to curl at the edges. Volumes must be kept closed until the moment at which it is necessary to film the text. The effect of light on textiles or paint is measured by the widely used Blue Wool test, which uses eight levels of colour with increasing resistance to fading to determine the degree of damage. Any archive with textile holdings, especially if they are on display, should monitor them carefully.

Measuring and monitoring pollution levels

Pollution often refers either to air quality or to particulate deposit, or both; the implications for archives, particularly for photographic, audiovisual and electronic materials, are serious. Additionally, the risks posed by pollution from outside a building, from within a building and from the air inside storage containers differ. In general the damage caused by pollution to archives which are well stored is unlikely to be as great as flood or fire, but it is often more insidious as it is less obvious to the naked eye. The particular circumstances of each archive must be assessed to determine the level of risk.

Air quality and the particulate deposit level inside an archive building, whether within the storage area or more generally, is very dependent on the location and prevailing weather conditions as well as the quality of the construction. Pollutants may include car exhaust fumes, industrial contaminants or prevailing climatic conditions such as salt-laden winds. The last-named can introduce pollutants from some distance so must be taken into account when a site is chosen. The HVAC (heating, ventilating and air conditioning) engineer rather than the archivist will be the expert as regards air-conditioning plants and will undertake technical measurement and monitoring; the archivist will need to develop a close liaison with the building specialist to ensure effective consultation and input. The archivist must understand about the dangers posed by poor air quality and particulate deposit, but is more likely to have to argue for a construction site away from pollutants, to monitor the use of appropriate building materials or finishes and to ensure the quality of display cases. Poor air quality and high particulate deposit levels inside containers are likely to result from the materials themselves or from the materials used to construct the container or display cabinet.

Effect of oxidizing gases on photographs

At the Norwegian Museum of Photography – Preus Fotomuseum – an exhibition of the Norwegian photographer Marie Høeg's work was curated in 1997. The prints were copied onto contemporary fibre-base paper, after the original glass-plate negatives from around 1900. The exhibition travelled to other museums and galleries in Norway, and at one museum a frame glass broke, and therefore was completely removed. For unknown reasons, instead of replacing the glass the picture was simply exhibited without glass, which is why this print was openly exposed to the surrounding air while the other prints were protected by their framing. That exhibition took place during a hot summer, and after a few weeks all high-density areas in the openly exposed print were faded to a brown/yellow colour. It turned out that the gallery walls were newly painted with oil paint, and a high concentration of oxidizing gases had probably been present in the air.

(Ryhl-Svendsen, 1999, 211–15)

Those measuring pollution in an archive are likely to concentrate on the quality of the air in the main storage area. If film or photographic materials are stored separately it is worth measuring the oxidizing gases, including acetic acid and nitrogen oxides, which may be the result of a breakdown of either cellulose nitrate or cellulose acetate film. If they are stored with the other materials the levels may be more difficult to detect.[5] In a modern building, the BMS will monitor air quality, its movement within the archive building and its regular replacement. If the building is in the UK and is air-conditioned, the specification for the storage areas should aim to comply with PD 5454: 2012. Pollution sampling, another method of determining the extent of damage being caused, is usually carried out by experts, as it requires laboratory equipment for analysis. Recommended exposure levels for heritage institutions have been published (Blades et al., 2000; Thomson, 1986)[6] but archives are usually better protected than libraries or museums, since items are normally stored in containers or wrappings. Pollution within boxes or enclosures has been proved to be lower than in the surrounding area. In general, the ambient conditions act as a buffer to external agents, strengthening the argument for enclosing and protecting all formats within the archive storage area.

IMPACT: Innovative Modelling of Museum Pollution and Conservation Thresholds

This major European research project, led by the Centre for Sustainable Heritage at University College London, set out to predict concentrations of damaging traffic-generated pollutants on the basis of publicly available pollution monitoring data outdoors and some basic data about the building envelope. The main outcome, a web-based indoor pollution prediction tool, available at www.ucl.ac.uk/sustainableheritage-save/impact, enables users with minimal technical expertise to quickly evaluate risks to their collections associated with SO_2, NO_2 and O_3.

Recent collection management guidance (BSI PAS198) requires collecting institutions to seasonally assess the risk due to pollution. In situations where there is publicly available traffic-generated pollution data from local monitoring stations, the IMPACT approach is very suitable as the first step in the assessment process and it may even remove the need to make actual pollution measurements. These may be necessary, however, if a real risk is identified, and local, time-consuming and often resource-intensive monitoring may need to be put in place. However, effective environmental legislation led to significantly reduced pollution levels across much of the UK, and long-term predictions are that these will continue to decrease.

How can pollution levels be reduced?

Avoiding the causes of pollution is the best policy; however, if a strategy is required the most appropriate measures for the degree of pollution experienced must be selected. Many of the measures are common-sense and should be part of an overall strategy to maintain good environmental conditions.

Assess the risks, including:

- the orientation of the building
- wind direction
- location in relation to industrial activity or major roads with heavy traffic
- proximity to the sea or river
- existing types of material within the archive
- indoor plants within the building.

Test:

- any building construction materials for possible emission of pollutants
- any new materials used for enclosures for archives
- any incoming material for possible risks – photographic materials are both potential polluters and at particular risk, so always examine them on arrival and separate any materials which might off-gas.

Decide on an appropriate strategy, such as:

- achieving passive control with natural ventilation
- blocking up gaps round windows, doors, pipes, ventilators, etc.
- fitting mesh to any windows or openings which cannot be closed
- ensuring that fresh air intakes are not adjacent to polluted areas or heat
- increasing the reactivity of surfaces by using different finishes
- boxing or wrapping all items
- controlling ventilation and pollution with carbon dioxide sensors and variable speed fans (the concentration of CO_2, largely produced by people, indicates the degree of ventilation required)
- using portable or temporary filtration units in small defined areas
- introducing localized air conditioning with carbon filtration to storage areas only
- providing air conditioning with carbon filtration for the entire building (installed plants will automatically have facilities for washing the air to clean it, both from exterior and interior intakes, the latter forming the re-cycled air, but they will not necessarily have carbon filtration; particulate matter can only properly be controlled by a filter system[7] with coarse and fine filters to catch particulates and activated carbon filters to reduce gaseous pollution).

Air conditioning comes last on the list as the most expensive and complicated solution; it is not advised in any area where the power supply is unreliable or the technical expertise is not available to maintain it. Additionally, the investment in energy-hungry plant, which also has environmental impacts, is unsustainable, especially in existing and future economic climates. In many parts of the world, archives have to manage without it.

Special arrangements

Specialized storage, particularly cold temperature storage, is increasingly used for rarely accessed material. The most notable example is the Norwegian National Library Legal Deposit Department at Mo I Rana, just south of the Arctic Circle. The store has been created within a mountain where a constant temperature of 8°C/46°F and rh of 35% is maintained, albeit with mechanical intervention to ensure the stability and cleanliness of the area. While paper undoubtedly benefits from such conditions, the benefits for photographic and film materials are even greater. Research by the Image Permanence Institute in Rochester, NY, has shown that reducing the storage temperature of moving image film from 20°C to 14°C (68°F − 58°F) can double its life expectancy. Similar conclusions led the English Heritage Archive (owned and managed by English Heritage) to build a dedicated cold store for its photographic collection at Swindon; no direct access is allowed and any materials required for copying are slowly acclimatized to room temperature over 24 hours. Conversely, they are slowly re-acclimatized to the cold conditions before being returned to store, thus minimizing the danger of condensation and consequent damage to the material.

Shared accommodation is a possibility, especially for material which requires special conditions such as the cold storage outlined above, or simply as a means of releasing space in collaborating institutions. To undertake this requires a degree of trust between partners (Dumbleton, 2005), but it can be very beneficial if undertaken in the right spirit and with adequate safeguards. It may ensure the survival of vulnerable materials, which can thus be stored in the right conditions rather than put at risk by continuing incorrect storage conditions. CAVAL,[8] a consortium of libraries in Victoria, Australia, has been operating a number of joint services for over 25 years, including a Centre for Archive and Research Materials – a single-copy repository for low-use research materials owned collectively by the store. Kept at a constant temperature and relative humidity, it offers a model for shared storage.

TNA and DeepStore, Wilmslow, UK

Pressure on space in the UK's National Archives after the closure of its off-site record store at Hayes in 2003 led to consideration of off-site storage in disused salt mines in Cheshire. The space available was remote from current mining operations, was environmentally stable (the natural conditions are 14° C /57.2°F and 62% rh, brought closer to BS 5454 – now PD 5454: 2012 – standard by mechanical intervention) and was very secure. A pilot study suggested that although rarely used material, or that which was available in other formats, would form the main bulk of the deposit, it was possible to provide a three-day service for readers despite the distance from Kew, the main archive site for public records in the UK. Other archives and libraries, as well as organizations such as hospitals requiring storage for semi-current records, had already made use of the facility, which had proved very reliable. Accordingly, 25 km of shelving of records were transferred to the safekeeping of DeepStore, the owners, overseen by the staff of The National Archives.

Off-site storage is another solution adopted by some archives and libraries and is likely to become increasingly popular as remote access becomes cheaper and more feasible. High costs in inner-city areas can be reduced dramatically if rarely used material, or material which has already been copied, is stored in cheaper areas of the country. Care must be taken to ensure that the normal requirements of a repository are specified and adhered to and that the environmental and security provisions of the storage facility are to the appropriate standard, to avoid the assumption that lower grade accommodation is acceptable. Disaster planning specifications will need to include this type of facility and the institution's expectations appropriately specified in the contract.[9]

How can comparative costs be assessed?

Costing storage is a notoriously tricky business but, as indicated previously, is becoming a significant factor as archives have to store greater quantities of material in an increasing variety of formats. This issue has become more urgent as the vast quantity of digital material requiring storage grows rapidly. Allied to this is the cost of storing multiple versions of original material, a factor rarely taken into account when surrogates are created.

Stephen Chapman (2003) compared the variables in the cost of storing different types of surrogates at the Harvard Depository and the OCLC (Online Computer Library Center) Digital Archive in the USA; both are managed storage facilities with accompanying services, not just storage areas. He concluded that storage costs for digital images were 1.5 times higher than for original volumes and 2.5 times higher than for storing microfilm.

Jonas Palm (2006) looked at the costs of storing and servicing electronic data in Sweden (checking on data integrity, backup procedures, restoring information, automatic transfer to new tapes, etc.); his conclusions were similar to those of Chapman, since the element of servicing, which involves the unpredictable future cost of employing staff, must be included in the cost of storing digital material. These two studies, while not necessarily replicable everywhere, should lead to a sober reappraisal of comparative costs elsewhere.

Other aspects of storage costs, involving rent and the purchase of storage units or shelving for traditional types of material, are more predictable.

Shelving, racking and plan chest specifications

Shelving issues in archives are more complicated than perhaps they appear at first sight. Accurate measurement of holdings is surprisingly difficult given the variation in the size of the materials, whether boxed or not, and many archives only come to grips with these issues when they are required to move from one repository to another. Issues needing resolution when assessing shelving include:

* decisions on the measurement format – linear or cubic metres
* the orientation of boxes

- the spatial implications of reboxing/repacking
- the necessity to leave space for accruals
- the potential effect of an electronic location database to rationalize space requirements
- variation in size of boxes or volumes
- ease of shelf adjustment
- the width of aisles to accommodate trolleys
- the width of aisles to ensure that outsize material can be extracted safely
- the height of the shelving
- decisions on the installation of static or mobile shelving.

Shelving

This must be stable and accessible – self-evident perhaps, but not always achieved, particularly if it has not been designed for the storage area but imported from elsewhere. Opinions differ on the merits of steel or wooden construction; steel is more common but will fail in a fire if the temperature rises above 500°C/932°F; wood may emit harmful volatile acids but can be treated with an anti-inflammatory coating and sealed to prevent gas emissions. It is more likely to char than burn in a fire, given the density of material stored on it. An inert polyester powder coating as a finish to steel shelving to avoid off-gassing from oil-based paints must be specified. All shelving or racking should be at least 75 mm away from any outside walls to avoid damp and increase air circulation; bottom shelves should be not less than 150 mm above floor level to avoid damage in case of flooding.

The choice between static and mobile shelving will be determined by the need for additional shelving, the load-bearing capacity of the floor and the shape of the storage area. Weight imposed by mobile shelving is proportionately heavier than that imposed by static shelving, and one square metre of records can weigh 500–600 kg, plus the weight of the shelving itself. In terms of force exerted this can equate to 10–12 kN/m². Manufacturers claim that capacity is increased by up to 50% due to the need for gangways being minimized. Clearly this varies according to the height of the shelves and type of materials stored, and the choice will often be dictated by circumstance. Estimate the total weight per metre (the standard shelving length) by weighing a sample of full boxes or volumes.

In accordance with most national standards, both mobile and static shelving should be made from carbon steel, with rolled edges and sufficient strength for the anticipated load; the details should be agreed between the archive and the manufacturer according to individual requirements. The uprights should not impede withdrawal of the material (avoid angled uprights for this reason) and the shelf ends should be open, or consist of perforated panels to permit air circulation. The shelving should be divided into bays 1m in width and of sufficient depth to avoid the stored material protruding over the edge, with cross-bracing at the back. Several different depths of shelving are likely to be required to maximize storage space; double-depth shelving can be created by placing bays back to back, but cross-bracing must be installed carefully to avoid damage to items when they are extracted. Standardizing on box sizes should make it possible to reduce the variety of shelf depths to two or three.

Static racking for film of any sort, or audio or photographic materials, is desirable, as the weight is considerable; if mobile shelving is used this must be taken into account. Mobile shelving is not recommended for shellac discs or glass plate negatives due to their fragility; they should be placed vertically on the shelf in appropriate packaging (see below).

Small items such as wax cylinders, CDs, DVDs, mini discs or tapes are best stored in boxes within drawers in steel cabinets, which support them and prevent too much movement.

Mobile shelving runs on tracks which are best installed when the storage area is constructed, but can be a later addition if another floor is laid on top of the structural floor to support the track. The penalty is that the former may be higher than the latter and therefore makes the use of trolleys more difficult. It is essential that the track floor is level to permit a smooth run for the shelves, carrying as they do a heavy load. The load must be determined in discussion with the manufacturers to ensure that the tracks are sufficiently strong and will not deflect in use. The operation can be either manual or electronic, although many archives and libraries prefer the manual system since it is less prone to faults. Anti-tip devices should be fitted to prevent damage to the documents or boxes stored on the shelves if there is any danger of shaking. Section 6.12.5.3 of PD 5454: 2012 recommends fitting such devices to all shelving. The whole of section 12 in PD 5454: 2012 provides detailed guidance on shelving. It is particularly important that the boxes or contents of the shelves do not protrude beyond the edge of mobile shelving, to avoid damage when the mobile shelves are closed up. Safety devices between the bays prevent injury to staff if an attempt is made to close the bays while others are retrieving material. If a sprinkler system is fitted as a fire suppressant it will be necessary to have an automatic parking mode for the bays, positioning them not less than 25mm apart, so that the system will be effective should a fire break out when the archive is unstaffed. Shelving should be positioned so that it is at right angles to any strip lighting, to ensure illumination in all the aisles. The need for future servicing and possible additional components should be considered when choosing a manufacturer.

Volumes can be stored on either type of shelving, although the stability of any mobile shelving needs to be tested before using it for this purpose. Store volumes of the same size together to avoid light or flood damage to unprotected covers. Ensure that volumes are upright, using book ends to support the last volume if they do not fill a complete shelf; this avoids distortion of the binding and of the text block (the *National Trust Manual of Housekeeping*, 2005, provides more detailed guidance; section 42, 6.8 to 6.11).

Storage for flat and rolled items

These can be stored in different ways according to the available space and budget. Plan chests are preferable as they support large flat maps and documents, but are risky if the drawers are filled too full. Racking for rolled items is an alternative, provided the rolled items are not piled up too high and that the depth of the racking fully supports the roll length.

Steel plan chests (see Figure 6.6) with shallow drawers should be sited as close to the consultation area as possible, to make production of maps and plans to the public easy and prevent damage when they are moved around; special trolleys can be used for transport if necessary. Vertical hanging cabinets are not normally recommended for archival material, as they do not provide adequate support, introducing the danger of distortion. They may be used if no other solution is available but full-length support must be provided at the

Figure 6.6 Steel plan chest

top of the item with attached guards. Plans, posters and large flat items can be further protected in archival quality or, at the very least, acid-free card enclosures/folders or in inert polyester sleeves.

Chests should be fitted with an anti-locking device to prevent more than one drawer being opened at the same time, and the drawers themselves should have safety stops to prevent them being pulled too far out. Preferably each item should have its individual drawer, but if that is not possible the number of items in each drawer must be limited; ensure that an integral restraining flap keeps them flat. Chests can be banked on top of one another but the difficulty of extracting material safely from a height normally precludes more than a double banking; special safety measures must be introduced for any higher stack. Wooden plan chests may present problems when stacked one on top of the other, as most carcasses are not rigid enough to offset the combined weight, which causes the lower sections to bow; this can result in drawers that cannot be opened and/or closed. Wide aisles are needed to enable the drawers to be opened fully.

Racking for rolled materials should support the material fully. Store the item parallel to the front of the shelf if it is too long for storage at right angles; racking such as this can be at an angle to the wall of not more than 10° to prevent items rolling off. Alternatively troughs can be constructed, also running parallel to the front of the racking since extracting any item as large as this will probably require more than one person for safety. The back of the racking should be solid and not less than 150 mm high.

Figure 6.7 Wall-mounted racking © London Metropolitan Archives

What kind of boxes and enclosures should be used?

Archives need to budget for boxes and enclosures on a regular basis, whether for new accessions being brought in or for the replacement of torn or damaged containers. If a large number of boxes are required it is worth discussing the economies of space and bulk ordering in using flat packs, which can be made up as required. The main requirements for boxes are that:

- they are appropriate to the size of the material they will contain
- they are sturdy enough to withstand constant handling
- they are constructed from inert or non–damaging materials
- they offer protection without adding unacceptable bulk to the total shelf length of the storage area.

They should be constructed from materials which are acid–free, lignin–free and undyed; if these specifications cannot be met any covering or box is better than none but a budget should be established for replacement items of better quality over time. All should be capable of being marked clearly and permanently for identification, especially if they become immersed in water.[10] Inside the boxes folders should also be archival quality (acid free as a baseline); ideally these should have been used by the parent body when the records were created but may have to be replaced if they are sub-standard. If there are spacers in upright boxes they should also be of an archival quality to ensure that no degrading products are stored close to collection materials.

Boxes for unfolded paper and parchment with separate lids offer better protection and are usually more durable than those with flaps; opinion is divided as to whether they should have ventilation holes but for strength and better protection from water those with solid sides are preferable (see Figure 6.8). The micro-climate created within the box acts as a significant buffer for the protection of the contents from fluctuations in temperature and relative humidity in the storage area. To avoid rust there should be no metal closures or stapling; solid brass stitching is, however, acceptable.

Maps and plans should be stored flat if possible but if they are too long they must be rolled and supported along their whole length (see Figure 6.7). They should be rolled freely but not too tightly round the outside of a tube made of archival quality board (never inside), and then protected by a dust-proof wrapping or bag. Alternatively, square section acid-free cardboard tubes – 'cube tubes' (see Figure 6.9) – can be used to store rolled materials as these have sufficient space for the item to be extracted safely; these stack neatly on top of each other.

Seals are a problem if they are attached to documents; individual boxes with recessed Plastazote[11] or inert foam supports for the seals are the best, if

Figure 6.8 Archival boxes

Figure 6.9 Archival cube tube

most expensive, solution (see Figure 6.10). Protection for the seal can also be provided by inert wadding and individually made polyester envelopes.

Microfilm spools should be chemically inert (polyester, poly-ethylene or polypropylene) and canisters for cinefilm should be of tin or inert polypropylene plastic. Cinefilm spools should be as for

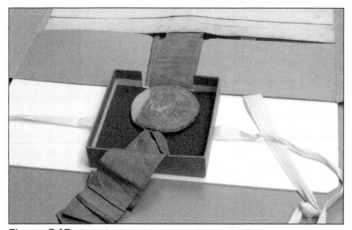

Figure 6.10 Attached seal in protective packaging

microfilm and the diameter of the core should be 75 or 100mm to reduce cold curl (adjustment of the polymer film base to shape over a long period). Place the canisters flat on top of each other, in piles no more than 300 mm high.

Research on storage of cellulose acetate film

In the 1990s Jean-Louis Bigourdan and James M. Reilly from the Image Permanence Institute (IPI) worked on a preservation strategy for acetate film based on an environmental assessment and condition survey. They investigated the effectiveness of both the climate-controlled macroenvironment and the microenvironment. At room temperature they found that tight enclosures had a detrimental effect on film stability. However, open enclosures did not significantly reduce the acid content of the acetate base film. Microenvironments created by absorbents or low preconditioned rh were found to extend the longevity by a factor of three to four. Macroenvironments using low temperatures showed greater potential to improve film stability than did microclimates. The studies demonstrated the utility of the TWPI (Time-Weighted Preservation Index) in evaluating the efficiency of a storage area.

(https://www.imagepermanenceinstitute.org/environmental/research/preservation-metrics)

Wax audio cylinders should be stored in their original containers, vertically; they are very fragile and at risk of deterioration, especially in high relative humidity. Audio and video discs should also be stored vertically, supported by frequent shelf dividers, in their original sleeves or a replacement; never stack them horizontally more than five high, or mix discs of varying sizes in a pile.

Tapes should be stored vertically in their original cassettes, away from any magnetic field source. The original advice given by sound archives was to avoid metal shelving and cabinets due to the danger of magnetic interference; this is now discounted, as any residual magnetic impulses in the shelving are thought to protect the tapes from greater interference from outside fields.

The black moulded plastic used for inserts in the jewel cases used for CD and DVD storage has been shown to cause oxidation of the reflective metallic layer of the disc. The danger can be neutralized by replacing the inserts with Corrosion Intercepts™ or putting a MicroChamber CD-Saver disc below each disc to prevent contamination. These can be purchased from conservation suppliers. The discs should be stored vertically in appropriate boxes.

Photographic materials are best stored in inert polyester envelopes; these are available commercially in several sizes or can be tailored by conservators to individual requirements using an ultrasonic welder. Avoid paper or glassine envelopes where an adhesive has been used, since this may affect the photograph inside.

Ensure that magnetic materials are not stored close to any strong magnetic fields. Keeping or using electrical equipment in a storage area is strongly discouraged for this reason.

What kind of equipment is needed?

Moving materials around safely and securely, both in the storage areas and within the building, needs planning. Routes and procedures are important and staff should understand them and abide by them, allowing for periodic review and change. Try to avoid any items being carried individually; trolleys are much safer for horizontal movement and also reduce personal health risk. If material has to be moved vertically, between floors, a book lift may be easier and cheaper to install than a passenger lift. Less room is required and restrictions are fewer since it is not used by people. However, safeguards to prevent material falling out of it are necessary and should be specified accordingly. A few large archives and libraries have automated track carrying systems for moving material round the building in computer-controlled containers, both horizontally and vertically. This is only suitable where the distance to be covered from storage to reading room would result in unacceptable delays in the production of the material to the user. Such systems are similar to the automated retrieval systems used by some large banks and insurance companies.

It is almost impossible to have too many trolleys. The main constraints will be the space to store them and the budget, but be generous; they save damage to archived material by proper support, they prevent personal injury and they can save time if used for temporary storage of material overnight for a reader the following day. However, the trolley will need to be stored in the strongroom to ensure that the collection material is both safe and secure. Specify lightweight steel construction with no sharp edges, large swivel rubber castors and no upright lips to the shelves. In some cases the latter can be helpful to restrain small items which might otherwise slide about, but in general they present the danger of tearing unprotected items or preventing easy placing of boxes on the trolley shelves. Double-sided trolleys, often constructed from steel but with angled wooden shelves, large swivel rubber castors and protective corners, are used to transport volumes and prevent them falling out or off. Books should be vertical and the trolley should be loaded to maximize stability. Never pile books horizontally on a trolley except for single outsize volumes on the trolleys intended for archive boxes. Specialized map trolleys assist in the transport of outsize flat sheets by curving them gently (see Figure 6.11 overleaf). Scissor trolleys (see Figure 6.12 overleaf) can be used for moving large heavy material from high shelves, but the operational procedures need to be carefully drawn up and adhered to if injuries are to be avoided. Staff will require appropriate training in the use of any specialized or automatic equipment.

Figure 6.11 Map trolley

Figure 6.12 Scissor trolley

Stepladders are used in most storage areas unless the height of the shelving is consistently about 2m; access to any higher shelves must be by ladder as it is difficult and hazardous to extract or return boxes above head level. Even if the height is uniform it may be necessary to provide ladders for shorter staff. Ladders should be stable and of lightweight construction, with lockable wheels and a railed platform at the top (see Figure 6.13). The steps should also have a railing. Often described as warehouse ladders, these are more appropriate for use in archive storage areas, being attached to a rail at the top of the stack, than library rolling ladders, which are not designed for the removal of more than a book or two at one time. Most archives will need a selection of ladders and staff should be trained to use the appropriate ones to ensure the safe removal of material from shelves and their own health and safety.

Three-wheel kick stools help with the safe removal of material from shelves that are only a little too high for comfortable reach where there is little or no danger of overbalancing. Provide adequate numbers so that they are not difficult to find when needed. They should be two-step, with spring suspension and instant set-down once weight is applied. Rubber castors enable them to be moved easily by foot.

Ensure that tables or pull-out shelves are available in the bays for removing files or documents from boxes if they are to be produced individually. Balancing boxes while attempting to extract material is likely to be disastrous.

Figure 6.13 Ladder

Inert plastic wallets, portfolios or folders which support documents may be required if they are to be carried any distance to the user.

Possible future developments

Archival and library storage has much to learn from other storage developments and increasing pressure on space is dictating the need to find economic solutions. Warehouse technology is already extensively used in some archives, notably bar-coding; warehouse equipment is also used for racking and transport and more developments are being scrutinized for adaptation.

High-density storage facilities for libraries are becoming increasingly common in the USA – maximizing storage space with containers for volumes, and utilizing bar-coding and warehouse software for retrieval. Fully automated systems rely on cranes and conveyors to retrieve material from within the warehouse, with the result that, as staff are not required to work within the store itself, the temperature can be kept lower than normal; low-oxygen environments[12] can also be introduced to minimize the danger of fire (Olney, 2005).

Preservation issues loom large when considering this type of storage solution but the suggestions do offer a major improvement on current practice, namely the separation of stored items from people; until now solutions have had to compromise on the environmental conditions required for the comfort of both.

Security and identification of stock are both of concern to warehouse owners; bar-coding has its place for location identification but the development of radio frequency identification tags (RFIDs) for commercial storage has made it possible to identify tagged items using hand-held monitors and to link product – or document – information to the inventory or automated catalogue in addition to location. Libraries in the USA are using the technology to track stock and it is being installed in the Vatican library in Rome.[13] Since archives are already commonly stored in boxes, unlike the majority of library materials, it seems likely that the same technology could improve archive storage in the future too.

Summary

Good storage is one of the most important features of a preservation strategy; gradual realization that this is one of the best – and cheapest – methods of ensuring the survival of archival material has led to the development of a range of standards, benchmarks and guidelines covering all the issues from environmental control to good shelving. This chapter has outlined these, including those highlighting aspects such as mould prevention, and has also suggested possible future storage developments that may ease some of the current constraints, such as the maintenance of low temperatures.

The next chapter looks at managing the risks associated with disasters, often incurred in storage areas or exhibitions, where archives are particularly vulnerable.

Notes and references

1   In April 2012, two significant standard guidance documents were produced in the UK to extend and review common storage practice. This resulted in some important changes to the previous tolerance levels for the storage of heritage materials. Three key drivers for this change were the need to reduce the overall costs of storage, that the science of materials had advanced and that there needed to be a move to manage the wider environmental impact of HVAC systems and so develop a more sustainable approach.
     PD 5454: 2012 *Guide for the storage and exhibition of archival materials*
     PAS 198: 2012 *Specification for environmental conditions for cultural collections.*
2   See PD 5454: 2012, section 0, Introduction, page 2:
     'It has also been recognized that the long term conservation of archives and other heritage collections is not to be achieved at the expense of the earth's environment or through unrestrained energy use. This guidance has been produced in the light of these changes in scientific knowledge and the awareness that a protective environment needs to be achieved sustainably by passive means, wherever practicable.'
3   FFP = Filtering Face Piece.
4   Some conservation suppliers offer hire deals for this equipment.
5   The University College London Centre for Sustainable Heritage explores many

areas of managing pollutant levels, both from the environment and resulting from the deterioration of collections materials:

www.bartlett.ucl.ac.uk/graduate/csh/research/projects/teach

www.bartlett.ucl.ac.uk/graduate/csh/research/projects/heritage-smells.

6   Current research at: www.ucl.ac.uk/sustainableheritage-save/impact/intro.htm.

7   The details are within the European standard BS EN 799: 2002.

8   See www.caval.edu.au/carm.html.

9   The UK National Archives have published guidance in 2009: www.nationalarchives.gov.uk/documents/information-management/considerations-for-developing-an-offsite-store.pdf.

10 The UK National Archives evaluation of archival boxboard: www.nationalarchives.gov.uk/documents/information-management/evaluating-archival-box-board.pdf.

11 Plastazote is cross-linked, closed-cell polyethylene nitrogen expanded foam which is chemically inert and very stable; widely used for the protection of delicate items in museums and archive conservation.

12 Ignition cannot take place if the air contains only 15% oxygen; this is compared to the standard percentage of 21–22%. The ignition point is 15.4% and stores need to be sufficiently airtight to ensure that sufficient time is allowed to enable material to be evacuated should the equipment fail. See recent presentation on British Library's Boston Spa low oxygen storage: www.ifla.org/files/pac/British-Library-low-oxygen-case-study.pdf.

13 The International Federation of Library Associations (IFLA) recognizes the importance of RFID technology and has created a group to monitor and comment on developments: www.ifla.org/en/about-rfid.

7

Managing risks and avoiding disaster

Introduction

> Disaster planning is truly not for the faint of heart.
>
> (Wellheiser and Scott, 2002, iv)

Avoiding disaster is an aspiration shared by many archives but disasters are adequately guarded against by few. Even after well over 20 years of publicity about the benefits of taking precautions, the value of risk assessment and the ultimate cost to an organization that suffers a disaster, embryo plans still lie unfinished, staff are still untrained and mutual help partnerships have not been forged. Articles, websites and manuals abound, but taking the first initiative still appears to be difficult in too many archives, as the above quotation hints. Little recognition is given by those in responsible positions to the long-term damage that could be caused by a disaster, not only to the documents in physical terms but also in terms of the effect on the staff, the users and the depositors. For businesses the result can be catastrophic; why should it be any different for archives?

This chapter includes:

- the reasons for developing disaster planning
- definitions
- responsibilities
- priorities for salvage
- development of a disaster control plan
- implementation of the plan
- insurance
- partnerships.

Why undertake an 'operation-hope-not'?

The goals must be clear to all those involved, otherwise confusion will take over. They include:

- knowing, assessing and mitigating risk
- the maintenance of service
- avoiding or minimizing loss and damage to the holdings
- knowing who to call on for necessary assistance.

Recent experiences in many countries have emphasized the value of speedy recovery of information to those whose vital records have been in a disaster. But the success of these operations depends on the professional skills of those brought in to rescue the documentation. It must be remembered that a disaster is a disaster; it is not going to be cheap or easy to return to the previous status quo.

Flood disaster recovery, York, UK

Unprecedented flooding in the autumn of 2000 resulted in vital files being inundated but then rescued and air-dried at the Borthwick Institute of Historical Research, in order to allow the owners to resume business as fast as possible. The successful elements of the operation included

- a good understanding of the needs of the stricken organization
- adaptable planning and innovative solutions
- willing teams of staff to help when required but not to crowd the recovery operation
- plenty of space to lay out the documents
- lots of good humour

and resulted in a prompt return to the owners and good publicity for the Borthwick Institute (Webb, 2001).

Definitions

Some of the difficulties in developing disaster planning are caused by failure to understand the meanings of various terms used.

Risk assessment and management

This is a modern description of an activity which has been carried out over decades – but is now a highly developed science with a whole methodology behind it,[1] to the extent that one firefighter from Hampshire County Council (UK) is quoted as saying that 'risk assessments and management save

Electrical fire disaster in a chartered surveyor's office

Working documents from filing cabinets and archive files were unusable due to smoke and water damage. Files contained original material and were required for immediate business use, otherwise the reputation and survival of the company was at risk. A commercial rescue company:

- acted fast
- retrieved the documents
- categorized them all into priority requirements
- cleaned the urgent files within one day
- removed the surface smoke and smell
- dried the wet documents to prevent mould growth
- consolidated them as necessary.

All the files were returned within two weeks and were usable for business purposes (from www.documentsos.com).

far more than any salvage exercise' (Forbes, 2003, 197). Documented risk assessment and avoidance is now so common in all project work that the concept is unlikely to cause headaches at a senior level in an organization, although junior staff may require training and assistance. On a practical level it involves:

- identifying risk
- deciding on the level of its significance
- ensuring that it is minimized to the extent that the likelihood of occurrence is small.

Emergency

An emergency is an unexpected occurrence, usually restricted in scope and unlikely to result in major loss to holdings. It can turn into a disaster but if adequate precautionary planning has taken place this is less likely.

Disaster

A disaster is 'a sudden or great misfortune' (*Oxford English Dictionary*), more likely to result in serious damage or loss to the archive – or for that matter to any heritage organization – in which it occurs. Major resources will almost certainly be required to return to the pre-disaster position.

Disasters can be divided into those which occur as the result of natural phenomena, such as earthquakes, volcanic eruptions, tsunami (tidal waves) or hurricanes, and those which are man-made, such as floods, fires, building collapse, arson, vandalism or theft. Many natural disasters will cause the same effects as those which are man-made, but on a larger scale. The areas of the world in which they are likely to occur usually have detailed national emergency plans to limit the damage. Plans drawn up for an archive – such as the installation of shutters on the windows in hurricane areas – will necessarily be co-ordinated with any such national effort. A major disaster involving a wide geographical area will seriously affect the ability of an archive to carry out its own disaster procedures, through lack of power and external assistance. In these circumstances a disaster will assume much greater proportions, and the archive may have to do the best it can in the face of much greater problems for staff and infrastructure. In many cases, heritage organizations will have to look to the international community for assistance and support. The establishment of the International Committee of the Blue Shield has provided specialist assistance and enabled fact-finding missions into areas of unrest or conflict where heritage collections are at significant risk.

International Committee of the Blue Shield

A convention for the protection of cultural property in the event of armed conflict, it acts as a focal point for local, regional, national and international initiatives, promoting awareness of risks to cultural heritage objects. It is cross-sectoral, covering archives, libraries, museums, galleries and the built heritage.
www.ancbs.org

Disaster planning

Disaster planning is the activity covering all aspects of:

- assessing and managing risk
- planning and co-ordinating response
- developing procedures
- writing a manual
- organizing appropriate training
- ensuring that after any incident, simulated or real, the appropriate lessons are learnt and incorporated into future plans.

In many cases, and especially to avoid the loss of electronic data, insurance companies now require evidence of such planning before they will issue cover. This follows widely publicized figures about the small proportion of organizations which actually recover after such an experience; one estimate is only 57%,[2] resulting in a staggering 43% going out of business within six months.

IRA bomb disaster in City of London 1993

A massive bomb ripped through the heart of the City of London in 1993, killing one person and injuring more than 40. The explosion shook buildings and shattered hundreds of windows, sending glass showering down into the streets below. A medieval church, St Ethelburga's, collapsed; another church and Liverpool Street underground station were also wrecked. The damage caused by the Bishopsgate bomb cost £350m to repair. The huge payouts by insurance companies contributed to a crisis in the industry, including the near-collapse of the world's leading insurance market, Lloyd's of London.

Disaster control and reaction

This will ensure that, in the case of a disaster, the documents suffer minimum damage and that the archive can resume business, either for the public or for the parent organization, or both, as soon as possible.

Who is responsible for disaster planning?

The short answer is that the organization, and senior management in particular, have to take responsibility for disaster planning. Such planning must be business-wide, the first concern must always be for the safety of the staff and all preservation disaster planning must co-ordinate with this overall policy. In planning to avoid damage to the archives the choice is between:

- developing and using expertise within the organization
- hiring professional assistance from experienced disaster reaction companies.

If the former is chosen it is essential that responsibility is clearly spread across the whole spectrum of staff, to demonstrate a shared commitment. Everyone has something to offer, but the plan must be rolled out in a controlled manner.

If the latter is chosen the capabilities of different companies, and their ability to match the potential needs of the archive, must be discussed and agreed in advance. Several such organizations exist but it is essential to negotiate with them before any emergency, to discover what services and equipment they can provide and what they charge. They do not all deal with every type of material, but in an emergency it is tempting to assume that they are all-round experts. Although they will have the immediate interests of the organization at heart, remember that they are essentially providers of a commercial service.

Additional expertise may also be found within an over-arching body, such as the local authority or the organization's head office, since considerations of personal safety and the security of the building will be part of general business recovery plans. Planning the survival of the holdings must, however, be undertaken by the archive (whether in conjunction with a specialized company[3] or using its own professional expertise), ensuring that the two plans dovetail and do not confuse lines of responsibility. It is sensible to follow well known guidelines to ensure that no vital part of the plan is accidentally omitted.

What should be saved first?

Each archive must attempt to draw up a list of priority items for salvage, however difficult that might be. Some, such as cathedral archives and libraries, have to draw up lists of their items of outstanding value for other purposes; the Cathedrals Fabric Commission requires this and the experience of doing so has led one archivist to conclude that salvage is made much easier if these items are subsequently shelved together, particularly if fire crews have to be directed towards salvaging priority items (Forbes, 2003, 192). Other items of particular importance in most archives, though not necessarily of monetary value, include:

- finding aids and catalogues
- vital records of staff and organization management files
- accession registers.

Some maintain that published, microfilmed or digitized documents stored elsewhere in that format should have a lower salvage priority than those which exist only in their original format; this is worth debate. Also, some formats are more vulnerable to water than others – e.g. old film and magnetic tape or coated papers – which may make them priorities for salvage and treatment.

Development of a disaster control plan: where to start?

Getting the agreement and co-operation of senior management is the first and essential point; no plan will be successful without senior backing and involvement. It is best to assume that plans are starting from scratch; in practice that is unlikely, but it may well be that an incomplete or out-of-date plan has to be resuscitated and re-worked. Presenting it as a new plan with fresh ideas will be more effective than simply re-issuing the previous plan.

Disaster control project

Outlining a project for developing a disaster control plan is a necessary first step to raise staff awareness of the risks and their potential involvement. It can also draw attention to issues which are sometimes overlooked and offer opportunities to support and encourage initiatives.

Not all the actions required for successful disaster control need to take place consecutively; the order will depend on individual operational practice and how much work has been done before. The project document does not need to be long but if the staff are to be involved it should suggest the following commitments by the organization as a minimum:

- to undertake regular risk assessments of the buildings and operations within them, and ensure that remedial work is carried out to specification
- to make financial provision to enable arrangements for recovery to be carried out in case of need
- to maintain a checklist of staff and contacts who may be required to assist at a disaster scene
- to ensure the maintenance of appropriate contracts for assistance
- to train staff in recovery techniques
- to provide necessary equipment to maximize the efficiency of any disaster recovery operation
- to review any disaster recovery operation and incorporate recommendations into a revised plan.

The choice for the next step should be made clear. Basically it is between:

- doing nothing and hoping for the best
- employing an outside disaster recovery specialist
- undertaking the planning and management of the scheme in-house, probably with some outside help as required.

The first is extremely unwise and the consequences should be spelt out in stark detail. If the second option is chosen a contract must be negotiated and financial provision must be available (see above). If the third option is chosen the draft project document should be agreed and distributed, and action taken under the following headings:

- prevention
- preparation
- reaction
- recovery
- evaluation.

Appoint a co-ordinator and a committee

Before anything else happens the plan co-ordinator must be appointed, tasked to manage the whole operation, to ensure that finance and equipment are available and to organize staff training. These responsibilities must be clearly defined as part of a job description. Since cross-departmental co-operation may be required, it is important that the level of the appointment is sufficiently high to give the post authority. A small committee will be needed under the direction of the co-ordinator, to ensure co-operation between all those involved. Ownership of the project is crucial to guarantee commitment to minimizing the danger to the holdings. In a small archive committee members may have to fill more than one role but it is important that functions are recognized and allocated as follows:

- the co-ordinator for managing the project
- team leader(s) for salvage/cleaning operations
- security staff
- the press officer or equivalent
- building maintenance staff and possibly administrative staff in a large organization
- conservator(s) for air-drying material or preparing material for blast freezing.

Prevention

Risk assessment of buildings, both inside and outside, must be a routine measure undertaken regularly and particularly before the onset of winter or rainy seasons. As a minimum, it should include investigating:

- drains and pipes
- gutters and gullies
- exterior and interior electrical installations
- door and window frames.

Sort out responsibilities, and remind staff of good health and safety practice.

Necessary repairs, replacements and maintenance procedures must be carried out, and a regular timetable for further surveying drawn up. As a basic safety measure all electrical equipment should be documented with its date of installation and its estimated length of working life. Replacements should be made, as appropriate, to avoid the danger of electrical fires. Reminders to staff and readers of their responsibilities relating to fire prevention should be issued annually, together with a smoking policy applicable to all.

Partnerships and regional co-operation

Disasters are not to be tackled alone. The first partner needed in the event of a disaster is the local fire service, which must be able to act efficiently and fast. Liaison on a regular basis is essential, not least to explain the nature of the archival holdings and their location within the building. The benefit of such contacts has been amply proved where firemen have helped to minimize the danger of soaking unaffected material or the even more insidious smoke damage.

Testing a disaster control plan at Lanhydrock House, UK, 2003

A damage limitation exercise at Lanhydrock House, Cornwall (owned by the National Trust) proved the importance of contacting and working with the emergency services:

> The results were very promising and much was learned by all parties involved. From our point of view two factors stood out. First, the success of the plan relied on sound understanding and co-operation with the fire service. Regular liaison, therefore, is essential.
>
> (Holden, 2004, 31–2)

Without a planned and practised strategy, access in the event of disaster would be extremely hazardous and the safety of the collection would therefore be severely compromised. Additionally, good housekeeping and active maintenance of equipment are essential in avoiding any incident.

The provision of detailed floor plans is a necessity for both the archive and the fire or salvage operator; these should be drawn up as a priority if they do not already exist. These should indicate the location of:

- keys or the controls for an electronic security system[4]
- vital records for business continuity
- priority archival materials

- stop-cocks
- gas mains
- any other hazards
- a priority route to be followed in the event of a power failure.

Most buildings with public access will have a fire panel offering sophisticated information to the fire service (see Chapter 5). The disaster co-ordinator and committee should be familiar with the panel and be able to provide any necessary additional information to the emergency services.

Mutual help partnerships are worth considering at the same time, whether regional or local. In the UK the East Midlands Regional Emergencies and Disasters Support Service (REDS)[5] was formed in 1991 as a museum initiative to co-ordinate pre-planned responses and specialist support for museums, libraries and archives in the region. More locally, in Canterbury, staff from the cathedral archive and the cathedral itself, archivists from elsewhere in Kent, museum curators and administrators from other organizations have formed a disaster-planning group to help each other out. The M25 Consortium of Academic Libraries provides a Disaster Control Plan template that is available to all from their website.[6]

Insurance issues

The extent of any insurance cover must be clear; arguments in the midst of a disaster over what is allowable add to the misery of the situation and can be avoided with adequate preparation. Crown properties in the UK are not insured for either the buildings or the contents; this is Treasury policy to avoid massive insurance premiums. Instead, payment is forthcoming as and when necessary, but it is wise to discover who would authorize what payments, and how. Taking out insurance against the cost of restitution, however, is sometimes permissible and it should be clear whether this would cover the cost of trucking soaked material to a blast-freezing depot, the cost of storing the material at such a depot or the conservation costs for the final rehabilitation of the material.

Other organizations have their own forms of cover, but it is essential to discover whether they are adequate; calm discussion of the extent of any policies before a disaster occurs is time well spent. As noted above, some insurance companies will not guarantee cover unless a disaster recovery plan has been formulated. The general advice for insurance is to ensure that provision for conservation after the disaster event is included in the policy.

Georgetown Library, Washington DC, USA

Sometimes the best laid plans can be undermined by unforeseen or uncontrollable events.

The Georgetown branch of the Washington DC public library suffered a fire in 2007.

The library roof was ablaze in flames when the firefighters came to put out the fire. Due to complications in the area with water pressure and fire hydrants not working, the fire quickly spread and the roof collapsed down into the building onto the second floor.

What equipment is needed and where can it be obtained?

Suppliers of emergency services and equipment, together with contact telephone numbers and business details, should be identified and noted. The list should be in the disaster manual and easily available to those who might need it. Any of the following might be needed, depending on existing supplies and the extent of the disaster:

* crate, trolley and folding table hire
* mobile phones and/or a walkie-talkie system[7]
* emergency generator hire
* emergency lighting hire
* emergency pumping equipment hire
* canteen equipment and catering services
* plumbers
* carpenters
* structural engineers
* additional suppliers of polythene sheeting, archival boxes, etc., for protective purposes
* blast-freezing and vacuum-drying facilities, together with refrigerated trucks if necessary, to remove soaked material for chilled storage or freezing.

Wherever possible, engage with local services, since regular and emergency contact will be easier and quicker.

Preparation
Action manual

The draft action manual can be drawn up by the co-ordinator while preventive and preparative plans are being developed. It is likely that particular issues will be discussed during the preliminary stages and it is helpful to write them down, even if they are later changed. A timetable should be one of the first considerations of the committee, with target dates for completion of different tasks, including the manual. It is not, however, a task which will ever be finalized; after each training practice or real disaster, the instructions will need to be reviewed and amended.

The manual should be entirely familiar to all staff or volunteers, as they will have helped compile it and used it in training. It should be designed as an aide-mémoire in a stressful situation. One person should be given the specific task of checking telephone numbers and contact details on a regular basis (e.g. every six months); staff and suppliers, or their circumstances, change and an out-of-date list is useless. Since every disaster is different there is little point in outlining complicated plans; better to have a short loose-leaf manual (for ease of updating) with essential information and rely on trained staff to be flexible according to the situation they are dealing with. The contents of the manual should include the following:

- telephone numbers of trained staff arranged as a cascade (see section on Reaction, below)
- telephone numbers of suppliers of services and equipment
- floor plans
- outline instructions for the co-ordinator (deputies may sometimes have to take charge)
- outline instructions for teams for removing material from the disaster area
- outline instructions for those dividing material into what can be dried on-site and what will have to be blast-frozen
- outline instructions for documenting any material going off-site (labelling crates, listing reference numbers, etc.)
- outline instructions for documenting any material air-dried either on- or off-site (lists of files and locations)
- outline instructions for security if material has to be taken off-site
- outline statements for press or other media.

Additionally it may be prudent to compile a summary (printed on two sides of A4) and laminated (to be waterproof) for each member of staff. Some organizations issue numbered task cards to staff as they arrive at a disaster scene, preferring to assume that there is no guarantee that staff with specialized training will be available when needed.

It is likely that staff may have to respond to a disaster out of normal hours – most disasters occur when there are fewer people around to notice the warning signs. It is therefore essential that staff are happy to become part of a team and that any out-of-pocket expenses or overtime will be paid. Disasters are not cheap events and the staff and their skills are the greatest asset for any organization.

Equipment

Equipment must be provided (see Figure 7.1) in boxes at suitable locations around the building, or even off-site in a lockable storage area. The scale of provision depends on the ease with which additional supplies can be obtained. Not all equipment needs to be in the same place; it can be helpful to store rolls of polythene sheeting and scissors in the strongrooms, to protect undamaged material immediately if a flood or leak is detected.

Disaster storage boxes must be clearly labelled and should be secured with tags to avoid items being 'borrowed'. Their contents

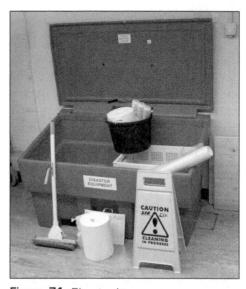

Figure 7.1 Disaster box

and whereabouts should also be checked regularly by the co-ordinator or a designated member of the disaster committee. Wheeled containers are convenient, as they can be moved to a disaster area. Most archives will need at least two to avoid the possible danger of the only equipment being in the disaster area. Many will also have back-up and additional materials stored in the conservation workshop if there is one, or elsewhere in store.

Protective clothing and essentials such as torches and batteries may well be best stored close to a building entrance for immediate availability. Alternatively it may be preferable to issue staff with clothing to take home, to avoid the potential problem of the clothing store being within the disaster area. Disaster response staff should wear layers of clothing, easily removed or replaced. Some buildings may be very cold if electricity is unavailable; others, due to good insulation, may heat up.

Equipment for disaster boxes

The boxes should contain the following as a minimum:

- mops
- buckets
- sponges
- tie-on labels
- string
- tape
- sticky tape
- hazard tape
- scissors
- polythene bags
- torches
- absorbent paper
- pens and pencils (indelible)
- disaster recording sheets
- crepe bandages (for wrapping volumes for freezing)
- safety pins (to secure crepe bandages).

Protective clothing for staff

As a minimum all staff should be supplied with, or bring, the following:

- reflective jacket or strap (buildings can be very dark)
- apron or other protective overalls
- waterproof boots
- torch, or helmet with torch attached
- plastic and cotton gloves
- facemask.

Training

Training is the last vital part of preparation. Disasters are frightening and threatening events. The objective of the training is to ensure that staff are sufficiently confident of their roles to avoid panic. For this reason it is important to stress that only trained staff should be called out to an emergency; other volunteers will undoubtedly want to play a part but are likely to be more hindrance than help. Stressing the importance of training also emphasizes the value of being prepared and raises the profile of disaster planning within the archive or the parent organization.

Each individual or team should practise so that members are clear about their own responsibilities. They should understand where these coincide or overlap with the responsibilities of others. Typical training might include:

- removal of boxes from one place to another in the dark, making allowance for the fact that wet material will be twice as heavy as dry material
- packing material for freezing (even if it is not wet)
- erecting drying lines
- setting up tables with fans to dry volumes
- outlining the situation to ensure information about the disaster is accurate
- indicating and setting up the designated assessment area for the rescued material
- indicating and setting up a rest area for staff
- preparing press statements of a non-specific nature to reassure outsiders.

Sample pre-prepared press statements

- 'The archive/organization has suffered damage from flood/fire/earthquake and the extent is currently being assessed; further information will be available shortly.'
- 'The damage caused to the archives/organization by the flood/fire/earthquake has been limited and services will resume shortly; please await further announcements in the press or on the local radio.'
- 'Anyone wishing to use the archives should ring 000 1234 before visiting to ensure that the material they wish to see is available, following the recent fire/flood/earthquake.'

A full-scale practice should be carried out at least once a year to test the operation of the plan and the skills developed by those involved. Gaps in the planning process are frequently discovered during such practices, which are much easier to rectify at that moment than during a real emergency. Include an observer to provide objective feedback – an invitation to the pre-appointed insurance loss adjustor to observe a training exercise in Canterbury in the UK resulted in much greater understanding of the type of disaster which might occur in a cathedral library (Forbes, 2003, 195). Make certain that the views of all the staff about the operation are taken into account; those involved are the ones who know where the gaps are. The practice activity may best be provided as a regional exercise and therefore bring together likely partners and help develop a network. Commercial disaster companies offer this service and provide a practical scenario.

Reaction

Many archives rotate the task of acting as call-out officer to avoid one person always being on duty; using mobile phones makes this much easier than it was 20 years ago, but the responsibility is still one which should be shared, if not remunerated.

Once a disaster has occurred the co-ordinator must take control as soon as permitted by the emergency services, if they have been called. No one will be allowed within the building until the fire service or police deem it safe. The overwhelming priority for everyone is to avoid loss of life or personal injury. This is the point at which the value of a well thought-out and practised plan becomes clear.

The initial task of the co-ordinator is to assess the extent of the damage and to call out as many staff as necessary. In the first instance it may only be a few, and perhaps warning others to be on stand-by. Having organized the telephone numbers in a cascade system will cut out the need for the co-ordinator to spend too much time on the phone; at each level a designated member of staff can ring an agreed group of volunteers. Alternatively, a comprehensive telephone tree can be placed with a security company with instructions to activate it on the receipt of a single call from the co-ordinator. This activity could also be carried out by a designated member of staff to prevent the stress of the moment resulting in staff not being called. This reduces the time taken ringing round and can be organized to ensure that those living closest to the archive are contacted first (Holden, 2004, 29).

Communications between those working to rescue the archival materials can be difficult; two-way walkie-talkies or other 2-way devices can be used but successful communication requires practice in advance. Consider also the possibility that the phone lines to the organization may not be working, making communication dependent on mobile phones; giving out a pre-determined off-site number for enquirers as part of a press release can alleviate this problem.

On arrival staff should be issued with badges and a register should be kept of all those who enter and leave the building. In a confused situation, probably in the dark, opportunities are offered for unauthorized entrance and security breaches.

An assessment area away from the scene of the disaster, to separate material which has suffered minor damage from that badly affected, must be identified but sufficiently close to avoid wasting time moving materials. The site of the disaster will determine whether a pre-selected area is suitable; flexibility of choice is important. Remember that carrying wet files any distance is arduous and can slow down rescue operations. This applies particularly if different levels of the building are involved and lifts are out of action. If the available space is small, consideration should be given to using an external site, close to the archive, where a temporary secure shelter can be established.

The area should be spacious and preferably well ventilated; this is where decisions will be made on whether to air-dry or freeze the material and where many damaged boxes may be discarded.

A rest area must also be designated so that staff can be briefed as they arrive and have regular breaks; tea and coffee should be provided if possible. If the salvage operation is likely to take a long time it may be necessary to organize emergency catering on-site. On arrival staff should be warned of any potential dangers and should wait for a partner or team before starting work; individuals working alone could be a safety hazard. A range of these support and ancillary services may well be included in the organization's business continuity plan and this emphasizes the importance of liaising with other departments when compiling the archive's disaster plan. This sort of provision may also include counselling in the event of staff becoming upset by the disaster event.

The suppliers of emergency equipment should be contacted and rescue firms, or suppliers of refrigerated trucks for transit off-site, should be alerted, even if subsequently they are not required. Insurance firms should be notified as soon as possible and a statement prepared for the media. Photographs of the damage should be taken immediately for insurance purposes.

At the same time, efforts should be made to air and dry out the building; appropriate action will depend on the scale of the damage and the facilities available but opening windows and ensuring that smoke vents are operational will assist the flow of air and help reduce the threat of mould.

During the course of a disaster control programme many staff will be acting in groups of two or three to:

- remove material from the damaged or threatened areas
- erect protective polythene sheeting on unaffected areas
- establish drying areas on-site
- prepare material for blast-freezing or air-drying
- list material according to destination
- pack material to be blast-frozen.

If the archive is large, staff are usually best employed in their normal roles: repository or storage staff are familiar with those areas and with techniques for moving heavy boxes; conservators are accustomed to assessing the condition of archival material and handling it when fragile; other staff are well used to documenting materials, or dealing with administrative matters relating to supply. Smaller organizations will have to adapt to the resources available but partnerships may be helpful in providing specialist assistance.

If possible all media enquiries should be dealt with by someone familiar with the press, able to issue calming statements in a fraught situation. This may best be carried out by a senior manager or the head archivist, who needs to be fully briefed by the co-ordinator; it is important that all trained disaster staff are available to enact the practicalities of the plan. Prior preparation of statements will help. Most archives, other than private organizations, will also have access to a press officer – e.g. within the local council – or the fire service can assist.

What happens next?

The first task is to move the material away from the damaged area, leaving cleaning up until later. The material needs to be brought to the assessment area, where there should be normal or emergency lighting. Designate routes for removal staff, using temporary lighting and hazard tape, so the flow to and from the disaster area is unimpeded. Conservators, or specially trained staff, will assess the extent of the damage. This, however, is not the only criterion for deciding what to do next. Each situation has to be judged by:

- the extent of the damage to the building – how soon it will be able to function again and the temperature and relative humidity levels
- the extent of the damage to the documents
- the urgency with which material is required for normal use
- the availability of assistance
- any insurance considerations.

Air-drying paper can be very effective if sufficient space is available and the temperature and relative humidity can be controlled. Listing and marking up the location of the material is still very important if this option is chosen, as it is all too easy for the water-swollen contents of files, bursting out of their folders, to get mixed up. Files or papers can be hung over temporary lines erected in the drying area if the contents are not too heavy. Volumes can be stood on end and the leaves fanned out to promote air circulation if the boards are strong enough to support the text block. If at all possible the contents of files should be kept together to ensure the security of individual papers. Cold-air fans must be used in preference to heated appliances, and dehumidifiers can help to reduce the overall relative humidity (but always remember to ensure that they have sufficient bucket capacity if they are left on overnight). However, they will only work efficiently in relatively confined areas. The window of opportunity for drying material is about 48 hours; if it is left damp longer than that the danger of mould growth increases rapidly, adding to the problems already experienced.

Experience of air drying at the Borthwick Institute, 2000

Back at the Borthwick, before the [soaked] files arrived, we laid our plans. We had a cool, ground floor room with ample floor space. We had portable dehumidifiers and cool air fans. We raided our disaster boxes for protective gloves and aprons with health and safety in mind, and covered the floor with blank newsprint as an absorbent material. We also rigged up a series of drying lines, using the metal supports of the room. Then, the files arrived. . . . We mobilized as many of our staff as could be spared. . . . Half the team carted the files to the drying room, and the other half hung them on the drying lines and spread them on the newsprint. In no time at all, the room was full, so we spilled over into the nearby corridor. That filled up too and we still had about half the files to find room for . . .

(Webb, 2001, 249)

If the decision is to blast-freeze some or all of the material (likely to be that which is not required immediately) it will then be stored in a freezing facility, being vacuum-dried later when the facilities and time to undertake the necessary conservation work are available. This is an invaluable assistance to the immediate rescue work, but success depends largely on meticulous documentation and management. If there are no records of which documents are where within the freezer, it is not possible to return them to the archive in the priority order in which they may be required.

Certain materials should not be frozen, because of the damage which may be incurred as they are dried out:

- Parchment should be carefully air-dried on absorbent paper, using weights round the edges to keep the shape. This is specialized work for conservators. Illuminated material requires very specialized treatment and should always be treated by conservators.
- Seals should be washed with clean (preferably purified) water and carefully wiped dry with a lint-free cloth. Take care not to spread the water if the seal is attached to a parchment or paper document.
- Photographic negatives and prints can be soaked in clean water for up to 24 hours and then carefully separated by hand, preferably under the direction of a conservator.
- Cine film dampened during a flood should be kept damp in clean (preferably purified) water before being taken as soon as possible to a specialist film laboratory where it can be chemically rewashed and dried

by experts. Film damaged by smoke and high humidity should also be treated in a specialist laboratory.

- Nitrate film should be left to burn, as it is almost impossible to extinguish. It gives off highly toxic gases so evacuation is essential. Insurance problems may arise as a result of this material being on-site.
- Magnetic tape should be rinsed in clean (preferably purified) water, then hung up to dry using the spool as support. It is likely to need recopying as soon as possible. Specialist advice is highly preferable to do-it-yourself techniques.
- Sound and video materials should be decontaminated by spraying with clean (preferably purified) water before controlled drying or specialist treatment. Freezing has been undertaken successfully but this again should be done by experts (Lee, 2001, 19).
- Optical discs can be rinsed in clean water and dried with a lint-free cloth, always wiping in a perpendicular angle to the grooves, not in a circular motion.

If the disaster has caused massive amounts of dust very considerable care will be needed in cleaning audiovisual material, because of the damage even tiny specks can cause. Thorough vacuuming should be carried out before any canisters are opened or equipment used.

The reaction may take several days or even weeks to complete; it will certainly be some time before the archive can return to normal operations. The co-ordinator should be making notes at every stage on what happened, so that, ultimately, the plan can be evaluated.

Recovery

Recovery is the slowest part of any plan. A co-ordinator must be prepared for this to take months or even years, which is dispiriting for the staff and readers and may prove a difficult message to convey. Once the immediate action of saving the material from complete destruction is over there may be an expectation that the archive will soon function normally. To counter gloom once the immediate emergency is over, and to move the project on, it is important to start planning the recovery of the documents at the earliest opportunity.

Priorities for document salvage will be determined by the nature of the archive; some may see the restitution of current records as most important, while others may require more immediate access to material used by researchers. Depositors may be concerned to see the documents they had placed with the archive in the expectation that they would be safer there than

The Cologne Archives Building collapsed on 3 March 2009

The archive and two neighbouring residential buildings collapsed. The emergency evacuation procedure was handled by local police in co-operation with the fire service, the German Federal Agency for Technical Relief, General Health and Hospital Care and the City of Cologne. Due to a co-ordinated and well managed plan, within 29 months the archive had recovered 95% of the archive collections.

elsewhere; considerable diplomacy is required in dealing with this situation.

Material already copied (microfilmed or digitized) may be low down the list for restitution and conservation since, provided the copies have survived, these can be used instead. It is likely that these will include some iconic items, but they will be both safe and secure if frozen and need not be a priority.

Using the lists of material in different locations (some may be elsewhere for air-drying, others may be frozen), and taking into account available skills and resources for conservation, re-boxing or re-wrapping, a recovery plan should be drawn up, following discussion with colleagues. This will be equally necessary if an emergency recovery organization has undertaken the work, as the priorities for recovery must depend on the decisions of the archive. Insurance companies must be involved; an independent assessment of the situation will be needed and if insurance claims form part of the recovery plan, time must be allowed for this.

While planning is taking place for recovery the premises must be returned to normal conditions – dried out or, at the very worst, replaced until appropriate accommodation is available. If it is necessary to use temporary accommodation for storage, the new premises must be checked for environmental stability and security. Under no circumstances must the archives be returned to sub-standard accommodation likely to cause further damage. Monitoring the storage environmental conditions at this stage is essential.

Once the plan has been drawn up, resources for recovery have been agreed with the insurance company or the organization itself and suitable accommodation has been provided, the painstaking conservation work can begin on frozen material. Air-dried material may well have needed treatment as it was spread out – removal of anything likely to rust and separation of pages which might stick together being the most likely. The advice of an archive conservator is essential; the local record office or library might offer help with this. The Institute of Conservation in the UK maintains a list of accredited conservators (the Conservation Register) who can be called on for assistance.[8]

Evaluation

Documenting the course of the disaster and the successes and failures of the reaction and recovery plans is the responsibility of the co-ordinator, with the assistance and additional observations of others involved. These may include those observers who played no part in the actual operation; their comments will also be valuable. Call a meeting to discuss the disaster and gauge reactions to the effectiveness of the plan as soon as possible without interrupting the work. A final report should evaluate the success or otherwise of the plan and make recommendations for changed procedures, provided these have been thoroughly discussed and agreed by those who were present at the disaster.

International disasters

In recent years there have been some terrible and significant international disasters: the Asian Tsunami of 2004, the Haiti earthquake of 2010 and the Japanese Tsunami of 2011.

The future for Japanese archives disaster recovery was best emphasized by the President of the National Archives of Japan, who outlined the priorities as follows:

* Restoration of records contaminated by radiation
* Review of disaster prevention methods
* Pass down the records of the disaster.

Summary

Drawing up and implementing a response to a major disaster is time-consuming at first and must be followed by dogged determination to maintain a level of commitment and understanding. But the rewards will follow, in the shape of absence of a disaster – or mitigation of the potential damage if a disaster does occur. This chapter has shown how to draw up such a plan, outlined what is needed in the way of equipment and training and emphasized the importance of support at all levels.

The presence of conservators on-site is not essential, but some trained staff will need to be involved.

Notes and references

1   See, for instance, Ashley-Smith (1999).
2   www.documentsos.com/whydocsos.shtml.
3   See, for instance, Forbes (2003, 189).
4   See Chapter 5 – particular security measures will be required if the security system

is electronic and therefore doors remain open because of the emergency.

5   See http://emms.org.uk/reds.

6   See www.m25lib.ac.uk/m25dcp.

7   'In an emergency an effective communication system is essential' (Kennedy, 1995, 4).

8   See www.conservationregister.com.

8

Creating and using surrogates

Introduction

Surrogates – the production of a user copy of the original – have a major role in preservation management, as they reduce the wear and tear on originals and in many cases enhance access. Developing a programme should therefore be an option for all archives, but it must be recognized that all interests, including those of the readers, should be taken into account. Policy decisions will have to be considered if surrogates are to be offered to readers; will it be obligatory to use them and are there copyright issues, especially if they are available online? These issues need to be debated and agreed by the archive, since they will undoubtedly be raised at some point by readers.

Debates about different methods, the reasons for copying, and the associated costs of creation and upkeep have ranged widely over the past 50 years. Until recently such discussions have been centred largely on copying for the purposes of preservation. Access issues, however, have always crept in, emphasizing the difficulty of isolating one from the other. The development of digital methods of copying information has given increasing prominence to access issues, leading to change and enlargement of archive and library access policies, plans and costs. These are issues which are likely to loom larger in the future. Preservation is no longer the main focus.

This chapter looks at:

- the different types of copies
- the preservation issues surrounding the creation of surrogates
- the changing policies of archives on copying
- the actions needed to ensure that original materials are treated appropriately if they are copied.

It does not describe the technical requirements or standards for equipment, which can be found in the appropriate manuals.[1]

Copying archive material

> Reformatting for preservation whether utilizing analog or digital technologies is a series of choices all affected by economics, legal or social conventions, and decisions about risk management.   (Bellinger, 2003)

Decisions to copy, as Bellinger states, involve a host of choices, all of which require judgement about condition and access, and some of which may be controversial. Nevertheless, they must be made and priorities established; the alternative could be the total loss of information and therefore access to it. Risk management looms large in debates about copying.

The publicity surrounding the creation of a surrogate frequently sparks off renewed interest, leading to greater demands to see the original; this trend was very noticeable when a new photographic facsimile of Domesday Book was produced to celebrate its 900th anniversary in 1986. Since then, the development of digital methods of copying information has given increasing prominence to access issues, leading to consequential change and enlargement of archive and library access policies (Jefcoate, 2003). Such changes are not to be underestimated; Stephen Chapman (2003) and Jonas Palm (2006) have highlighted some of the problems that stem from this enlarged role, including the changes needed to overall strategic plans and the very necessary calculation of the cost of making, accessing and storing materials in different formats (see Chapter 6). These are issues of which all archivists involved with copying programmes should be aware, and need to ensure that senior management fully appreciates the impacts on the service. A digitization project is not a panacea; it includes many complex and detailed decisions. However, managed well and appropriately planned, such a project can be an exceptional example of preservation in action.

What copying techniques are available?
Hand copying
Historically, and even today in some parts of the world, manuscript material, usually iconic or decorative, has been hand copied for wider distribution or exhibition purposes. Before the invention of printing this was the only method of ensuring the survival of texts; more recently the technique has been adopted for the purpose of exhibition when security is an issue or long exposure to light might damage the original. The quality of some of these

facsimiles is very high, involving many hours of detailed work and producing a result very close to the original. The costs however are enormous, and many users would question the archival authenticity of such material.

Photographic copying

Photographic copies are still made, but not in the quantity of earlier periods when it was the only realistic copying technique available for access purposes. Created very largely for publication purposes or for use by readers at home, it was never a large-scale copying technique for preservation, owing to the expense of creating negatives and prints. The development of digital photography has led to much wider use of photography as a copying technique, but it is still largely used for access reasons. Any digital copies of documents used for preservation purposes will need the same rigorous preservation care as any other digital material (see below and Chapter 3). In both cases, the accumulation of, and care for, the surrogate resource needs to be included in the planning process.

Microfilming

Microfilming techniques were developed as early as 1839 by John Benjamin Dancer, resulting in slides visible via a microscope. Then 20 years later the first patent for microfilm was taken out by René Dagron, who demonstrated its use for transferring messages by carrier pigeon during the siege of Paris in the Franco-Prussian war of 1870–1. Realization of the value of this method resulted in large volumes of ephemeral newsprint being microfilmed in the 1930s and led to further filming of cultural materials at risk, and of captured documentation, during World War 2. From the 1960s it became the preferred method for archives to safeguard fragile originals from overuse, although it was not necessarily the favourite option for those who had to read them in that format. Nevertheless, the process is cheap and simple, with additional access benefits for those unable to visit the archive in person. Microfiches (16mm film) were developed in 1961 as an alternative format, using the same techniques; this offers a sheet, as opposed to a roll, of (35mm) images, usually covering 100–130 pages of text. For some types of material such as census enumerators' returns or parish registers this is an easier method of access for readers; pinpointing individual items on a complete roll of microfilm is time-consuming and potentially damaging to the film, which is constantly being rewound.

The potential income generation from selling copies made microfilming all the more attractive to those archives in a position to undertake the work in-house. For those without such expertise or resources, commercial companies or the Church of Jesus Christ of Latter-day Saints were often willing to undertake the necessary work. In the UK, by the 1990s many projects, not least NEWSPLAN (a national project to microfilm rare newspapers), obtained funding from the Heritage Lottery Fund and other sources to preserve and make collections available, often with the proviso that microfilming for preservation was undertaken, and to national standards.

These standards were developed[2] partly as a result of a major grant from the Andrew W. Mellon Foundation to microfilm endangered materials in the UK copyright libraries, the previous lack of some technical standards having resulted in many poor-quality films in both libraries and archives. The defects included:

- physical breakdown of the film base (cellulose acetate)
- poor image quality due to inadequate filming techniques
- lack of focus for the same reason
- fading or darkening due to inadequate processing.

Replacing damaged diazo film[3] with new copies from films designated as masters was sometimes impossible, negating the original intention that the latter would remain as the definitive preservation copy. An increasing need in the electronic age to digitize some film, to make it both more widely available and searchable, has frequently proved difficult or impossible, due to any one, or any combination, of the above factors.

However, microfilm does have many advantages. If the storage and use conditions are suitable (see Chapters 6 and 10) it has a potential life of over 100 years and all the benefits of simplicity of production and use; it is relatively cheap to create and it is also a well used technique in countries where the availability of electronic communications is unreliable or not widespread. It is essentially stable; the process is primarily photographic and these processes have been refined over the last 160 years. The volume of material which can be stored in a very small format is an additional factor that leads many organizations, such as hospitals, to use the process for storing large volumes of current and semi-current records.

A further benefit is offered by the ability of readers to print copies of material from the film or fiche themselves. Strain on the original is reduced but the importance of filming to a high standard is reemphasized; illegible hard copy from a poorly created microfilm is not satisfactory for the archive, the on-site reader or a potential purchaser. The archive world has accepted microfilm as the main surrogate format despite its perceived drawbacks. The use of microfilm is viewed as very old-fashioned and the equipment is bulky and basic, but the standard of image, when produced to archival standards, has proved a very effective preservation strategy.

Photocopying

Photocopying has been used as part of the preservation strategy of many archives. It has a value, particularly for preserving material which was transferred on to very unstable carriers. The early thermofax copying process used heat to transfer the image, by means of infrared radiation. Both the paper and the transferred text proved to be very unstable over time, and in many cases the material is now unreadable. The best solution for retaining the information is to transfer such copies on to stable, or if possible archival, paper, using the facilities of modern copiers to enhance the image. Thermal paper, treated with a heat-sensitive thermal coating, continued to be used in fax machines and electronic whiteboards until quite recently.

Photocopying can also be a useful method of reducing the use of material such as original manuscript indexes, or making additional hard copies of material which the user would expect to access in a conventional format. In general, however, the additional bulk created is a serious disincentive to adopting it as a solution for more than a few pages at a time.

Digitizing

Digitizing is an increasingly popular method of copying archival material, with all the advantages of access via the internet and of opportunities for searching and indexing electronically. Seized on by organizations and funding bodies in many countries in the later 1990s as the answer to government policies for access and inclusion, the development of digitization techniques coincided with a subtle shift away from core funding for public archives and towards project funding as a substitute. The result has been a vast increase in the number of documents now accessible worldwide, but these are usually selected on the basis of their relevance to particular projects rather than on the need for a surrogate due to condition or to the completeness of the archival

Digitizing collections means much more than taking images. Common perceptions of digitization projects requiring a scanner, a scanning operator and an item to be scanned, do not do justice to the often highly complex process of planning and preparing for digitization, image capture, quality control and metadata creation, eventually leading to successful online delivery of content.

[Bülow and Ahmon, 2010]

fonds (holdings). Archives will never digitize all their material – there is too much and the costs of storing the digitized images and preserving them are too great (Palm, 2006).[4]

What problems arise?

Much of the damage caused by copying is due to the difficulty of handling archival material. Originally microfilm cameras were not suited to the type of archive and library materials they were required to copy, being manufactured for business or large-scale copying purposes where the original documents were uniform in size. Few if any concessions were made to the needs of fragile materials. Copying large volumes, where the text continued right into the central gutter or presented a serious curve, was difficult. The results were often poor, even if specialized machines were used where the volume could be held in a cradle or supported at right angles to the machine. However, developments in the 1990s led to the use of cantilevered, padded and adjustable platens for the material to rest on, and shuttles for the book cradles to permit large or fragile items to be moved safely while being filmed with cool lights. Cameras designed especially for archives and libraries are now available, offering a greater degree of protection for the original materials, and enabling hybrid images (both microfilm and digital).

Most damage has probably been inflicted by photocopiers. The mere fact that the material has to be placed on a platen upside-down prevents careful handling and leads to damage due to the difficulty of adjusting the original to get the best copy. Large documents such as maps or plans, which are oversize for the photocopier platen, can be strained or even torn as a result of failure to support them. (Using a large format copier, such as those owned by legal firms or architects, is not an option, as they usually require the original to pass through rollers in the machine.) Volumes are likely to suffer spine damage from being forced down on the platen to get a good reproduction of any text which might be close to the gutter, or from pressure applied to the lid of the machine to get the same result. In addition the heat generated by the machine can cause irreversible damage to parchment, photographs or documents with attached wax seals or wafer seals.

There has also been concern over the level of ozone produced by the photocopying process and therefore the proximity of the machine to the collections.

The process still attracts controversy. Some libraries, however, have taken a rather different attitude to mass copying and expect that the copy will become the definitive version and that the original will not survive the process. Many bound volumes of newspapers have thus been destroyed after filming due to the poor quality of the paper on which they were printed, the physical difficulties of storing them and the perceived life expectancy of the microfilm. This led Nicholson Baker (2001) to decry the habit very publicly, in particular the tendency to destroy originals. Archives are not in the same position, since original materials selected for permanent preservation are precisely that, even if they have been duplicated in some way.

The advantages bestowed by flat-bed scanners, on which the material is scanned from above, are substantial – they offer much better protection for the originals and although preparation is still necessary they permit material in poor condition to be copied much more easily. However, some organizations have developed specialist facilities to copy large flat material and so address the access issues of the original.[5]

Commercial filming by television companies presents issues of preservation which are often acute. Television companies frequently request that material is exposed to the heat of very strong lamps, focusing on the quality of the image rather than the needs of the paper or parchment. Clear handling guidelines are necessary to avoid damage being inflicted in the name of greater access (see Chapter 11).

Developing a preservation copying policy: why do it?

Before embarking on a copying programme, or perhaps when reviewing current programmes and considering alternative methods, a clear idea of the purpose of a preservation copying policy is essential. At the least this will help to tease out the various reasons driving such a policy, and may assist in allocation of resources. Three preservation motives are key:

- to ensure continued access to archival documents where the information is in danger owing to the materials used or the condition of the document
- to preserve the originals against over-use, where they are fragile or where they are of such importance that security is an issue
- to provide back-up copies for analogue material in the event of a disaster or as security for digital material against electronic failure.

Additional rationales mostly focus on access, but it must be recognized that the increased emphasis on digitization for access often leads to materials being copied which might otherwise not need copying – they may be part of a project but in perfectly good condition, or they may have been copied already in another format. Subject-based projects tend to cherry-pick appropriate items for digitization, with the accompanying danger that materials lose their context or are not copied in their entirety; for access reasons this may be fine but the result can lead to a patchy preservation picture.

How can the copies themselves be preserved?

Organizations must also focus on the preservation requirements of the copies. For preservation purposes the first copy must be that from which any subsequent copies are taken; to subject the original to repeated copying defies the initial objective of reducing wear and tear. Two issues are particularly difficult. How many copies should be made, and should the same policy be followed for both large collections and individual items ordered by readers?

The issue hardly arises for hand-copied materials or analogue photographic prints, which will have negatives stored appropriately, preferably in separate low-temperature conditions (see Chapter 6). Microfilms require more thought. Ideally the first copy – often referred to as the master – should be recopied immediately to provide a resource from which further copies can be taken if required (the working copy). The master should be stored appropriately (see Chapter 6) and accessed rarely, if ever; there is even a case for storing the masters at an alternative site. The working copy will then itself be copied to provide a low cost diazo, or reading copy which readers will use. This can be replicated as necessary for further distribution or substitution when the original diazo copy is worn or scratched. Not all archives aspire to three microfilm copies but, for security purposes, and to avoid recopying originals, this procedure is regarded as best practice, although the costs are often prohibitive. To avoid recopying by mistake, an accurately maintained list, or preferably database, of all such negatives and microforms must be consulted before any orders are accepted.

Few archives have been able to adopt such rigorous procedures for photocopies. By their nature most orders put in for these by readers will be for individual items or a few dozen pages. Keeping copies of these to avoid possible further copying in the future has been difficult and uneconomical. The effect would be simply to create a duplicate archive with all the associated costs and problems. The development of digital copying, however, has made it more possible to maintain a master copy of individual documents in a database on a hard disk. As long as the digitized image has a means of identification (metadata) and the proper procedures for preserving it have been observed (see Chapter 3) it can be used to generate further copies as required.

Selecting correct copying methods

As is clear from the above, several options must be considered for creating surrogates. However, the key issue is that most archive material will need preparation in advance of digitization to ensure access to the information. It is essential to use the most appropriate method for the material. Damage can be done, and has been done, by copying fragile materials inappropriately. Although copying methods vary, most of the criteria for selection and initial planning work will be similar, whatever the final decision on the method to be adopted. Copying single items for readers is a different activity from undertaking a copying project with a large budget, but many of the criteria for selection listed below will apply to both; any staff undertaking routine copying should always be aware of the criteria and advise the public accordingly.

Criteria for selection

Any or all of the following should be taken into account:

*   the preservation policy of the organization and whether the proposal fits with it – e.g. if it has been decided not to copy material unless a certain level of current use can be demonstrated or future use projected
*   the condition and format of the item(s) to be copied
*   the type of material – e.g. whether paper or parchment, whether with or without attached seals, whether hybrid or any other combination which might make one method of copying a safer option than another
*   any existing copy, even in another format, which it might be possible to recopy
*   likely type of future use of the surrogate – e.g. whether or not it needs to be of high, medium or low quality; this will also have an impact on file sizes and therefore on digital storage costs
*   the availability of a budget for copying, whether in-house or by an outside agency
*   in-house facilities for copying – purchasing, or more likely leasing, equipment is expensive; it requires ongoing maintenance or maintenance contracts and, if purchased, may not be the most up-to-date model.

To ensure that full and effective information on the collections is available, the selection of material must be preceded by a survey. This survey will:

*   identify appropriate collections; those that are:
    — popular
    — sought after

— have low condition issues
— have low preparation needs
- assist planning
- enable the apportioning of resources
- aid the compilation of funding applications

Much of the above suggests that further information is required for making informed decisions on what to copy and how. Some should be available as routine management information, such as:

- any registers or electronic requests for items
- condition surveys or assessments indicating the types of material likely to be at risk and consequently good candidates for copying
- registers of copies of originals kept in the archive from which additional copies can be taken.

Marshalling and analysing this information is not always straightforward and the complexities should not be underestimated. Most archives have methods of accessing such copying data currently but may not have kept records in the past. A conscious decision to maintain information and use it to decide on priorities for copying for preservation may be needed. A simple matrix awarding points for use and condition is a useful way to sort out what is most heavily used and in poor condition, though do not expect the issue to be always clear-cut.

Preparation of material

Preparation time for both large and small projects should not be underestimated. A long run-in is necessary to ensure that the originals are selected appropriately, checked for condition, checked for completeness and documented. It is not unusual for the preparation stage to be underway 12 months before the image capture stage, to ensure that each item is ready and that handling is reduced to a minimum. If an application has to be made for funding, that will add considerably to the timetable for the whole project, although putting the proposal together will clarify the time and resources required. Decisions have to be made about whether the project will be staffed from existing resources, including both the staff to undertake the preparation work and staff to do the actual copying, or whether the selected and prepared material will be sent off-site to an agency; the security implications of that decision must be addressed from the outset. Workflows must be discussed and, for a large project, all those with an input – including repository staff, conservators, reprographic staff and even finance and human resources staff – consulted. The project must not be derailed because of unexpected workloads or failure to tie it into existing corporate and business plans.

A further consideration will be the packaging of all the material to be digitized. This is an opportunity to ensure that once digitized, and therefore technically out of use, that each item is then packaged to archival standards. This ensures a key element of preservation. Careful planning and purchase of packaging materials will then need to be included in the timetable and resource plan.

Preparation space

Preparation space will be required, whether it is decided to undertake the project in-house or use an outside agency. Any copying project involves considerable quantities of documents or volumes being moved from one area to another within the archive, with all the necessary equipment such as:

- trolleys
- adequate table space for examining and checking items, noting missing items within a series, identifying material unsuitable for filming before remedial treatment and noting additional material in files, such as photographic materials, seals or accompanying three-dimensional objects
- equipment for supporting fragile items such as foam wedges and lead-filled snakes for restraining pages
- computers for listing project documents, logging items in and out of the preparation area, documenting any existing damage, and charting progress; creating a database of the material involved in the project has many advantages, both for ensuring that locations can be checked at any time and that targets and milestones toward the completion of the project are met. The choice, evaluation and updating of software will need to be included in the management of the timetable and resources as the project could be spread over a number of years.

It is not a good idea to select, examine and document the material in the storage area, although it is clearly important to reduce movement to a minimum. If conservation facilities are available on-site, material may be most conveniently examined in the workshop prior to undergoing any necessary remedial work before copying.

A separate area must be provided for eating and drinking, as it is not acceptable to have food or drink in proximity to the archival material.

Staff training for preparation of material

Staff checking material prior to copying must be trained; the following issues will need explanation:

- removal of paperclips/pins to avoid damage to the copying machines and any damage through tearing or imprint on the originals
- policy on loose pages; these will need to be inserted in the correct place if known or copied at the end as a subsidiary series
- page numbering policy; if the items are to be filmed and are not copied sequentially readers may assume material is missing; digitized material does not present the same problem, but equally does not provide the same security; filmed images remain in the numbered sequence in which they are copied, providing evidence, if needed, of the existence of the material at the time of filming; the same is not true of digitized material which can be moved or altered in some cases
- policy on whether file covers are to be copied and whether blank pages should be numbered and copied
- policy on what to do about accompanying material which is unsuitable for the chosen copying method
- documentation of any damage – this is particularly important if the original material is to be sent to an outside agency for copying; such documentation must accompany every item while it is being copied, either in paper form or as a computer record.

Staff packing material for transfer to an outside organization or copying bureau must be trained to pack it securely in crates, using bubble wrap to line the crates, and secure lids. The crates should be filled comfortably with any space being packed with bubble wrap or corrugated card. They should have lockable lids and, if the quantity is sufficient, should be placed in wire carts or on pallets for moving off-site (see Chapter 9). Schedules for regular dispatching and returning of material will be needed for any large-scale project.

Preparation for particular copying methods

The above refers to all preparation for copying, whatever method is adopted. Additional precautions are required for specific methods to ensure the preservation of the originals and the copy.

If photocopying is adopted as a preservation solution the process must ensure the survival of the surrogate for as long as possible while access is still required. The following should be required:

- the paper used for the copy must be of suitable permanence and durability (ISO 9706)
- carbon black toner must be used
- the copying machine must be well maintained and serviced
- staff must be trained to ensure maximum quality of the surrogate
- an automatic checking process must be in place for proper adherence of the print to the paper, legibility, completeness, contrast and accuracy
- the storage conditions for the surrogate should match those for originals.

If microfilming is the preferred method a number of other checks must be made during the preparation. These include:

- conformity of the film itself to BS ISO 18906:2000 (35mm, unperforated and with silver gelatine emulsion on a polyester base)
- conformity of the processing to national or international standards
- ultrasonic splicing to ensure the archival quality of the film and the security of the information on the film
- use of lint-free gloves by everyone handling the film to avoid damage by scratching or grease.

If digitizing is selected as the means of creating surrogates many of the above apply; the JISC Digital Media website includes a wide range of guidance and online tutorials.[6]

Copying of material in-house

Any in-house copying area must be well organized to avoid material staying too long in environmental conditions which may not be as good as those in which they are normally stored. Every effort should be made to keep the temperature and relative humidity as stable as possible, but the likelihood is that cameras or other machinery will expose the materials to conditions which can become hot and dry. A good workflow, efficiently managed to minimize the time spent in such conditions, and care taken to re-box material as soon as possible after copying will reduce the potential for damage.

Reprographic staff should be trained (by conservation staff or an external conservation consultant) to handle the material properly, including:

- careful removal and replacement of papers from files, particularly those which are overfull
- careful opening of bound volumes to minimize strain on binding

- use of padded camera base boards to limit damage caused by moving material on and off them
- use of padded book cradles or foam wedges to support covers of bound volumes
- use of lead-filled snakes where necessary to restrain pages, sheets of Perspex or glass platens counterbalanced on cameras
- minimizing time that the material is out of its box; this is also a security precaution especially where some of the material is not marked with a reference but has merely sequential numbering – this problem is rarely encountered in libraries but can be common in archives where cataloguing backlogs exist for large collections
- procedures in case of finding unidentified material or material unsuitable for copying
- procedures for liaison with conservation staff, or a local specialist, over issues of condition and/or appropriate handling or packaging
- training of staff and operators
- targets and programme reviews
- liaison with digitizing agency.

Use of outside agencies

Most reprographic agencies are commercial businesses undertaking copying processes for non-archival purposes. Usually any contract with an archive will be carried out off-site, although on occasion – e.g. the filming of the UK World War 1 service records at The National Archives – the contractor can bring staff and equipment to the site. In either case it will be necessary to ensure that the agency understands what is required, has experience in preservation copying and, if the work is to be done off-site, has the necessary capacity to store archival material overnight securely and to operate a secure system for the packing and transport of material to and from the archive. A detailed specification will need to be compiled and this will underpin the key issues outlined in the contract.

The following is highly advisable:

- Visit several agencies to talk to staff and discuss the preservation issues arising from the type of material to be copied. Ensure that they are aware of the necessary standards and are able to conform to them. Discuss training and discover whether permanent or temporary staff would be used for the contract; the latter could be a major difficulty if they have to be trained from scratch or the turnover is such that repeated training is necessary.

- Inspect samples of work done for other archives or libraries and, if possible, submit some work from the archive to test the quality of the result. Vary the type of material to cover the range for which copies are required.
- Spend time drawing up a contract which covers all the points required from the service, including monitoring and quality assurance. Documentation of the entire process of copying and transfer of material must be required to ensure that if mistakes are made – and with big copying contracts something is bound to go wrong at some point – they can be easily and quickly rectified.
- Take up references from similar organizations to ensure that unexpected preservation issues have not arisen.
- Institute additional checking procedures either within the archive or with a third party if the expertise is not available.
- Ensure that one member of the archive staff is responsible for the project and contract and that contacts at both the archive and the agency are clear. Communication issues are often the cause of unnecessary problems, resulting in poor quality work and possible damage to originals.

Additionally, the specification from the supplier should include detail regarding:

- equipment to capture images
- insurance and risk
- the use and management of metadata
- files for use on websites
- storage and security of digital data
- access to data/information.

Creating and using surrogate materials for preservation purposes is very worthwhile but it is not a quick or easy solution. Well carried out, however, it offers many advantages and can provide a more secure carrier for information where the original is failing.

Since 2004, commercial partners have invested an estimated £53 million in The National Archives UK's digitization programme, delivering more than 80 million images online, but this only represents 3–5% of the entire collection.

[Bülow and Ahmon, 2010]

Summary

This chapter has outlined the options for copying and the preservation issues related to creating surrogates; the need to choose appropriate copying methods, the need to carry out a survey of potential material for copying and the need for adequate safeguards for the originals. It has also covered the issues relating to the use of in-house or external agencies, which have implications for budgets and accommodation.

Copying, especially digitization may well be one of the options to consider when an archive is required to move. The very fact of changing location should prompt discussion about whether alternative methods of access for readers should be a factor in determining a new site. The following chapter covers the issues which arise when planning a move.

Notes and references

1   Detailed information about digitization projects can be found on the JISC Digital
     Media website (www.jiscdigitalmedia.ac.uk/stillimages/docs/category/managing-a-
     project), which outlines project management issues as well as case studies.
     Two other key resources:
     National Preservation Office, *Guide to Preservation Microfilming,* National
     Preservation Office (2000)
     Bulow, A. E. and Ahmon, J. (2010) *Preparing Collections for Digitization,* Facet
     Publishing.
2   See Bibliography for a full list. The manual produced by the Mellon Microfilming
     Project Working Group (National Preservation Office, 1992) was also responsible
     for raising standards.
3   Diazo film is a low-cost option for viewing using ammonia gas or liquid instead of
     silver during processing.
4   Further information is available on the JISC Digital Media website,
     www.jiscdigitalmedia.ac.uk/stillimages/advice/digitising-microfiche-and-microfilm.
5   For example the Coal Authority's scanning service,
     www.imat.cimtech.co.uk/Pages/IM@T_Online/2006/December/1206_NewsTrack_
     03.htm.
6   See www.jiscdigitalmedia.ac.uk.

9

Moving the records

Introduction

Moving all or part of an archive is a daunting experience and one which needs to be approached in a very organized way. It is highly likely that many archivists will have to organize a move at some point in their careers. A successful move will ensure that:

- the material is undamaged by either the move or the new surroundings into which it is put
- access to the materials is interrupted for as little time as possible.

That said, any move is a serious risk which needs to be minimized as far as possible by good planning and efficient execution. This chapter looks at:

- the risks involved in moving archives
- managing the move
- briefing a removal firm
- the equipment required
- preparing for the move
- the move itself.

What are the risks?

Listing the preservation risks offers a good way to identify those which can be reduced and those which will have to be monitored throughout the process. Any of the following might be a problem:

- If there is a lack of clarity about the scope and purpose of the move it will be very difficult to retain control over the operation. Both scope

and purpose should be spelt out in detail to inform those who are
involved and clarify their roles.

- The parent organization – e.g. business, university or local authority –
  may not fully understand the requirements of the archive for moving.
- A complete move of an archive involves many factors and requires
  logistical expertise which may not be available in-house. Even a small
  move within an archive is complicated.
- The decision to move may not leave sufficient time or budget for the
  operation to be undertaken in the optimum way. Skimping on time for
  planning will affect the success of the outcome and introduces
  additional hazards. Poor budgeting will lead to risks that essential
  preservation procedures, such as boxing and wrapping, are not
  undertaken or too few staff are involved to guarantee the safety of the
  archive.
- If the material is in poor condition or is not adequately protected it risks
  additional damage in transit, and subsequent inaccessibility to readers.
- The new accommodation may not be completed in time for the
  planned move; predicting the timetable for the completion and fitting
  out of a new storage space is not easy and can be affected by many
  exterior factors such as bad weather, poor contractors and poor
  management. In consequence the material may have to be moved
  before all arrangements are completed and the building has had time to
  dry out.

Planning the project

The objective for the first phase of planning is to scope the project and to
draw up an outline requirement for staff and resources, preservation standards
for the move and a timetable.

If the size of the archive is not known – and many archives do not have a
clear idea of what they hold and in what format – the first part of the plan
must be to determine the scale of the proposed operation. An agreed unit of
counting (boxes for the most part, although some individual items will be
included) is essential and calculations must be made on that basis; the final
meterage and volume of shelving to be moved will influence the timetable
and the budget. At the same time the condition of the material can be noted,
although this is not the time for detailed examination.

Staff

Moving the records may be part of a larger operation to move the whole organization to completely new premises; on the other hand, part of the archive may be moved to another location or material may be moved around within the existing archive. Whatever the scale of the operation, it is vital to employ the right staff and allow adequate time to plan. A project manager is essential. Appoint someone who:

- is thoroughly conversant with the records and their current location
- knows about preservation standards
- has a good track record in project management
- has good leadership and communication skills.

The appointment must be made as early as possible to allow time for adequate planning and determining how much extra help will be needed. For a large project, such as building a new facility, the appointee will be required to work within the whole framework and so must be included from the outset in wider discussions and meetings to ensure that all information relevant to the move is passed on. If it is a small internal move it is still necessary to ensure that comprehensive information from all those involved or affected is available to those in charge.

Staff involved in the move will include those currently employed by the archive who have a detailed knowledge of the records and their locations. The ICA's *Moving Archives: guidelines for preservation* (Albrecht-Kunszeri and Loescher, 2001, 364) recommends that these staff should be given the skilled tasks, as their experience and knowledge will be vital to the success of the operation. They may be required to act as project managers for parts of the operation if the move is large-scale.

Temporary staff can be given more routine work, as appropriate; this might include packing and labelling material or monitoring the move and the logistics. Students can be employed during vacation, as can personnel on secondment from the armed forces; the latter are particularly skilled at logistics and can offer considerable insight into methods of moving. Professional removal contractors may be required on a temporary basis, as may additional administrative staff, depending on the scale of the operation. The commissioning of a removal contractor requires careful planning with a tightly worded and comprehensive contract. The contractor may be able to offer a range of services over and above the actual move and the client will need to view this element of the project with a flexible perspective. In some cases, removal staff have had to be on-site a year before the move, attaching barcodes and compiling a corresponding database.

Volunteers can also be helpful but it is essential that they are given the same training as temporary staff, since they will require the same commitment and stamina as those who are being paid. For some organizations, the use of volunteers may be the only way that the move preparation can be achieved, so a detailed programme of training and timetabling will also form part of the project manager's (large) remit.

The move should be controlled, preferably requiring fewer people for a longer time than more people for a short time. While preparation is taking place, such as the packing of records or the labelling of boxes, more staff may be required temporarily.

Budget

The budget will be high on the agenda; at the least the costs are likely to include:

- temporary staff and any overtime required
- professional services of removal contractors
- packaging and preservation materials
- any equipment not provided by moving contractors (crates, trolleys, etc.)
- any hardware and software required to log the move or create a database of new locations
- remedial conservation.

It will be difficult to assess the final figure at the outset but generous provision must be made to ensure that the preservation requirements of the organization are met. The converse, the failure of the archive to ensure the security and wellbeing of its holdings during the course of the move, is the very reverse of what every director of archives wishes to experience. Frequent revisions to estimates, clarifications and elaborations will be needed all through the planning process; ensure that one person has an overview of all the budgets to prevent over-spend (Bendix, 2012, 2).

Access during the move

Make a clear decision on whether the archive will be open to all readers at either the old or the new location, or both, while the move is taking place. The risks to the material are reduced if it stays closed; staff can concentrate on the move and less outside assistance may be required.

Experience at the British Library suggested that the move of the Manuscripts Department was easier than the move of the Printed Books Department; the former was closed, while in the latter the material was available to readers throughout, apart from the immediate weeks while it was being moved. Political decisions will also play a part; continued access was important to the British Library, which had suffered a very negative press campaign during a protracted building period.

Remaining open has a serious impact on planning, as it involves absolute assurance to users that stated material will be available on a predetermined day at either location. Given the scope for slippage in the move, this necessitates very precise planning and a commitment to success that must be sustainable over a long period of time. It also affects the budget, as additional staff may be required, as well as more vans and moving equipment; this is where the contract is vital to ensure that appropriate compensation sanctions are available to the client for changes to the agreement. Overall, staying open reduces flexibility but if it is successful has considerable public relations benefits and is likely to build up support from users. Some archives opt for access during the move to a limited number of users – this may be more appropriate for a business where access can be crucial for some but unnecessary for everyone.

What standards should be applied?

To ensure a successful move, preservation standards must be determined and agreed at a very early stage. It is not possible to outline a budget until the organization has committed itself to standards which are clear and unambiguous and ratified by senior management. These should be drawn up irrespective of the budget to start with – compromises may be needed later but the highest standards should be aimed for. Standards must apply to all the record formats, an added incentive to keep them simple. The following should be a minimum:

- All items in transit should have protective packaging – this may be temporary or permanent but must be sufficiently rigid to support the material inside during movement. Decide on the standard of boxes/packaging materials/crates/three-sided moving trucks, etc. and ensure that everything purchased or provided meets that standard specification for construction strength, movability, weight, availability of replacement parts where appropriate and smooth construction without sharp edges.
- Containers must be the correct size for the material inside so that they do not shift in transit; this involves providing a variety of sizes of container on-site and packing them out where the contents do not fill the container.

- All boxes or housing must have a facility for fixing on labels securely; this is especially important if a bar-code system is being used to manage the move.
- Any permanent packaging must be of archival standard; if new packaging is included in the plans for the move ensure that the manufacturer can provide the required amount on time and that any boxes either come flat or can be stored on-site conveniently. Phased delivery may be the answer.
- Training in preservation must be given to all temporary staff as part of their contracts; permanent staff may need refresher training, especially if they are required to act as trainers for others. The standard of conduct must not drop due to fatigue or preoccupation with other aspects of the move.
- Temporary staff working directly on the archives must be supervised by permanent staff at all times; the expertise and skills of the latter to maintain standards will be better used in this way.

Fixing a timetable

Timetabling the move will require consultation with the whole organization and dovetailing with any other plans. Factor in as many of the proposed activities as possible to ensure that none are overlooked; including them later will be difficult as the date for the move gets nearer. Plan for the maximum lead time that the total project will allow – a great deal of information will have to be collected at speed, the records will have to be packed up and the management of the project must be planned in detail (see below). Setting up contracts and identifying appropriate suppliers also takes time. Factors such as building operations at either location, traffic restrictions, availability of lifts, capacity of removal trucks or any requirement to maintain a service to the public will influence the timetable; some of these factors will be beyond the control of the archive. Time should also be allowed for days off when, due to illness, bad weather or other emergency, the move has to be halted. Breaks in the programme should be scheduled (at least monthly) for reviewing progress, deciding on alterations to the schedule or catching up if the project is behind time.

Other planning factors

A database of locations at either end, if one does not already exist, and a computer tracking system so that it is possible to locate any record at any time (see below) will need development and may involve other experts who are not permanent members of the archive team. Since moves are frequently not straightforward this will assist security and planning.

Disaster plans must be reviewed before the move to ensure that they are up to date and that they reflect possible difficulties during the project. This can be done at any time and ensuring that they are completed well in advance prevents panic if something goes wrong.

Good and regular communications with all the staff are an essential part of ensuring that the move safeguards the records. The move may not be popular and the new location will involve some in longer, more difficult or expensive journeys to work. Change is rarely welcomed, however good the new premises may be. Counter a negative attitude by involving all staff, consulting and talking to them and ensuring that they have accurate and timely information. Attention to their concerns and needs at the outset should help to ensure that the move takes place in a co-operative atmosphere, conducive to best preservation practices; the converse, a rushed job with unco-operative and resentful staff, could be disastrous.

Briefing a suitable removal firm

In some archives staff will move the materials themselves but the majority will hire expert removers. Expert they may be but, unless they normally deal with fine art or antiques removal, they are unlikely to know what is required for a move of archives. When drawing up a contract the archive must make all the key decisions; stating these in advance will assist planning and ensure that the archive maintains control over the move. These issues must form the core of the tender specification and it is vital that the project manager assists with the compilation of this document and takes part in the evaluation of the submissions in advance of awarding the contract. This decision needs to be based on the tenderer's fitness for purpose and ability to fulfil the brief, not to be unduly influenced by price/cost. However, avoid unnecessary restrictions which will hamper the move or alienate the removal staff through being unworkable. Start by outlining:

* the complete move and the objectives
* responsibilities of the archive and of the removal firm (e.g. packing/moving fragile items/replacing materials at new location, etc.)
* responsibility for damage procedures
* any logistical hazards (e.g. low ceilings, small strongrooms, restricted vehicular access, awkward parking arrangements, etc.)
* the special preservation requirements of particular types of archives in detail

- standards for protection of the material once packed, including orientation of the crates (e.g. to be kept flat), maintaining order of crates as loaded, special arrangements in bad weather, etc.
- prohibition on removal staff handling individual archives in the event of a spillage or disaster
- standard of removal staff behaviour required in the archive (e.g. no smoking, drinking or eating)
- handling training required for removal staff; remember that they may need to know about more than one type of archival material
- arrangements for handling training for replacement removal staff if the move is likely to last several months
- expected communication arrangements, such as intervals of meetings, timetables and emergency arrangements in the event of things going wrong
- special arrangements for loading and removal needed for any mobile shelving, map racking, three-dimensional objects or specialized storage areas
- travel routes
- monitoring role of the archive staff.

Require:

- specifications of equipment to be supplied (removal trucks, crates, metal or wire rolling carts, packing materials as appropriate, etc.)
- compliance with prohibition on transporting mixed loads – e.g. not taking archival material and office furniture in the same van
- references and security checks for staff; this may be difficult if staff turnover is high but must be complied with to ensure security: factor in additional time if this is likely to occur within the timeframe
- time built in for training in records handling
- rigorous contract staff management procedures – e.g. punctuality and responsibility for any damage caused by the removal firm; this requires a clear idea of the condition of the material before it is moved, something which is not always possible (in which case the issues must be discussed and agreed before any contract is signed)
- procedures and responsibility for dismissal of staff not complying with archive requirements
- security procedures, especially in relation to:
  — locking the vans on departure
  — unlocking at the end location
  — keys for each location

— any storage of materials in vans overnight
— special arrangements in the event that the van(s) break down or are involved in an accident between locations

- visits to both sites for any potential contractors with a detailed meeting/tour on the problems likely to be encountered
- a session for the archive staff to watch the packing techniques of the removal firm; staff should be on the look-out for poor handling and understanding of the material being moved
- insurance cover to outline what can be carried per van load.

Further considerations for the owner of the collections:

- Make contact with corporate finance and insurance teams well in advance of the start of the move to ensure that all issues are communicated to the insurer; some elements may be covered by general terms of existing insurance.
- The move contractors will require 'Evidence of Insurance' if insurance has been arranged by the client; there will be no need then for transit insurance from the move contractor.
- Plan for risks and develop appropriate responses; risks during transit; risks from any temporary accommodation; wrapped and packaged collections will require more space than originally.
- Be sure what you are moving; uncatalogued collections are always a risk; a clear identification methodology will need to be in place for tracking and auditing purposes (barcodes or RFID tags).
- Keep a record of what has been moved each day; the move contractors must be able to provide a list and locations at the end of each day.
- The value of the loads should never exceed the insurance maximum arranged; if high value items are to be transported then the client will need to increase the cover or use smaller vehicles.
- It may be prudent to ensure that staff are always accompanying the collections during transit in case of vehicle breakdown and for added security.

Minimum removal equipment specifications

Draw up specifications for the equipment to be used; this will be useful whether the archive has to purchase such equipment or it is provided by the contractor. In either case the specifications will provide a checklist for standards and quality. Take the likely length of the move into account when drawing up the specifications and remember that equipment will wear out.

Replacements and/or more robust varieties should be budgeted for if necessary. Remember to budget for the money and time spent on providing adequate training for all staff unfamiliar with some of the equipment. Start with a list of what might be needed:

- removal van(s)
- ramps
- trolleys
- dollies
- pallets
- three-sided rolling carts
- tough plastic crates with lids (with no holes)
- packing materials
- boxes
- ladders.

As a precaution, more than one removal van will be needed, even for the smallest move outside the original building; vans can break down. Each should be covered, with lockable doors and no access to contents from the driver's side. It should be well insulated so that the interior conditions are stable; if very sensitive material is to be transported the van should be climate-controlled. No indication should be given on the outside of the contents being carried. The interior should include bars to which straps can be attached to restrain items in transit. A van with an air-ride suspension system should be provided for fragile materials such as glass plate negatives, shellac discs or delicate objects.

Ramps may be required if the material has to be moved down short flights of stairs or into vans without automatic loading. They should be stable and well constructed while being light enough to be moved easily; it is likely that they will be moved several times a day. Ensure that the dimensions tally with those of the trolleys or rolling carts which will be wheeled directly into the van.

Trolleys are normally used by the archive but the wear and tear inflicted during a move will be considerably greater than daily use. They should be strongly constructed from stainless steel without projecting edges or ledges and should take a known weight. Make sure that replacement wheels are available. Some specialist trolleys will be required to transport large items, and any used for moving glass plate negatives or fragile items should have pneumatic tyres. Ensure that sufficient are ordered to keep a supply at both ends and some in transit at any one moment for the duration of the move; replacements may be necessary. Ensure that they will fit into available lifts and any corridors or passageways.

Dollies should be steel-reinforced, lightweight and have a standard flush deck protected with carpet or other soft covering; the castors should be non-marking and double-ball with replacements easily available; the load bearing must be known and observed. Various sizes are required to accommodate different needs.

Boxes can be stacked on pallets and then shrink-wrapped to avoid any movement. This may be a feasible method of transporting large numbers of boxes if a fork-lift truck is available to move the pallets at either end. The pallets should be rigid platforms, constructed of wood or plastic. If they are to be used as a temporary base for the boxes the construction material does not matter; as long-term supports (e.g. for material which is rarely, if ever, consulted) they should be made from inert materials. Do not stack too many boxes on top of each other; specify the number which can be safely transported per pallet.

Piles of boxes may also be transported conveniently in three-sided rolling carts which provide protection and support, with the same caveat as for the pallets; too many boxes piled up will cause damage to those at the bottom and to their contents. The base and frame should be sturdily constructed from stainless steel with either solid or wire sides. Mesh reduces the weight overall and also offers visibility of the contents and its labels. Replacement wheels may well be required for longer moves. Many different types of cart are available, some with detachable or folding fourth sides. The contents can be secured with straps or stretch film.

Flat-sided crates with folding lids are likely to be the basic movable unit; they provide protection and are easy to move, provided they are not too large. The size should be dependent on the ease with which they can be carried when full. Many varieties are available: stacking (but not nesting), flat-packed, open-sided, with or without handles. Sturdy construction in tough/high-density plastic should be specified, with a known weight load.

Packing materials may include:

- blankets
- bubble wrap of different sizes
- foam or Plastazote, an archival alternative (see Chapter 6)
- shrink film
- heavy duty polythene sheeting
- straps
- tapes
- corrugated card
- acid-free tissue or paper
- any materials which are used to ensure the safe transit of the archives.

None of these materials are likely to form permanent packing or covering and so they do not need to comply with archival specifications. However, should the proposed new storage location be temporary or short-term (over six months) then a higher standard of archival packaging will be required for all formats. Ensure that supplies are ample, in particular of anything used to cushion items in transit.

Boxes will be required before the move to replace those which are defective and those which are damaged during the project (see Chapter 6 for detailed specifications). If a boxing programme is undertaken in association with the move, ensure that the supplier can manufacture the required number to the given timetable. Specialized boxes will be required for the protection of fragile items such as glass plate negatives or shellac discs. Large or oddly shaped items may need either specially made boxes or to be wrapped in bubble wrap or acid-free paper.

Ladders must be sturdily constructed from steel and, other than very short stepladders, must incorporate a platform; moving boxes to/from shelves above head height requires stability and room to move. Ensure that ladders can access storage areas where space is constricted – e.g. in narrow rooms, through narrow doors, through winding corridors, etc. Scissor-lift platforms may also be useful.

Preparing for the move

Preparation includes developing a number of plans; allow as much time as possible if they are to be drawn up in-house, and a detailed presentation of the proposed timetable and process should be given to senior managers. It is vital that management understand and appreciate the significant impacts of a move on day-to-day activities. It may be more efficient to bring in outside help for these specific tasks, remembering that permanent staff with intimate knowledge of the current situation will need to offer considerable and time-consuming assistance.

Do floor plans for both the old and new buildings exist?

If a location plan for the existing accommodation does not exist draw one up; many archives will already have this information but possibly not in electronic form. An important factor is identifying floor loadings, as this can have a direct impact on the move plan (Bendix, 2012). A database will enable more precise planning, particularly if material is to be moved more than once, or from more than one location. Efforts should be made to avoid multiple moves, but sometimes it is just not possible. In order to ensure that the right records are moved at the right time carry out a complete location check and return items to their original location. Specify a date at which items in use must be back in their correct location before being moved. If a bar-code system is to be used to track boxes during the move it is essential that the database is correct.

The location plan for the new accommodation must be precise and accurate; the move will only proceed smoothly if the records are put straight on to the correct new shelves in the right order; security will be compromised if this does not happen. If mobile shelving is installed remember that only one aisle can be accessed at once – this factor can seriously undermine a removal company's calculations and timetable. Weight loading must be established at the outset – archives are heavy, as is mobile shelving. Avoid stacked crates where possible, to minimize the risk of overloading particular areas.

Move plan

The move plan – the order in which the material is to go to the new location – must tie in with existing and new location plans. Most importantly, the timing of the move itself must be controlled; plan for a maximum number of movements a day, based on how many metres of shelving can be safely loaded into trucks, transported and placed in the new location a day.

Ensure that access at both ends is logical so that the operation can proceed smoothly. Consider what time the material is to be moved from the original location; should it be moved the previous evening and stored overnight in a secured van or in the early morning so that it can be transferred into a van first thing? Will the first van be followed by subsequent vans to be filled or will the next load have to wait for the return of the first van from the round trip? Where will any material wait? Will it get in the way of users at the current or new location? Will the security be adequate? The logistics are complicated and a register outlining the risks and the best means of mitigating them must be drawn up.

Develop a tracking system for all material to ensure no loss of intellectual control during the move – at the least this should be a card system. No records should be moved without being checked at the old location, moved with an identifying tag and checked and reshelved at the new location. A master plan will need updating every evening to check that the planned moves have been completed satisfactorily. For large moves most archives will adopt a more sophisticated electronic solution, usually in conjunction with bar-coding all the items to be moved, either individually or per crate. Checking movements and automatically updating the location plans at both

University College London (UCL); Special Collections move 2011

The process to physically move (including barcoding) 7000 linear metres, consisting of many complex elements, took just 10 months to achieve.

Due to advanced planning and robust project management, including accurate assessments of the volume of material to be moved, it was possible to move 240 crates (each crate measured 1100 x 380 x 300mm) per day of pre-packed collections. While the actual move to The National Archives, Kew, was completed in the months of July to August 2011, the first planning activities started in 2008, with pre-move assessments of all the collections and barcoding starting in November 2010.

The key factors that contributed to the success of this ambitious project were:

- the availability of a temporary secure space in which to decant processed material in advance of the actual move
- the additional availability of a large secure warehouse space to store packing boxes, crates and conservation supplies
- a mezzanine office space that was free and available; the space was able to accommodate 7 conservators and over 150 volunteers carrying out cleaning, wrapping and mould removal
- a very significant input from volunteers, taken from both inside and outside UCL; on one day it was recorded that there were over 40 different individuals involved in various aspects of the preparatory programme
- a close working relationship with the removal contractor during the planning stages and throughout the whole move
- the commissioning of two specialist external project consultants to assist in planning, advise on best practice for moving library and archive materials and to keep track of progress during the move itself.

ends of the move is made a great deal easier this way. It ensures greater security and enables staff at both ends to know exactly where all the material is at any moment. The methodology is the same as that adopted by warehousing companies; it is not new and can readily be adapted. The process of using barcodes needs careful consideration and planning with the removal company. There are very specific preservation issues inherent in the use of self-adhesive barcode labels and this must be appropriately assessed, a detailed methodology compiled and compliance rigorously monitored.

Draw up a route plan for the vans between the locations involved in the move; this may involve multiple buildings with consequent complications of timetabling. The route plan should be as direct as possible and minimize the likelihood of hold-ups in traffic. Enquire of relevant local authorities whether any major road works are planned during the period of the move, and ensure that the highway authorities and police are aware that regular van journeys are planned over the course of the coming weeks or months. Establishing good communications with all these to promote partnerships will result in benefits for all. Try out the route at several times of day, and an alternative for use if necessary, to determine the average journey time. Insist that the removal vans use the approved route and do not deviate from or stop on it.

Moving the archives
Moves are rarely straightforward . . .

We couldn't just move A to B – boxes came in from the outstore to St Luke's, half of them were put on one side, boxes came in from County Hall, the Records Management Team in County Hall moved their stuff to the vacated strongrooms, and we then sent the outstore RM files into County Hall from St Luke's to be put in their vacated strongrooms. . . . Sometimes the lorries were moving empty, and sometimes they were full both ways.

[Carl Boardman, County Archivist of Oxfordshire]

Considerable pressure may be exerted on those planning the move, from management and external agencies commissioned to assist with the process, to draw up a precise timetable. Resist the temptation to be too specific too early; the safety and security of the archives depends on all the preparations being complete and many factors will remain uncertain for some time during the preparations. Choose a suitably representative selection of the archives with which to carry out a pilot move; this will reveal valuable information about unanticipated hazards or difficulties to which solutions can be devised more easily in the planning stage than once the main move has started.

What will be the best way to communicate progress?

The decision about access to the material during the move will have been taken already; if the archive proposes to offer access during the move, devise a user communications strategy, both in advance and at the time the material is actually moved. Users will be dependent on that information for decisions on when and where they plan to use the archives. Some, however, will remain unaware of the dislocations planned; draw up contingency plans for communications if material is late in being relocated. Issue early advance warnings in:

- appropriate journals and professional literature
- the original location
- the future location

- the website
- office communications internally and externally
- mailing lists.

Keep these communication routes open throughout the move and ensure that users have a means of direct communication with the archive by phone and in person to check availability. Decide on how to cope with demands for access from those with influence. Indicate how complaints can be made, and deal with them speedily to minimize the inevitable discontent caused by the disruption.

Continue regular communications with staff, both those directly involved with the move and those who are affected but not necessarily part of the operation. Glean valuable information from staff during pilot studies; ensure that everyone knows their roles for the major move; encourage sharing of problems and listen to staff who are finding the process difficult. Ensure that everyone knows the timetable, the consequences for them personally and the final objectives of the move. Remind them regularly of the overriding need to ensure the safety and security of the archives during the whole operation and reiterate the preservation standards and requirements frequently.

Protecting documents for the move

For the move itself the objectives are to avoid multiple handling and ensure adequate protection when the material is packed into the van, when it is in transit and when it is finally unpacked and reshelved at the new location.

The damage caused to archival material by poor environmental conditions is well documented, and moving it from one environment to another and finally to a third will almost certainly subject it to stress. Equalizing the old and the final destination levels of temperature and relative humidity will help if that is possible. Minimizing time spent in transit will also help, particularly if the outside conditions are extreme. If much parchment is to be moved it is worth considering using vans with climate-control or air conditioning. Otherwise, the archives will be best protected by boxing or wrapping, using as much as possible to insulate the materials in rapidly fluctuating conditions.

Packing the archives securely is a major part of the strategy to ensure a successful move with all the materials arriving intact. Much depends on the current protection offered in the old location. Assume, as a basic, that current packaging will be used during the move but identify as priorities any items which are not already boxed or wrapped. Follow this with an estimate of the number of existing boxes or wrappings in such bad condition that they do not offer sufficient support and protection to the contents for a move. The budget (see above) will need to be adjusted once this estimate has been made, since it is likely that an overall figure will have been needed before this more detailed analysis can be undertaken. If this seems the wrong way round, accept that this happens frequently and try to be prepared in advance.

Provide a large, well ventilated space for staff and any temporary employees or volunteers to do the packing or wrapping in the original location, with tables of an adequate size, chairs and sufficient equipment to give very dirty material a basic clean. It is unlikely that time will permit more detailed work but it is important to avoid taking dust, dirt and the accretions of centuries into a new, clean repository where air conditioning ducts can get blocked and new premises polluted. Provide:

- brushes
- low-suction HEPA filter vacuum cleaners[1] or air suction cleaning tables if necessary
- face masks, gloves and overalls, which will provide basic protection to staff – but additional health and safety measures may be necessary should the material be found to be contaminated.

It is vital to ensure that all staff have received full training to enable the appropriate use of the Personal Protective Equipment (PPE). Preferably all documents would be boxed but some archives will have too many bundles of papers for a boxing budget. Wrap these in acid-free paper and ensure that they are placed in crates with bubble wrap or foam protection on the bottom and sides. Cut this just oversize and put in place – it can be re-used if clean – with the flat surface facing inwards (bubbles away from the object).

Packing and cleaning is boring work and a rota for dealing with different types of material will offer some variation. Set targets for completion against a reasonable timetable; requirements that are too tight will result in poor protection or dirty material being moved and causing subsequent problems. Any untrained staff should be required to attend at least one training session on how to maximize protection to material while it is moving, as well as personal health and safety.

Do not overfill the crates with boxes or bundles and pack any space at the top with additional foam or bubble wrap to ensure the contents do not move during transit. Standard boxes can be moved in and out of the vans in three-sided carts with protective foam or carpet on the base to prevent too much shaking or disturbance. Alternatively, they can be placed on pallets and shrink-wrapped for the duration of the move; if shrink-wrapping is adopted as a measure for protecting material it will be necessary to install the equipment in a well ventilated room and away from smoke detectors, as it generates non-toxic fumes and smoke. Advice is available on using shrink-wrapping as a technique from the National Archives and Records Administration in Washington.[2]

Rolled maps and plans need special long crates – sometimes known as coffins – for transport, lined as above. These crates are often moved on dollies, which should also have protective covering on the base to minimize disturbance. The maps themselves may require wrapping in bubble wrap if they are fragile; be generous in allowing for overlaps and tuck-ins and ensure that there is a pre-layer of acid-free tissue or paper between the object and the bubble wrap. Alternatively they can be wrapped round tubes and protected with acid-free paper on the outside. Flat maps and plans may be more easily transported in the drawers in which they are normally kept, even if these plan chests are not going to be used in the new accommodation. Ensure that the drawers are not overfilled and that a securing flap is in place to prevent maps falling out, and place protective bubble wrap or foam on the top. Dollies may be used for these too; the removal firm will have techniques for moving large items of furniture.

Bound volumes, whether of archival or printed material, can be transported on protected library trolleys with angled shelves, shrink-wrapped to avoid volumes falling out; this enables them to be moved directly from the shelves at one end to those at the other end. Alternatively, they can be placed in protected crates; ensure that they are placed either spine downwards to avoid the text block pulling the joints, or flat. Special collection items can be wrapped in acid-free tissue and should be transported flat. Outsize volumes will require particular protection to avoid damage; wrap them securely in bubble wrap (after pre-wrapping in acid-free tissue or paper) before packing in crates.

Wrap three-dimensional material – models or items too large to pack in boxes – in bubble wrap and pack into large crates with sufficient additional packing to ensure that they do not move in transit.

Electronic or magnetic materials will need additional protection to prevent damage in transit and to ensure that they are not in contact with any magnetic fields. The vans in which they are moved must be climate-controlled.

Fragile items such as intact glass plate negatives or shellac discs must be securely packed and transported on trolleys with appropriate weight loading and with pneumatic, air-filled tyres. Vans should have an air-ride suspension system to cushion against shocks. Move glass plates in their storage orientation, i.e. resting on the longer side, and ensure that they are all held tightly in the container in which they are packed. Likewise, shellac discs should be orientated on the edge, not stored flat. Minimize any movement by placing the flat planes of the glass or discs parallel to the sides of the trucks.

Broken glass plates should also be moved in the packaging in which they are normally held; this should be in protective sink mat enclosures made from corrugated card or Plastazote. Test moves of items deemed difficult – using, for example, window glass in the place of negatives – will smooth out problems when the main move takes place.

The move itself

If the preparations have been well thought out and co-ordinated between the parties involved the actual move should proceed smoothly and in a regulated manner. In practice:

- Reiterate the roles of every individual, as it is essential that everyone knows what they are supposed to do and where they should be.
- Maintain communications with both staff and users, informing the latter exactly which archives will be available when and where.
- Ensure that documents in use are returned to their location according to timetable so that they are ready for moving.
- Allow time for mistakes to be rectified, as even the best preparations go awry on occasion.
- Check, maintain and if necessary replace equipment.
- Keep a log of progress and problems and ask all those involved to report any difficulties or damage to you immediately.

And afterwards . . .

Once the move is complete it is important to start the process of replacing all the boxes or containers damaged during the operation. It is inevitable that some damage will have been sustained but, with good preparations, it is likely that only some of the protective coverings will need attention or replacement. If there is any need to negotiate with the removal firm or insurance company over costs for damage or loss it is essential to have documented evidence, such as photographs, to hand. Enter into any negotiations on this as soon as possible.

Write a report of the whole project as soon as possible, culling additional information and assessments from those who were involved. Despite the assumption that this was a once-in-a-lifetime experience, it is quite likely that the archive will undertake a further move in the future or that other archives will ask for advice. Having a report to hand will be invaluable.

Summary

Moving an archive successfully is a highly skilled job, with substantial risks attached to it. Consequently the more planning that is undertaken in advance the better the result is likely to be. This chapter has outlined the necessary steps to achieve a successful outcome, and has highlighted some of the pitfalls. Choosing the right removal firm, briefing temporary staff fully, packaging all the archival material to minimize the risk of damage in transit, ensuring that appropriate equipment is used, and planning the re-location meticulously – all take time and thought.

The next chapter moves on to the subject of exhibiting archives, and charts the further risks involved in this, again emphasizing the importance of forward planning for a successful display.

Notes and references

1   HEPA stands for high efficiency particulate absorbing.
2   See also Stagnitto (1992).

Exhibiting archives

Introduction

Why put irreplaceable material at risk? The main answer to this is that exhibitions are a major way of promoting access to archival material and involving the public and staff in a topic of mutual interest. All the activities connected with exhibitions, such as the publication of catalogues, production of facsimiles for sale, group visits and publicity, are major concerns of those involved with outreach. For those involved with preservation the essential requirement is to match these needs with adequate security and preservation standards, while not inhibiting or dampening the enthusiasm and talent of colleagues. The crucial factors are collaboration and understanding; exhibitions involve planning and co-operating, compromise and change. Once others understand the concerns of all, the process becomes easier but communication in the first instance is vital. If the parameters relating to standards of exhibition are laid out at the very beginning much less can go wrong. This chapter covers:

- minimizing the associated risks
- policies, standards and guidelines for exhibitions
- managing the care of documents in exhibitions
- planning and preparing for an exhibition.

How can the overall risk be minimized?

The easiest way of minimizing the risk is to set out an exhibition policy and procedure with which everyone agrees. This may involve not only a simple statement of aims for internal use but also a more detailed policy and set of procedures for external loans. The organization will benefit from being very clear about what it will and will not display, outside borrowers will understand the limits of what can be borrowed and why, and staff will appreciate the concerns of other colleagues. Drawing up such a document may take some time, but plenty of examples are available to suggest the main headings. It is very unwise to wait until an exhibition is suggested; policies developed in a hurry under the pressure of a particular project are never satisfactory. Consider:

- the purposes of exhibiting archival material and the authority by which the archive does so
- the scope of exhibitions and the capacity of the organization to mount them
- whether the policy of the organization is to display originals or facsimiles
- the location – whether on the premises or elsewhere
- the best conditions for safe display and the mandatory requirements
- the conditions under which material will be lent to other organizations
- who bears what costs – both for internal budgets and for external borrowers.

Conditions for loans to external exhibitions need additional detail, as they are intended to clarify the responsibilities and obligations of each party in respect of the loan; the potential for misunderstanding – especially if to an overseas borrower – is high. National archives, libraries and museums usually have a written document which outlines the details: The National Archives of the UK publishes its loan conditions on its website (see Appendix 1). This clarifies all the immediate issues about which borrowers might be uncertain. An agreement form should accompany, or follow, the loan conditions document, for signature and return to the lender. Alternatively the same sort of assurance can be issued in the form of a letter to be signed and returned.

Other organizations often use the authority of their governing body, their board or even the responsible government minister to make a final decision on requests for loans. This protects the archivists or conservators most intimately involved with the proposed loan, whose role is to provide appropriate advice.

Additional requirements are sometimes included in loan conditions, such as:

- the necessity for all material to be couriered by the owner to and from its destination, the costs being borne by the borrower
- the need for the lender to use shipping agents for overseas loans
- the requirement for the borrower to pay for a security copy/microfilm
- the stipulation that the loan is to a single institution, and not intended

Exhibition policy

The following points should be considered for inclusion in an internal exhibition policy:

- The XXX Archive is committed, by the authority of the XXXX, to the widest possible access to its holdings and will hold regular temporary exhibitions to promote and publicize them.
- It will provide adequate time for the staff to research, prepare and mount the exhibitions and adequate funds for mounting the displays.
- It will hold at least XX exhibitions a year at the Archives for a maximum of three months each.
- It will display the items in a responsible manner to ensure that they are not damaged as a result, and it will provide the necessary environmental conditions to safeguard them.
- It will provide appropriate security.
- It will ensure that all visitors understand the need to avoid eating, drinking or smoking in the exhibition area.
- It will treat any items loaned for exhibition purposes in accordance with the wishes of the lender and to at least the same level as its own holdings.

Extracts from reports by couriers to exhibitions

'I arrived at the proposed exhibition location to discover that the cases were still being constructed, painters were all over the floor finishing the decoration, flimsy security was planned for the cases and no timetable existed for completion other than the opening date of the exhibition in two days' time. . . . I had to tell the organizers that I could not agree to the loan going ahead as planned, and departed home.'

'The security staff at the airport on the return of the loan insisted on opening the package containing the item in full view of all the other passengers, potentially displaying something of value unprotected.'

'The courier's van got stuck in traffic and we arrived at the airport too late to catch the plane; authorization for the purchase of new tickets needed to be negotiated, but could only be done through the lending organization although the cost would have to be borne by the borrowers. Meanwhile we were trying to ensure the security of the packages . . .'

'The borrower had persuaded an airline to sponsor the ticket, but after a lengthy wait it was announced that the plane was full and non-paying passengers would be delayed. After a fuss, since the loan was awaited at the other end, another seat was found but on a different plane, and the airline lost all track of passenger movements. As a result no one was waiting to meet the by-now frazzled courier, and the borrowing institution, being in a different time zone, was closed.'

for a travelling exhibition
* security precautions as to
  — who handles the loan item
  — where loans can be stored
  — under what circumstances an exhibition case can be opened by the
    borrower
* the environmental conditions which must be met
* the storage of packing material while the exhibition is open
* reproduction conditions.

External loans are a potential source of difficulty, and horror stories of loans which have been difficult to manage abound. The examples cited in the text box on page 161 reinforce the need for excellent communication between lender and borrower, for clear loan conditions and for responsible flexibility on the part of the courier accompanying such loans. It also makes clear the need for courier duties to be undertaken by senior staff with sufficient authority to act in an emergency.

Paperwork should include:

* the initial loan conditions document
* the signed acceptance by the borrower
* a signed receipt for the loan on delivery
* a signed return form at the point of collection
* condition reports for signature (see below).

Guidelines or standards on the exhibition of archival materials have been issued by archives in many parts of the world, displaying considerable unanimity on the subject. The range varies from the very detailed American standard to the basic guidelines issued by the Devon Record Office in the UK, which are quite sufficient to shepherd owners of archival material in the right direction (see next box).

Condition reports should always be compiled on items lent to exhibitions in other organizations. They provide a basis for agreement on the condition of each item between the owner and the borrower at the outset, and a check for any damage sustained during the course of the exhibition afterwards. All existing damage should be noted in writing, preferably by a conservator, and a digital photograph of the document should be taken before it moves from its normal location; this should be agreed by the borrower as a true record and can then be compared to the condition of the exhibit at the end of the exhibition. Any conservation or compensation necessary can subsequently be agreed. It is a safeguard for both parties. The initial report should be signed

Some standards and guidelines for displaying archival materials

Association of College and Research Libraries USA (1990) *Guidelines for Borrowing Special Collections Materials for Exhibition*,
www.ala.org/acrl/standards/specialcollections.

PD 5454: 2012 *Guide for the Storage and Exhibition of Archival Documents*.

McIntyre, J., Kirtley, T., Barratt, A. and Jones, I. (2000) *Guidance for Exhibiting Archive and Library Material*, National Preservation Office, London.

ANSI/NISO Z39.79.2001 *Environmental Conditions for Exhibiting Library and Archival Material*, American National Standards Institute/National Information Standards Organization,
www.niso.org/apps/group_public/download.php/6482/Environmental%20Con
ditions%20for%20Exhibiting%20Library%20and%20Archival%20Materials.pdf.

AFNOR CG36/CN10Z401L/2002 *Prescriptions de Conservation de Documents Graphiques et Photographiques dans le Cadre d'une Exposition*, Association Française de Normalisation,
http://infostore.saiglobal.com/store/Details.aspx?ProductID=646795.

Devon Record Office, *Exhibition of Archives*, www.devon.gov.uk/stopping_the_rot-5.pdf.

by both lender and borrower, and again when the item is returned, indicating acceptance of the document's condition at both times.

Holding exhibitions over many years has accustomed some archives to regard the cases they own, or the exhibition areas habitually used, as the only options for display. Question this: think differently and reconsider what is really required for the safety of the materials and to what standard. Displays mounted for a short time may not require the same conditions as those consisting of facsimiles only, or longer exhibitions of original material lasting a full three months.

Managing the care of documents in exhibitions

Curating, co-ordinating and running exhibitions is a major responsibility, involving many of the archive staff in different capacities. Conservators should be involved in the planning of an exhibition from the start, as the documents are at risk during any display. Their expertise extends to issues of environmental control, the effects of materials from which display cases may be made and the safest way to display documents. Skills in packing and securing documents for transfer may be required for loans, as may testing of light levels or conditioning display cases. Knowledge of national standards, and their recommendations on display, is essential if originals are to be used.

Environmental conditions

Visible light levels must be monitored in all exhibitions where the display materials are original manuscripts, paintings, drawings, textiles or photographs. It is common to reduce the immediate light levels to 50 lux to avoid fading, a requirement which appears to be reasonably well understood by the public. The cumulative effect of light on such vulnerable materials is less well understood; damage is proportional to the length of exposure and light intensity, and is irreversible. Even in unlit storage the effect of earlier exposure to light will continue to cause deterioration, albeit at a reduced rate. It is therefore imperative to limit exposure as much as possible, and many exhibitions are now limited to a maximum of 18,000 lux hours. Lux hours are calculated by multiplying the light intensity, as measured by a digital lux meter, by the length of exposure in hours. Thus 18,000 lux hours might represent an exhibition lasting a total of 360 hours (45 eight-hour days) while lit at 50 lux, or a total of 180 hours (22.5 eight-hour days) while lit at 100 lux.

A rough rule of thumb is that temporary exhibitions should not last more than three months. The alternative for longer exhibitions, or for material deemed too fragile to display, is to use facsimiles; this applies particularly to photographs, where the image is especially susceptible to light damage. Lightcheck strips,[1] which measure cumulative light exposure on individual display items – taking into account sensitivity and previous display – make it possible to decide on what it is safe to exhibit.

Ultraviolet light should be kept to a minimum in an exhibition area by placing film on windows or filters on fluorescent tubes; it can be measured using an ultraviolet meter. Electric light produces heat and bulbs should therefore not be placed directly in a display case; fibre-optic lighting, however, does not produce radiated heat or ultraviolet radiation and can be used when resources permit. The overall lighting should be dimmed to 50 lux; reassure visitors by providing a notice outside explaining that it may take a few moments for their eyes to adjust.

Temperature and relative humidity (rh) levels in display cases should be as near as possible to those specified in international or national standards for storage areas. It is difficult to monitor and maintain optimum conditions throughout a whole exhibition area, since visitors will bring in heat, relative humidity (particularly if it is raining outside) and dirt. Monitoring conditions within the cases and taking appropriate action is a more practical solution. The temperature will usually reflect the level within the exhibition room and can be difficult to control without localized conditioning. Relative humidity, however, can be stabilized using silica gel or ArtSorb, a moisture-sensitive silica material which absorbs and desorbs moisture to offset variations. Purchased in beads, sheets or packs for insertion into the cases, it also acts as a drying agent to remove moisture from air, since most exhibition cases are not sealed sufficiently tightly to prevent all air leakage. Indeed, some air movement is necessary, changing preferably once every 24 hours. The amount of space required within display cabinets for these preconditioned agents is calculated according to the inside volume of the case at the rate of 20 kg of conditioning agent for every cubic metre. This necessitates the construction of a large storage area below the display area. Before it is placed in a display case the agent must be conditioned, by moisturizing, to the desired rh, since it is shipped in a dry, inactive state.

Pollution of exhibition areas is likely to be caused by the materials used to construct the exterior or interior of the exhibition cases, rather than the outside atmosphere (Thomson, 1986, 85–102). In particular, lead and silver are affected by volatile organic acids created by using oak, birch or beech in the construction of the cases.

Where should exhibitions be held?

Successful exhibitions require a balance to be achieved between maximum publicity, adequate security and minimum natural light. Ideally the display area should be prominent within the building, capable of being protected from natural light, and easy to patrol or oversee as necessary. In practice many organizations site their exhibitions in entrance halls to achieve maximum

Great North Museum, Newcastle, UK

This museum was planned to take advantage of:

- an existing natural history museum (in a listed building requiring maintenance) which needed upgrading
- an antiquarian society whose library was inaccessible
- a natural history society library and archive which needed professional management and more space
- a very fine university collection of antiquities currently housed in an almost inaccessible part of the university
- a heavily used university museum collection relating to Hadrian's Wall which was in serious difficulty about display space.

By combining planning and funding the University of Newcastle, Newcastle City Council and Tyne and Wear Museum Authority together developed a facility more widely available to the general public, and better looked after than the constituent members could have achieved on their own. Moreover, the management of the new facility is in the hands of the Tyne and Wear Museum Authority, signifying the trust of the other partners in the ability of the professional body to care for the artefacts and materials previously in their own hands.

publicity, thereby introducing the risk of theft by having unique materials on display in an area where movement by the public is uncontrolled. The alternative, exhibitions tucked away in the interior of the building, may be more secure, but difficulty of access defeats the purpose of display. Compromises often have to be made and the risks identified. Joining forces with other organizations to provide specialized exhibition and research areas for museum, library and archival materials is one solution. This offers the visitor a one-stop opportunity for research or leisure and can result in much better public facilities, professional curation, environmental and security conditions and storage areas.

Should the display be of originals or facsimiles?

Facsimiles or surrogates, using digitizing techniques on to a variety of media, can now be made to a very high specification and are often difficult to distinguish from originals. However, if the decision is taken to use them, and in particular if the exhibition has a mixture of originals and surrogates, it is essential to label copies as such; the visitor to the exhibition must not be misled into thinking he or she has seen the original. Decisions on which to use are likely to be decided by:

- the proposed nature of the exhibition
- the timescale
- the condition of the originals.

Exhibition policy at the British Library

The British Library reviewed its exhibition policy in 2005 following concern about the permanent exhibition of some of the highlights of its collections, notably the Lindisfarne Gospels. The staff have adopted a policy of removing such items from display for six months within a two-year period. See www.bl.uk/aboutus/stratpolprog/borrow/index.html.

If the subject matter of the exhibition is important – a commemorative display or an item of national importance – it is likely that originals will be requested. Not infrequently an archive or an exhibition officer will be subjected to political pressure to show such original iconic materials for particular commemorations or business reasons. This often results in requests for extended display, or display in unsuitable circumstances; communication and understanding the purpose of the exhibition by both the promoter and the archive is crucial, since it may well involve issues to do with advocacy and pride in historic documentation. Compromises can be made, such as a limited length of display of the original followed by the substitution of a good quality facsimile, but not on principles of safe display.

Surrogates are particularly attractive as an option for travelling exhibitions, especially those out of the country. No security or environmental conditions need be attached to the loan of such material and the organizers can be free to use the material in graphic displays or as enlarged posters, providing all copyright issues have been ascertained.

Which cases are suitable for the display of archive material?

Many exhibition cases are on the market but the security features to look for include:

- an adequate thickness of anti-bandit glazing
- UV protection
- locking mechanisms and integral fittings as secure as a four-lever lock, e.g. case locks with cam or snap-in operation
- locking mechanisms out of sight and reach of visitors
- inaccessible hinges
- strong hinges to flat tops of cases to avoid damage to people or documents when the cases are being filled, or freestanding tops or glazed surfaces, lowered into place using suction pads once the display is complete
- piano hinges or approved security fittings for items displayed in frames.

In all situations the curator or conservator must be aware of the types of locks and the ways in which the cases operate. Any security staff employed, either permanently or in a temporary capacity, should know how the cases work in case of an emergency.

Case construction features should include:

- a sufficiently solid structure to prevent rapid changes in temperature and humidity and to prevent the case being knocked over or accidentally moved
- provision for a small leakage of air, which should be equal to one complete air change every 24 hours
- use of appropriate materials (see above)
- easily accessible space-conditioning chambers for silica gel, or its equivalent, to be moved in and out with ease

- separate provision for electric lighting or fibre-optic lighting; access to lighting mechanisms should be separate for easy replacement of bulbs
- sufficient depth for bound volumes to lie open on a cradle, at an angle of not more than 25° from the horizontal floor of the case.

How can disasters be avoided during an exhibition?

Disaster planning is of major importance before an exhibition opens. If the organization does not have a disaster reaction and recovery plan already, this is the time to implement one (see Chapter 7). Even if one is in place it may need revision, including the addition of the exhibition area as a potential source of disaster. Existing plans frequently concentrate solely on the storage areas, oblivious to the possible presence of documents in other parts of the building. If items have been lent by other organizations the owners will want to know that disaster planning is part of the exhibition preparation; think through the potential risks in an exhibition situation and ensure that they are covered by the procedures. As well as the normal risks, there might be a number of reasons for opening the cases during the course of the exhibition:

- for salvage of material not belonging to the organization after a disaster
- for relocating material following any failure to control environmental conditions or lighting in cases
- for repairing cases after any attempt to steal material resulting in damage.

Planning and preparing for an exhibition

The condition of the documents proposed for display must be assessed first; some will be too fragile, others too large or bulky for the cases. Ideally the curator or organizer of the exhibition will select a range of documents relating to the exhibition theme, from which the final choice will be made in consultation with a conservator. If it is likely that conservation work, packing or construction of stands or supports will be needed, this can be discussed at the same time. Planning will be all the easier if the exhibition organizer knows how much time to factor in for this work. This also applies to planning loan exhibitions, and is one of the reasons for requiring a long lead time.

Timetabling can be fraught, particularly when firm decisions on exhibits are not taken early in the process; large organizations, such as national museums, libraries or archives, often plan exhibitions more than two years ahead, necessitating a long period of preparation and communication. Dates for the resolution or completion of particular issues or tasks should be set at the very beginning, working backwards from the anticipated opening date of the exhibition. These should be agreed with all concerned and the exhibition organizer should ensure that they are adhered to. Some flexibility will be necessary at the end – no exhibition is complete without last-minute work – but the preservation status of the documents for display is compromised if preliminary work is badly organized or rushed.

Accurate budgeting is an essential factor for a successful exhibition where original material is being displayed, since ensuring the safety of the material requires a certain level of expenditure. For preservation purposes expenditure could include any of the following:

- conservation work, conservation materials and preparation undertaken on the documents for display
- fitting out the exhibition area with appropriate air conditioning, lighting, curtains or blinds, or upgrading security provisions
- new or upgraded exhibition cases and exterior fittings such as locks to the appropriate standard[2]
- new or upgraded interior case fittings, such as backboards, lining materials or permanent supports made from inert materials
- display stands made from Perspex or acid-free board
- mounts for facsimiles, pictures or photographs
- analogue/digital recorders for environmental monitoring in cases
- sufficient silica gel or its equivalent for case conditioning
- replacement bulbs for lighting whether interior (fibre-optic) or exterior
- inert bands of unbleached tape, Melinex[3] strips or other restraints
- packing materials for transport to exhibitions off the archive premises, such as insulated cases, boxes, bubble wrap or other protective wrapping
- travel and subsistence costs for any couriers bringing loan display items from elsewhere; the reliable provision of adequate funds and guaranteed seats on planes or trains is a major contributor to the confidence of any lending institution.

What about insurance?

Insurance details need clarity. In the UK the Government Indemnity Scheme is a non-commercial insurance programme to provide free cover 'against loss or damage to works of art and objects on loan to non-national museums, galleries and libraries'.[4] It is designed to encourage smaller organizations to mount more extensive exhibitions than might otherwise be possible, including material from other archives, libraries, museums and galleries. Any organization to which the public has access can apply to the scheme, which is now run by Arts Council England.[5] National institutions in the UK have their own arrangements whereby each bears its own costs, following a national agreement. Nail to nail insurance – full insurance from the moment of departure to the moment of return to the lender – for material travelling abroad must be covered by the borrower and be acceptable to the lender. This should be part of early negotiations but is often left rather late, since the borrower rarely wants to make the arrangements until all the other details have been settled. Insist on having a copy of the certificate, or make it a condition that the lender organizes the insurance.

Other countries have similar arrangements – e.g. the Montreal Museum of Fine Arts is able to organize exhibitions and present valuable works of art with support from the Canada Travelling Exhibitions Indemnification Program of the Department of Canadian Heritage.[6] Through this programme the federal government assumes financial responsibility for loss or damage to works of art presented in travelling exhibitions – very important in a country so large that only a small proportion of the population is able to access exhibitions held in the major centres.

In the USA the common practice is that the insurance is covered by the borrowing institution. However, there can be exceptions for archives that are part of larger organizations that will necessarily have more comprehensive insurance policies. Again, the key document here is the loan agreement and the important legalities that it outlines and formalizes; in some cases there will be the opportunity between the two institutions to negotiate terms.

Determining the insurance value of a unique item is difficult. Some organizations will want a full commercial valuation, while others only require insurance against damage; replacement is rarely an option for archives. Assessing the insurance value of material which is of iconic value to the borrower – for example an Act of Parliament granting accession to full statehood to a colony or the first map identifying the territory of a particular group of people – adds an extra difficulty, since some consideration for its importance must be made. A compromise is usually possible using a standard rule of thumb; detailed estimates are unlikely to be very helpful, given that the potential for damage is unknown.

Insurance for a courier against accidents should also be taken out if staff are not already covered. This needs to be checked, as many such policies are on an annual basis.

How should exhibition items be presented?

Display of the items selected should preferably be the direct responsibility of a conservator, since most documents will require purpose-made support to avoid stress. Archival items, for this reason, should never be displayed in picture frames hanging on the wall, since this position will cause strain. Exhibitors, however, frequently wish to use this available space and regard flat material, particularly maps, as ideal for such display. The issue needs discussion at an early stage.

Single sheets should be mounted in accordance with the instructions of the exhibitors (they frequently adopt a house style for all exhibits), but this must include support from an acid-free board at the very least, to avoid any danger of contamination of the exhibit from unsuitable backings. Such a board can be cut to the exact footprint of the document, and attached using Melinex strips, secured at the back. The document can then be safely leaned on an angled support, making it easier to read.

Volumes must be supported on specially constructed mounts, particularly if they are to be displayed open at a particular page. The mount can be constructed from Perspex, or more cheaply from board. It should provide a ledge on which the volume can rest, a back support angled to fit the degree to which the volume is open, and additional support on the ledge to support the text block. The latter prevents damage to the joints where the text is attached to the boards, particularly if they are constructed from paper. Alternatively the standard foam supports used in the reading room can be used, although these are usually too bulky to fit into cases.

Strips of Melinex can be used to restrain pages, fastened behind the volume, taking care that the band is not so tight as to risk cutting into the paper. Seals appended to documents must be supported so that the weight does not strain the document or the tag by which it is attached. Supports can be of Perspex or board, or the seal can be displayed in a Plastazote support. Particular care must be taken over any lead or silver items as above; if there is any doubt about the display materials it is safer to encase them in an airtight Perspex box.

Additional precautions for off-site exhibitions

Packing materials for items taken to exhibitions off-site should be robust and identifiable. Special carrying cases, with secure locks, should be used to transport materials leaving their own location. These are sometimes acclimatized if the archival material, e.g. parchment, is particularly sensitive to changes in the environment. Ensure that they have a strong outer covering and are lined with impact-resistant foam. The corners and rims should be reinforced with heavy-gauge steel to prevent damage. The interior should be flat, and can be lined with inert foam, shaped or cut to fit the particular exhibit on each occasion. Several such cases may be required to ensure that the archive can transport different sizes of document safely. It may also be necessary to have more than one of each size if material is to be lent to more than one organization at the same time; leaving the case at the exhibition deprives the lender of the ability to make further loans elsewhere unless a back-up has been purchased. Ensure that the name of the lending institution is easily read on the outside.

The conditions of loan should include the requirement that any packaging will remain at the exhibition site, and be stored in good conditions. Whoever picks up the material after the exhibition will then have the necessary materials to hand.

Transport for loans to exhibitions off-site should be clearly arranged beforehand. Most archives insist that their own staff accompany exhibits to their destinations, whether this is within the country or abroad. Additional conditions are needed for the loan agreement under these circumstances (see above) and the courier and receiving institution will need to communicate about:

- the date of travel – loans should arrive only shortly before the exhibition opens, since the facility is unlikely to be ready many days in advance
- arrangements for dates of travel of other couriers; many lenders will not want the cases (in which their materials are displayed) opened again to insert those of another organization; in consequence it is important that the arrival of couriers is co-ordinated, and this point will probably have to be explained
- the mode of travel – whether by train, car/van or air
- how many seats, whether standard, business or first class, are required for the courier and exhibition items (for a journey of any length business class should be the minimum; archival material should always remain with the courier in the carriage or cabin – larger museum and gallery items sometimes have to go in the hold of an aircraft or accompanying van due to their size, but, with the exception of maps, this is very unlikely in the case of archival material); some material will fit comfortably into overhead lockers in carrying cases while other items may have to be strapped into an extra seat purchased by the borrower (if this is necessary, be firm about the requirement, despite the cost, as it is up to the borrower to decide whether the additional expense makes the loan possible)
- who will supply the tickets; if it is the borrower, insist that the ticket is commercially purchased; sponsored tickets, particularly on airlines, are more vulnerable to change or delay, since the status of the holder is below that of a paying passenger

- where the courier will be met and by whom (further specialist travel arrangements beyond the initial destination should be provided by a recognized fine art carrier)
- what overnight arrangements have been made, if required.

During the exhibition

Although much of the work will have been completed before the exhibition, regular attention to the displayed material will be necessary. Monitoring the environmental conditions is crucial to ensure that the material does not suffer. Visible monitors inside cases make it easy to check on a regular basis. If there are problems with low relative humidity it will be necessary to humidify additional supplies of silica gel or other stabilizing agent to the required level to replace those in the cases before the level drops too far. Request records of environmental conditions from the host organization if items have been loaned off-site; this is not unreasonable and offers some remote control to the lender.

Instructions to exhibition warding staff should refer to the non-smoking policy and stress that food and drink should be kept away from the area. If the opening of the exhibition or subsequent private views include evening events, those stipulations may need to be re-emphasized. Security arrangements are often better observed at the beginning of an exhibition than subsequently, when the first excitement of the opening is over. Ensure that the agreed arrangements are maintained throughout the display period.

And afterwards . . .

Displays in frequently used galleries or exhibition spaces will often need to be dismantled to a fairly tight timetable. None of the exhibits should be handled until the conservator or representative of the lender is present; there is a danger that items might be stored inappropriately, or moved in a hurry under such circumstances, resulting in damage. Security arrangements for the exhibition should be maintained while the facility is being dismantled. Loan exhibition items coming off display should be checked by both the borrower and the lender, using the condition report as a means of comparison of condition before and after. Agreement on condition should be signed off by both parties to avoid subsequent problems. Packing materials should be re-used as necessary and all exhibition items should be returned to their original store as soon as possible. Individual archives will have their own arrangements for signing documents in and out and it is important that these procedures are carried out; subsequent disputes about whether or not an item has been returned are not unknown.

Evaluation of the success or otherwise of the loan procedures is important after the return of the items. Suggestions for improved procedures are easiest to remember at this stage and can be included in a manual. Experience of managing exhibitions is built up slowly but every one adds something which should make subsequent exhibitions a little easier to organize.

Summary

Exhibitions are important to an archive for promoting access. Properly planned and managed, they can be hugely enjoyable and present very little risk to the materials on display. However, careful advance planning is required, and this chapter has outlined the need for early timetabling, assessment of the condition of the documents to be displayed, responsible provision of exhibition equipment and environmental conditions, and good communications between all those involved.

The following chapter moves on to the subject of handling records, which also has a bearing on exhibitions, since the documents selected are heavily handled prior to the final setting up of a display. Care is needed at all stages.

Notes and references

1   www.lightcheck.co.uk/whatis.htm.
2   Collections Link; Attack Resistant display cases,
     www.collectionslink.org.uk/discover/security/516-specification-attack-resistent-
     display-cases.
     Preservation Advisory Centre: Guidance for exhibiting archive and library
     materials, www.bl.uk/blpac/pdf/exhibition.pdf.
3   Melinex is a polyester film made by DuPont Teijin Films.
4   www.artscouncil.org.uk/what-we-do/supporting-museums/cultural-property/
     protecting-cultural-objects/government-indemnity-scheme.
5   See www.artscouncil.org.uk.
6   See www.pch.gc.ca/eng/1268250082235.

11

Handling the records

Introduction

Archive material rarely handled is likely to remain in reasonable condition, even in an adverse environmental situation. In recent years, however, the rate of deterioration of some materials has increased owing not only to a diminution in the quality of archival materials, but also to increasing use. Visitor numbers at British archives have soared in the last 50 years. Archives and local history centres, previously the preserve of antiquarians and academics, have now become the destination for many seeking information of diverse kinds and are promoted for their seemingly inexhaustible supply.

The desire to promote access is irreproachable: the difficulty comes with the inevitable damage caused to the documents as they are endlessly extracted from storage, taken to a distribution centre or reading room, handed over to the reader and then returned.

Lack of resources to conserve every incoming document to the highest standard leaves the organization with no option but to train both staff and readers in the best ways of preventing further deterioration. This chapter covers:

- ways of encouraging and influencing staff and readers to handle documents carefully
- rules for the readers
- equipment for the reading rooms
- training.

The problem

Each time an original document is accessed by a reader, it is handled at least six times, and that will be in a small repository with few staff. In a larger organization it may be handled up to eight times on each occasion, not including the more detailed, page-by-page perusal by the reader. Archives have to take note of the damage being inflicted, often unwittingly. Much of the paper arrives in the archive already well used and in poor condition (see Figure 11.1). Maps are particularly at risk, often having been out in the field, stuffed into a pocket or traced on a drawing board. Photographs, which have become part of everyday life and are to be found in any archive, are equally at risk. Audiovisual material, tapes and optical discs are just as vulnerable to bad handling and poor care.

Figure 11.1 A tatty file

Improving the quality of care: how can it be achieved?

Any attempt to improve the quality of care of archives will require a number of different approaches. Training and refresher sessions will be needed, organized to fit in with other work and to inculcate good practice. Equipment will be required to assist with the support of documents and avoid too much touching, and vigilance throughout the archive and the reading rooms is essential to ensure that standards of care are maintained. Conservators, trained to handle fragile materials with care, are in the best position to initiate such training, although over time the training should be taken up by all those who handle documents. Good example is one of the best ways of passing on good practice. Much of it is common sense and can be implemented in any archive.

Many new users of record offices are unaccustomed to handling original material, and indeed are sometimes rather taken aback to discover that they are not required to use copies. Most archives and libraries warn readers in advance, by leaflets or on websites, that certain rules have to be observed in the reading rooms. These include basic precautions for security as well as exhortations for basic document care. The box below suggests the basic rules to be observed in the reading room; each archive must decide for itself the parameters of what it wants to achieve and how far it can control the handling of documents.

Example of reading room rules
Please:

- ensure that you have clean hands before handling documents
- handle documents as little as possible, turning pages carefully by the corner
- avoid disturbing the original arrangement of documents
- avoid creasing, folding or bending the documents
- avoid leaning on the documents
- use pencils only
- leave all sharp instruments in the cloakroom
- use pencil sharpeners away from the documents
- eat and drink only in the rest areas or restaurant provided
- report any damaged material to staff.

Why have rules?

A balance must be struck between the image of the archive as a welcoming and approachable organization, and the image of the archive as an organization that has a responsibility of care for its holdings as well as for the interests of future generations of readers. Rules are not in place for fun and staff and readers should be aware of their purpose. Care should be taken of new readers in particular; they may not have visited an archive before and may be unaware of the pitfalls in handling original material. Quite reasonably they may question rules that appear more draconian than those in other, more familiar public institutions. Established readers and staff may need reminders, especially if regulations have been tightened up or expanded; the solution is to ensure that the reasoning behind the rules is explained and understood. The advantage of this approach is that preservation of the materials becomes a joint responsibility for all; a feeling of involvement with the organization and its holdings, particularly for readers, is valuable.

Setting out rules inevitably suggests penalties for non-observance. Each archive must consider how rigorously to enforce the rules and what to do with those who persistently, or wilfully, break them. Exclusion from the

The reasons for rules in archive reading rooms

- Clean hands prevent the transference of dirt from documents to people and vice versa. Using a licked finger to assist page turning could be bad for health.
- Documents are unique items and handling them endangers their survival; minimum handling therefore helps to ensure that they are there for others to use in the future.
- The order of the documents may give additional indications as to how they were used in the past, even if it does not appear logical now. Such evidence needs to be kept.
- Creasing, bending, or folding the documents weakens the fibres of parchment and paper and may obscure valuable evidence. Documents which have been conserved will often have been flattened for this reason, although the original crease marks will still be visible. Parchment is particularly vulnerable as folding or creasing may cause the ink to spring off the surface.
- Leaning on the surface of documents, for instance on large maps or when tracing outlines, may cause abrasion.
- Pencils should be used in preference to ink, fibre tip or ballpoint pens for all transactions in the archive, not only in the reading room. This prevents the danger of spillage or leakage, causing ineradicable damage.
- Sharp instruments present a potential threat to the documents and to avoid any misunderstandings should be left behind in the cloakroom.
- Pencil sharpeners should be used well away from the documents, as the graphite shaving produced can mark or harm them. Continuous lead pencils do not present the same problem and are welcome.
- Food and drink not only pose a threat to the documents through spillage, damage from sticky fingers or crumbs being left behind, but the consumption of food in unregulated areas can lead to infestation by insects or vermin. The ban should include sweets and chewing gum; if readers need medication they should inform staff but in practice it is rare for this to be needed in the reading room.
- Damaged documents should be reported to staff and a note taken of the reference; seriously fragile material should be withdrawn. Readers may well expect instant conservation work to be carried out but should be informed that the reported items will be prioritized for treatment. Any urgent requests for access should be noted and the reader given some indication of how and when the material can be used. Sometimes this can be under special supervision or in the conservation workshop if the archive has one on the premises.

archive is the ultimate weapon but it must be practicable and other methods of attempting to get compliance must be tried first. Legal challenges from readers are unpleasant, time-consuming and damaging to the organization.

How can readers be made aware of the rules?

Archives have adopted different strategies to draw attention to their rules and it may well be necessary to vary the approach from time to time. Prominent display is most important, not least in the reading rooms. Doing this reminds regular readers of the need for care as well as promoting the image of the archive as a responsible organization.

How to publicize the reasoning behind the rules is a matter of choice for each institution; some may prefer to introduce readers to the requirements individually and answer questions, while others may provide an explanatory video for the first visit or a sheet which can be handed out as required. In some archives new readers are required to read and sign the rules when they register – occasionally being asked to read the list out loud. In others, attention is drawn to the rules when the reader is first introduced to the facilities of the archive. Few go to the lengths of the Bodleian Library in Oxford, where would-be readers are required to agree not to kindle fires in the library, but the regulation draws attention to the library's continuing concern for the need for care. Many archives place copies of the rules on the desks, sometimes in bold type, handwritten or in an otherwise distinctive format such as an arresting colour. Having a copy of the rules on the wall is often useful for reminding regular readers that they must observe them, however familiar they are with the archive. Including the rules in any publicity about the archive, whether in leaflet format or on a website, can be useful, though it might be regarded as a rather authoritarian approach.

What equipment is needed?

In addition to reading room rules and explanations, certain equipment will help to encourage good practice and will be a worthwhile investment to promote good handling.

Suitable trolleys should be one of the first considerations, not least to avoid staff, or readers, carrying documents round the record office by hand, with the consequent danger of dropping them or injuring themselves. Regular checks are needed to ensure that they remain in good working condition – damaged wheels or shelves can lead to accidents and damaged documents. (See Chapter 6 for specifications.) Several small trolleys are better than a few larger ones, to discourage staff from attempting to load on too much at once, affecting the balance. Staff will need instruction in how to stack boxes of documents on them safely, and how to shelve volumes. Careless handling of a trolley, or failure to control it properly, can lead to mass damage. Library-style trolleys may be suitable for volumes and will carry them in an upright position; the shelves should be angled to prevent volumes falling when turning corners. Flat trolleys are more satisfactory for boxed material. Maps which fit into stiff portfolios can be transported on a flat-bed trolley with high sides to keep the portfolios upright. Oversize flat maps require trolleys specially made, since they are at particular risk of damage in transit. Portfolios can also be useful for ensuring that oversize documents stay flat and secure in one position.

Some archives keep a stack of folders, of different sizes, in the strongrooms so that individual sheets can be inserted into folders before being handed over to the reader. This reduces handling but care must be taken to avoid damage when inserting and removing the document; at least two sides of the folder should be open. If the folder is transparent readers should keep the document in the folder, thus reducing the risk of damage.

Trays or shallow boxes covered in acid-free paper or inert material can be used to hand documents to the reader, reducing the number of times an item is handled in transit and on the desk, since the tray can act as a reading mat. This is particularly useful for small deeds or items that might otherwise slip under other documents and be lost. Readers must be told of the reasons for, and importance of, using the tray.

Book cushions or foam wedges should be available to support volumes in the reading rooms and at staff desks and tables. These are preferable to the old-fashioned type of book rest, which, while holding the volume at an angle for the readers to see, does not support the text block. This can be a real problem for the many large and unwieldy volumes found in many archives; the weight of the pages, when the whole is propped upright, can cause the text to tear away from the boards, since the joints are frequently the weakest part of the construction. It is generally recommended that no book should be opened at an angle of more than 120° and those with a tight binding at a maximum of 90°. Foam wedges (see Figure 11.2), however, can be built up under the boards to accommodate any opening, leaving the spine to operate without strain on the joints. They can be readjusted to allow for the changing need for support as the reader progresses from the front of the volume to the back. Beanbags or cushions are also used as supports; their shape moulds to that of the volume and reduces strain on the weakest parts. They should be loosely filled with inert materials and covered with a soft archival quality cloth. While the cushion type of support is popular, it does not effectively support the book and the cover easily becomes dirty (and then requires washing). On balance, the foam supports are recommended by book conservators. Collapsible cradles are another, more elegant solution, taking up less room in storage. These can be angled for easy reading.

Many readers need assistance in preventing pages from turning while they are reading a volume, or when additional leaves of a large document are obscuring the part they are trying to read or maps are rolling up when laid out. Chains or snakes of lead pellets, as used in the hems of curtains, are a cheap and easy solution to drape over pages of volumes or maps (see Figure 11.3).

Figure 11.2 Foam wedges

Figure 11.3 Chain of lead pellets

Alternatively, small beanbags can be constructed; these are better than rigid weights, as they mould themselves to the shape of the document and have no sharp corners to damage documents.

Transparent sheets of Melinex should be provided for those who wish to trace maps or plans; these should be sufficiently rigid to avoid pressure on the documents.

Cotton gloves should be supplied for handling photographic negatives and prints, which should be held by the edge and never in the centre. Some libraries and archives insist on the use of gloves whenever original material of any sort is used; there are both advantages and disadvantages to this (Baker and Silverman, 2005). Use of gloves inevitably leads to a loss of sensitivity, which can in turn lead to damage to paper when it is being turned or moved. Gloves can also transfer dirt from one document to another, which can be avoided if hands are washed in between. On the other hand, gloves do provide some protection from dirty documents and also protect the documents from any dirt or creams on the hands of the reader. The most effective glove is the Nitrile surgical glove. This has many advantages; it is possible to feel more acutely the material being handled, the Nitrile does not hold any dirt and on completion of the activity the glove can be discarded. Each archive will have to decide on its policy.

Appropriate furniture for reading documents and consulting maps and plans is usually provided for the reading rooms, but staff are sometimes less well served at their desks. Adequate space on which to spread documents out is essential, as damage is caused by trying to accommodate such material on already overcrowded surfaces. The use of computers for inputting information directly has exacerbated this danger, due to the need to accommodate a keyboard and monitor on a desk as well as the original material. Cataloguing or editorial staff should be encouraged to work in a way which does not pose any risks.

Appropriate equipment for playing audiovisual and optical media should be available in archives as needed. It is preferable for the materials to be handled by staff only, who have been trained in the proper procedures; readers/listeners may need special booths or screens linked to a central control panel.

Where and how can good practice be demonstrated to readers?

Training in the use of all the equipment above and in good handling procedures must be a major element in any programme to encourage staff and readers to adopt best practice. Example is one of the best ways of inculcating good habits, especially in the reading room if the staff have time for individual attention. Documents should be seen to be carried carefully and can be presented in different ways to the reader:

- in a box, carefully packed
- individually in a shallow tray
- individually in a transparent Melinex sleeve (see above)
- in fascicules;[1] since the fascicule pages are larger than those of the original document, readers can turn the pages without touching the original (this is an elegant solution, but fascicules take up additional

storage space and are usually impractical other than for very special items).

Readers can be instructed at the same time about untying and retying bundles of papers, and the need for care where original tags, e.g. of parchment, are encountered. Small items or individual samples of textiles can be laid out on shallow trays, and the reader encouraged to keep them *in situ*, rather than risking losing them among other items on the desk.

Demonstrations of how to remove reference volumes from shelves in the reading rooms can help to prevent spines being pulled too hard; these are frequently the most heavily used materials in the archive and suffer considerable wear and tear. They should always be grasped by the spine and pulled gently towards the reader rather than being pulled from the headband and jerked backwards to get a grip. The books should be shelved sufficiently loosely for this to be possible, but if they are too tight the books on either side must be pushed to the back to allow room to grasp the spine.

Photographic materials must be handled with cotton gloves and held by the edges only; stiff card to support the material can be helpful in avoiding finger contact on the surface. The surface of any discs or tapes should never be touched, and neither readers nor staff should attempt to open cartridges or cassettes in which electronic or magnetic media are stored.

Staff who are invigilating the reading room should walk round rather than always sitting at a desk; readers must be corrected politely if they are infringing the rules and it is important that this is done consistently and firmly. Established users of an archive can become lax through familiarity with the rules, and will need encouragement to care for the materials. Other staff, once trained and confident of their skills, should be encouraged to visit the reading rooms and observe and assist readers as appropriate.

Group training sessions for readers can be more problematic – readers have come for the purpose of consulting documents, rather than being trained. However, they often express concern about the state of the documents and instruction on first visiting the archive is well received. If sufficient numbers are involved it is sometimes possible to hold short briefings – for a pre-booked party or group for instance – or to include basic handling advice in a general induction tour.

Visitors such as journalists or film crews may need training; television is a powerful method of influencing viewers and programmes which include archival material should demonstrate best practice. Make sure that the ordinary rules for using documents within the archive are observed even if the programmes have to be put together at speed. It may be possible to insist that only staff handle the documents; it is certainly possible to insist that strong lights are only switched on for the actual filming itself. It is also essential to insist on food and drink being consumed only in designated areas (camera crews are notorious for needing coffee as they work).

Any contractors who will handle original documents must be alerted to the rules. These might include microfilming or digitizing agents working either in the archive or on their own premises. The best way to ensure compliance is to include a requirement for training in any contract and for trained staff to provide it. The compilation of detailed guidelines to underpin and inform any training is a vital part of preservation management. This links back to the compilation of the preservation policy and forms one of the outputs resulting from the sub-policies that flow from the main mission statement of the organization.

How can staff be best trained?

Staff training in good handling procedures is the essential backbone of good practice throughout the archive. Preservation or conservation staff may well be involved initially, although ideally best practice should be cascaded through the organization, passing the responsibility to each line manager. Several groups of staff will need specific training.

Search room and supervisory staff need to know:

- how to handle fragile materials with care to avoid further damage
- how to identify material which is too fragile for use
- how to unwrap and wrap material secured by tape or string and wrappers
- how to remove material safely from boxes or other containers, and how to replace it safely
- how to use the equipment provided, especially in the case of film, audio, magnetic or optical media
- how to explain the reading room rules to readers.

Security staff (or those involved in any bag searches) need to know:

- how to distinguish archival material belonging to the record office
- how to distinguish between originals and photocopies
- how to handle fragile materials with care to avoid further damage
- how to explain the reading room rules to readers.

Cataloguing and editorial staff need to know:

- that the rules for readers apply to them, too
- how to handle fragile materials with care to avoid further damage
- how to unwrap and wrap material secured by tape or string and wrappers
- how to remove material safely from boxes or other containers and how to replace it safely
- how to use the equipment provided.

Repository or storage staff need to know:

- how to move material safely to avoid damage either to the documents or to themselves
- how to handle fragile materials with care to avoid further damage
- how to unwrap and wrap material secured by tape or string and wrappers
- how to remove material safely from boxes or other containers, and how to replace it safely
- how to use the equipment provided.

Reprographic staff or staff doing copying need to know:

- how to handle fragile materials with care to avoid further damage
- how to unwrap and wrap material secured by tape or string and wrappers
- how to remove material safely from boxes or other containers, and how to replace it safely
- how to use the equipment provided
- when to ask a conservator for help if the documents are bound or unwieldy to manage with the copying equipment.

Cleaning staff need to know:

- how to move material safely to avoid damage either to the documents or to themselves
- which cleaning materials can be used in the storage areas.[2]

Volunteers need to know:

- how to handle fragile materials with care to avoid further damage
- how to identify material which is too fragile for use
- how to unwrap and wrap material secured by tape or string and wrappers

- how to remove material safely from boxes or other containers and how to replace it safely.

Contractors, especially removal firms, need to know:

- how to move material safely to avoid damage either to the documents or to themselves.

Training should be focused towards these different groups and should be delivered in different ways, to reinforce the importance of good handling procedures. Initial training should take place on induction, whether or not the new member of staff has previously worked in an archive. Further training and refresher sessions should be held regularly for all staff: this includes training in the use of new equipment with which they may be unfamiliar. Resistance from long-term staff has to be overcome, as familiarity frequently leads to bad habits, including infringement of rules which readers are obliged to observe. This might include eating or drinking at a desk where documents are being used. A number of techniques will have to be adopted in order to maintain interest – these might include providing opportunities to see conservation work being carried out, or handling different types of material to become familiar with them.

Good practice is built up slowly in any organization but can be lost very quickly if those using the documents are not careful to maintain standards. Staff and readers have a joint responsibility which must have a high profile to ensure that handling originals does not result in damage.

Summary

This chapter has covered the importance of engaging staff and readers in contributing to the survival of the archival documents. It has suggested ways of bringing the issues to their attention, it has outlined the guidance needed in the reading room, it has discussed equipment to make handling fragile materials easier and safer, and it has highlighted the need for both initial and refresher training sessions for all.

The co-operation needed over handling issues is no less vital for the subject of the following chapter, pest management. Staff and readers are ideally placed to notice infestations or damage and can make a major contribution to reducing this threat to archival materials.

Notes

1   Fascicules are gatherings of acid-free paper into which individual documents are interleaved.

2   Although this is not strictly handling training it is important that cleaners are given basic instructions on using only water-based cleaning materials and not solvents.

12

Managing a pest control programme

Introduction

Threats to materials in archives, libraries and museums include infestation by pests, defined as insects, rodents or mammals which find the warm, dark conditions attractive. The damage caused can be considerable and in some cases catastrophic; not only can pests devour the displays and the materials from which artefacts are created, they may also threaten the structure of the building in which they are housed. This chapter looks at:

- the most commonly found pests in the UK
- how to recognize them
- what damage they do
- where they are likely to be found
- the signs of an infestation
- how they can be prevented
- eradication measures
- integrated pest management.

In the UK the incidence of very rapacious pests is currently small (a colony of termites found in 1999 in Devon has allegedly been eradicated) but in less temperate areas of the world they can be very destructive. Changing climatic conditions are likely to increase the likelihood of such infestation in northern Europe. An earlier tendency to assume that such outbreaks can be prevented or eradicated by the use of chemical pesticides or fumigants has been largely superseded by the adoption of policies which aim to be proactive rather than reactive and to avoid the use of substances which may be harmful to people and to the materials held in the archive or library. It is unlikely that any building will be able to keep all pests at bay; concentrating on as much prevention as possible and making the inside environment unattractive is therefore a more workable solution.

It is fair to say that most institutions would view an infestation or a mould infection of their collections as an acute embarrassment; this may have implications on existing funders and depositors or have wider local political impacts. However, all organizations will be affected by these phenomena and the profession can only move forward by sharing experiences and formulating credible responses.

What are the common pests?

They divide into vertebrates and insects. The most common vertebrates to cause damage in archives and libraries are mice, rats, squirrels and birds. Occasionally other vertebrates such as rabbits gain entrance to collections, but it is unusual. Insects are all smaller and therefore more likely to access the building through small cracks, gaps round doors or windows, or open casements. The insect pests that are listed below are the most common in the UK; national professional associations will be able to advise on others found worldwide. Those presenting common dangers include:

- carpet beetles
- clothes moths
- biscuit beetles
- cigarette beetles
- spider beetles
- book lice
- silverfish.

Those which threaten the structure of the building or the woodwork within it include:

- woodworm
- death watch beetles
- powderpost beetles.

How do I recognize them?

Remember that the insect lifecycle consists of four stages: eggs, larvae, pupae and adults. Being able to identify these very different stages is important to ensure that they are all eradicated, although the major damage will be caused by larvae. Figure 12.1 shows common UK insect types for recognition purposes.[1] The types of insects will vary depending on the region of the world in which the archive is situated; advice should be sought from local authorities, professional bodies or entomologists.

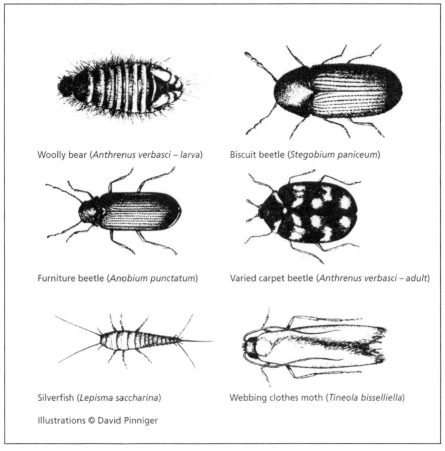

Woolly bear (*Anthrenus verbasci – larva*)

Biscuit beetle (*Stegobium paniceum*)

Furniture beetle (*Anobium punctatum*)

Varied carpet beetle (*Anthrenus verbasci – adult*)

Silverfish (*Lepisma saccharina*)

Webbing clothes moth (*Tineola bisselliella*)

Illustrations © David Pinniger

Figure 12.1 Common insect types

What damage do pests do to archival materials?

An infestation frequently indicates that the area affected is already dirty or in some way damaged; consequently the pests will be making a deteriorating situation worse.

Vertebrates such as rats and mice will damage archive and library material by shredding paper or textiles for nests, by harbouring insects, by urinating or defecating – causing degradation or mould – and by eating cellulose materials such as paper or textiles. Subsequent damage to text blocks will be caused if the bindings of volumes have been weakened by chewing or eating and the mechanical action of the volume is compromised. Wooden door frames, bookcases, cabinets or even the wooden boards used in older bindings may be gnawed by squirrels, rats or mice which need to wear down incisor teeth (or, if trapped without an exit, they may be using them as food). Bird droppings are acidic and can cause damage to both the contents and fabric of a building. Pigeon droppings often occur in loft spaces; the guano is very acidic and when it becomes desiccated the dust is harmful to human health. Birds also harbour insects in their feathers and nests, increasing the likelihood of infestation.

Insects are attracted by the cellulose in paper and textiles, by the starch and proteins in bindings (present in various cloth loadings and many glues) and by the wooden boards of some older volumes or the bookcases on which they are standing. Damage is largely caused by the insect larvae, which bore holes through paper and cause damage to the spines of books; they also sometimes graze on the surface of parchment or paper, thereby weakening the structure, and if there is a serious infestation they can reduce large quantities of paper to dust. Those which feed on wood bore through the structure, ultimately causing collapse.

The areas of damage may not be large individually but any unchecked infestation is likely to do substantial harm to a collection, since the conditions for breeding in an archive or library are good.

Where are they likely to be active?

Common habitats for vertebrates should be checked regularly and include:

- dark and dirty areas, especially if they are also warm and humid
- blocked chimney flues
- roof spaces and basements
- fireplaces, or eaves of older buildings
- unused heating and ventilation ducts
- areas of the building which are infrequently used and therefore unlikely to be disturbed
- areas of the building where food is prepared or eaten.

Vertebrates which die on-site as a result of poison or starvation are a potential breeding ground for insects and therefore an additional hazard.

Common habitats for insects include:

- dark, warm, humid and dirty areas, especially those which are rarely disturbed

- unused attics and basements
- cracks in the floors and walls
- old, undisturbed boxes
- folds in fabrics
- discarded materials left on-site
- areas of the building where food is prepared or eaten
- sources of water.

Indoor plants are also an attraction to insects, but it can be difficult to argue for their abolition (except for storage areas) given their perceived benefits of improving the atmosphere inside buildings, especially offices.

Temperature and relative humidity levels are important in preventing the reproduction of different species. Silverfish reproduce in temperatures of 16–24°C (60–75°F) but the relative humidity must be 70% (Pinniger, 2008, 37); termites require 26–30°C (78–86°F) and 97–100% rh, while beetles of various sorts thrive in a middle range of 20–28°C (68–82°F) and 70–90% rh.

What are the signs of an infestation?

All infestations leave traces, although those of small insects may be almost invisible to the naked eye. An additional problem is that because of the preferred habitat of most of the pests, the signs may not be detected immediately.

Sightings of vertebrates is an obvious means of detection, but they are frequently nocturnal pests. Mice, rats and squirrels will leave droppings and urine stains, all of which need to be identified. Points of entrance and exit are sometimes visible, but never underestimate the ability of small rodents to squeeze through tiny spaces under doors or window frames in search of food. Birds will leave droppings and sometimes feathers, especially if they are trapped and in a panic about exiting.

Insects are less visible but will leave small piles of frass (faeces) or fine dust from boring in little heaps close to the site of the infestation. Holes in the archival materials or furniture can be detected by close visual inspection. Occasionally an infestation is detected due to skin infections suffered by those handling material harbouring insects, but this is rare.

How can they be prevented from getting into the collections?

Understanding where the most likely entrance points are from the exterior of the building is essential to maximizing protection.

Vertebrates will usually enter through open doors or windows, through small gaps left round or under door or window frames, through gaps where round pipes or cables (especially those resulting from IT upgrades and computer network cabling) enter or leave the building, through drains or through cracks in the fabric.

Insects will use the same means, but will also be able to use much smaller holes. They may also enter the building in an already infested collection; this happens frequently when material has been stored previously in conditions which insects find attractive. All incoming collections should be checked for infestation before the documents are integrated into the rest of the archive.

External building management deterrents include:

- reducing foliage and plant cover immediately next to the building; open spaces are more threatening
- blocking up cracks and sealing gaps with barrier strips as part of good building maintenance and the result of routine inspection
- using sheet metal coverings to prevent wood being gnawed on doors and window frames
- placing mesh over windows, louvres or grilles which have to remain open
- fitting spikes on window sills and other perching habitats to deter birds
- capping unused chimney flues to prevent these areas being used for nests
- removing unused trunking.

Internal management deterrents include:

- cleaning the storage and display areas regularly
- regulating and cleaning any areas where food is prepared
- confining the consumption of food and drink by staff and readers to easily cleaned areas
- regular removal of rubbish and discarded items of equipment
- quarantining incoming collections from unknown sources until the material has been thoroughly examined and any infestation eradicated (an isolation room is best placed next to the loading bay or entrance through which new material enters the archive, to avoid spreading any infestation in the existing storage).

Why are previous eradication measures no longer used?

The development of chemical pesticides and fumigants in the 20th century led to their widespread use for many purposes, particularly by the food industry to eradicate infestations in grain stores. Further investigation has, however, resulted in health and safety regulations being tightened up. Many pesticides such as paradichlorobenzene, carbon disulphide or thymol crystals have now proved to be harmful, if not toxic, to humans; fumigants such as carbon tetrachloride are no less dangerous. Methyl bromide is a very powerful insecticide but as an ozone-depleting chemical it is no longer in use – neither is ethylene oxide for purposes other than the sterilization of hospital equipment under very strict supervision. In short, most of the methods or chemicals previously used have now been discontinued due to the danger they pose to those involved and the potential harm to the archive materials. Information can be found on the websites of national bodies concerned with health and safety, including the UK's Health and Safety Executive Advisory Committee on Toxic Substances.[2]

A good example of the use of associated practices (e.g. borrowing from other specialized professions) is the use of 'Santobrite' as a prophylactic treatment. This was a product name for a solution containing sodium pentachlorophenate, which had been widely used in the building trade to protect wood from fungus. The solution was used to impregnate paper sheets with a 10% solution in a mineral spirit and this was placed at the top and bottom of archive boxes to prevent mould. Over time it was found that this chemical broke down and produced a fine dust that was harmful to humans; the cost of addressing this was significant. Consequently, this treatment is no longer used.

Traditional pesticides such as camphor oil or neem[3] have been used in many parts of the world to deter insects in papers or textiles, and the latter has been the subject of considerable research as a natural product. While these may have some effect they are unlikely to reach larvae or pupae buried deep in the folds of textiles or in the centre of a volume.

Why is integrated pest management (IPM) now adopted as a strategy?

Earlier strategies for eradicating pests were essentially reactive – untargeted responses to a threat. Current thinking maintains that good pest eradication depends on knowing exactly which pest is infesting the archive and using appropriate means for eradication. Some approaches using chemicals are at best inefficient, and at worst dangerous to both staff and the archival materials if used indiscriminately. Commercial companies carrying out chemical fumigation may have little knowledge of the needs of archive collections and their users. A strategy which is based on real information about the nature of the infestation and with an emphasis on prevention rather than reaction is likely to be more successful, cheaper and less harmful to the organization and the environment.

What is an IPM strategy?

The aim is to:

- assess the scale of any current problem
- make one member of staff responsible for the co-ordination of IPM activities
- train staff to recognize and deal with infestations
- install traps
- identify the type of pest and its method of ingress
- treat any affected material with non-toxic methods
- avoid any recurrence by taking preventative measures throughout the building, especially by thorough cleaning
- review the IPM procedure regularly, adjusting the strategy as necessary.

David Pinniger (2008, 2) makes the point that IPM strategies must be appropriate to the building for which they are intended and that they should be simple; a plan which is complicated to implement will quickly fail.

Who needs to be involved?

Pest management is an activity frequently undertaken by conservators trained to recognize different types of pest within the archives. This knowledge can be transferred if there are other appropriate staff willing and able to become involved. It is important to establish who will take responsibility, since the issues are likely to require a consensus for action. Senior management support, if not involvement, is crucial, and sometimes lacking. 'It has taken two very expensive outbreaks to gain the attention of upper management' (Kingsley et al., 2001, 31). If, despite precautions, an outbreak of pests occurs, those in charge of storage, buildings maintenance staff and conservators will need to take action. An integrated plan of action will enable detection, and then solutions, to be implemented as quickly as possible.

How can IPM be introduced?

Introduction of an IPM may constitute a change of management style from the reactive style described above. Alternatively it may be a new initiative, without previous attempts at control; in either case communication is essential.

The key member of staff should have some initial training and then introduce a pest management policy, aligning the initiative with the overall preservation aims of the archive, and presenting it as part of the preservation risk management programme. Outline the philosophy briefly, describing the benefits of the approach and soliciting management support. The explanation of the thinking behind the approach should also be given to other staff as appropriate, in particular those who frequent the storage areas for access purposes, those who clean the storage areas and those who maintain the building. Their support and understanding is crucial to the success of any IPM scheme. Further training will be required at a later stage but the initial communication should focus on the purpose, the methodology and a timetable for introduction. It may be necessary to remove chemical sprays or aerosols previously used, explaining the reasons to staff.

Make an assessment of the vulnerability of the building and its contents. Regular building maintenance to prevent ingress is essential, and should be part of the routine assessment of risk. If there is no current quarantine area for new material or deposits consider the possibility of using a room close to the entrance. Ensure that identified maintenance problems are rectified.

Train the staff to recognize different types of pests and the evidence they leave behind them. Awareness may be low, particularly among staff who are not professionally trained. Basic training sessions may be required, with specialized training for those who may have to take decisions on remedial action in the case of an infestation. The cleaning staff, particularly if they are contracted in and not part of the regular staff of the archive, will require training to recognize the evidence of pests and to leave such evidence in place as part of the identification programme. Consider the value of adding a clause to any cleaning contract requiring staff to attend some basic training. The compilation of a cleaning specification (for the work required) will be vital for informing the contract. The specification should include:

- a timetable detailing the range of activities
- a map of the storage areas
- a specification detailing:
    — the extent of cleaning expected
    — the cleaning equipment to be used in each defined area
    — the frequency of the cleaning rotas
- health and safety issues, including an assessment of all chemicals and cleaning fluids to identify harmful materials.

Setting traps

Traps fulfil two functions; they catch the pest, thereby enabling identification, and they prevent the pest from causing damage. Traps should be placed strategically, the location should be noted and they should be monitored regularly; building up evidence over a period of time is crucial to ensure a successful strategy.

Non-toxic traps for insects covered in a sticky substance are available from conservation suppliers (see Figure 12.2). Place these on the floor in areas where insect movement is likely. Some are treated with pheromones as lures, aimed specifically at the furniture beetle (*Anobium punctatum*) and the webbing clothes moth (*Tineola bisselliella*). Cleaners and others using the storage areas should be alerted to ensure that they do not move or discard any traps. Research suggests that inspection once a quarter is sufficient to ensure that enough evidence is collected for casual infestations; if evidence is required for a current outbreak they should be monitored more frequently.

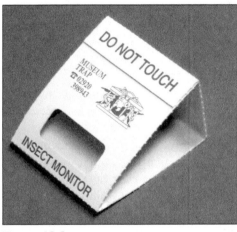

Figure 12.2 Insect trap

Traps for rodents should be inspected much more regularly to remove any corpses before they themselves become an attractive breeding ground. Rodent traps are best placed near any suspected infestation or in areas through which they are likely to enter the archive. Dark areas and peripheral areas around door and window frames, along skirtings or via storm drains are frequently favoured more than routes across clear ground.

Dealing with an infestation

If an infestation of either insects or rodents is identified, remove all the affected and surrounding material and place it in sealed polythene bags to contain the outbreak and prevent further spread. Store these bags well away from other collections until they can be examined in detail and a course of action agreed. Keep previously contaminated material under surveillance and do not return it to the previous location until both are clear of infestation.

Identification of the trapped pests or any that are found dead in the archive is a major part of the strategy; without this knowledge it is not possible to target eradication procedures correctly. For example, mice roam a much smaller area round their nests than rats. In consequence it is important to put out traps much more widely to catch the latter; the evidence left behind them, such as gnawed wood or shredded paper, might not allow for accurate identification. Be aware that adult insects may be found dead, but that eggs, pupae or larvae may still be present. Catching any pest is no guarantee that others are not still infesting the area. Use reference material to aid identification, and record the result.

Mapping the incidence and location of pests affords clues to the way in which they entered the building. Use this evidence to ensure that all holes are blocked up and that coverings over open gaps are sufficient.

Despite the emphasis on using non-toxic methods to control outbreaks of infestation it is necessary to have some means of elimination. If the problem has been identified as mice, rats, squirrels or other rodents it will be necessary to call in an expert exterminator to trap them in a manner which is safe for staff and the archival materials. Explain your concerns and ensure that poisons – which might result in corpses lying in inaccessible areas – are not used.

Insect infestations can be dealt with in several ways; they must be appropriate to:

- the type of material affected
- the type of infestation
- the severity of the infestation
- the value of the material being treated.

Consideration of these issues will determine which treatment is most likely to achieve the required result. It is important to remember that a serious infestation must be viewed as a 'disaster' and bring the same perspectives and methodologies into use as for a flood. Access may be impossible to certain collections and this will have impacts on users. It is important not to assume that aggressive treatment is always required. An extensive infestation will require the input and assistance of a specialist (a conservator and/or an entomologist). The following are some of the options:

- Insecticidal fluid can be used to treat structural timbers; this may need to be undertaken by a specialist firm. Be careful that the fluid used does not release vapour which might be harmful.
- Deep-freezing the items affected is an option. Blast freezing to $-30°$ C for at least 72 hours is recommended to kill all the stages in the lifecycle of insects. The materials should be bagged in polythene, labelled and placed in a freezer that can reach very low temperatures very fast. This

is beyond the capability of most domestic freezers, and it may be necessary to make special arrangements with a business with specialist freezing capacity.[4] The items should then be brought slowly back to room temperature while still bagged. If the infestation is extensive it may be necessary to freeze them again in the same way to ensure complete eradication. The advice of a conservator is necessary over which archival materials are suitable for freezing.

- Using anoxic methods will deprive a confined area of oxygen by chemical or physical means or by replacing oxygen by gases such as nitrogen or argon. This has to be done by specialists.
- Controlled atmosphere technology can be suitable for large infestations. It is carried out by specialist companies that erect a gas–tight bubble round the infested area and expose the contents to carbon dioxide (CO_2) for a lengthy period of some weeks.[5]

Ongoing management

IPM techniques must be adopted by the archive positively and carried out regularly to ensure effective control. Once the routine is in place the resources required are not substantial and are significantly less than those required for eradication once an infestation has occurred. Reviews of the plan must be scheduled to ensure that changes in the organization of the building, the issuing of new cleaning or maintenance contracts, the building of extensions or staff changes do not leave areas of the archive unchecked. Training will be needed on a regular basis to keep everyone involved up to date.

Summary

Combating pests in archives by use of management rather than chemicals represents a fundamental shift from earlier techniques, which merely eradicated the pests without considering preventative strategies. The identification of different types of pests, keen building maintenance standards, the use of sticky traps and, above all, good housekeeping are all the subjects of major initiatives which have been rehearsed in this chapter. The following chapter looks at preservation training issues and the use of volunteers in an archive; training in detecting and controlling pests is a good example of how non-professionals can assist in the care of unique material.

Notes and references

1   In the UK, English Heritage supply a free Insect Pest Identification poster (2010)
     www.english-heritage.org.uk/publications/insects-pests-historic-houses-poster/
     insect-pests-historic-houses-poster.pdf.

2   See www.hse.gov.uk/aboutus/meetings/iacs/acts.

3   Neem, or margosa, is a botanical cousin of mahogany. It belongs to the family
     Meliaceae and is found in Africa, India and China.

4   Some commercial companies provide pest eradication services, e.g.
     www.thermolignum.com. Some of the larger museums may be able to offer limited
     capacity to other institutions; it may be worth checking local provision.

5   For example: www.the-imcgroup.com/product/item/zer02-systems.

13

Training and the use of volunteers

Introduction

One of the key impacts on the success of collection care programmes is the availability of resources – these will vary considerably from institution to institution. Financial resources are becoming increasingly tight for heritage institutions and this presents many additional pressures and challenges. The preservation manager must continue to explore alternative means of addressing the significant needs of the collections. One particular resource that is vital to all elements of preservation is the people to carry out the activities, especially those who can physically process and/or package collections.

Two options are available:

- to extend the activities, capabilities and skills of all members of staff
- to develop programmes and systems to enable the use of volunteers.

In this chapter these two choices are addressed to ensure that they both may become integral elements of preservation planning.

What options for preservation training are available?

The manager has a number of different options for developing staff preservation skills and awareness. Most organizations will identify training needs via a staff appraisal process, but it will also require some knowledge of what is available, especially if specialist needs are identified. Alongside this commitment will be existing responsibilities for specific preservation activities among staff (not necessarily specialist) which might include pest management or environmental monitoring. These activities would ideally be included in individual job descriptions, which in turn presents a stronger imperative to provide training, and consequently to carry out the activity. This training may be provided in the following ways:

- Staff attend subject-specific external seminars and training events.
- Staff attend professional conferences (in the UK and abroad).
- Staff attend training at another organization, one-to-one with another professional.
- Staff who have attended a subject-specific or one-to-one training event provide cascade training for other staff within the organization.
- External trainers are commissioned to provide subject-specific training events.
- Staff attend subject-specific training provided by other specialist members of staff within the organization; this may be as part of a wider induction programme or as part of the preparation for a specific project.

The key here is how effective the training is and this can only really be assessed after the event; a gauge might be how preservation standards have improved after a set period of time. The use of the *Benchmarks in Collection Care* (MLA, 2011 – see Appendix 5) before and after a period of training would be one (independent) indicator of this kind of improvement. This could include a comparison of the levels criteria and/or a charting of progress from one level to another, or at the very least a record that a previous problematic issue had now been addressed (or partly addressed).

What areas of preservation should be covered?

The specific elements of preservation that require training will depend on the needs of each organization and on the types of collections and formats and the respective challenges that they present. However, the training areas that are most commonly required include:

- handling
- packaging
- disaster awareness, response and recovery.

These areas of preservation training are most logically included in staff induction programmes and also feature highly when developing project staff and volunteers. Additionally, there are a range of training opportunities provided by professional organizations, other institutions and professional training providers,[1] and these cover a more detailed brief, including:

- environmental monitoring
- disaster planning
- moving collections
- caring for photographic collections
- developing an insect pest monitoring (IPM) programme
- procedures for other non paper-based collections.

However the training is provided, preservation awareness needs to become embedded in the thinking and approach of the organization. Preservation must not be allowed to stand alone as an untouchable specialism that can only be dealt with by specialist staff (i.e. conservators). In the widest sense, the responsibility for preservation lies with each person who comes into contact with the collections, and it is via training that respect, understanding and skills are developed.

The use of volunteers

The use of volunteers is well established among both museums and libraries, but archives have been slower to fully realize the potential that volunteers represent. Museums have traditionally included more volunteer input and have accomplished much by the inclusion and integration of volunteers – unpaid people who assist with projects because they have an interest in caring for heritage collections or wish to develop new skills. Additionally, some conservation departments take on professional placements (both archivists and conservators); however, they would be managed by the overall principles outlined in this chapter. Placements will be governed by a wide range of other issues and objectives, but the principles remain the same. Indeed some museums are run entirely by volunteers. This has yet to happen on any scale within archives; this may be for a number of reasons, the key ones being the confidentiality of an archive or record, the security of the item and any preservation effects of poor handling.

Today, the challenges for the preservation manager have widened beyond the range of risks that need balance and evaluation to ensure long-term preservation. The objective of preservation can seem to some to be too altruistic and unrealistic – particularly the concept of preserving collections in perpetuity. This has put extra pressure on those with responsibility for collections to find other, and sometimes lateral, ways to extend existing capacity to care for collections. In a shrinking financial or funding environment more has to be done with less. The impact on preservation services is significant as posts are frozen and staffing levels reduced. In such an environment, the concerns regarding the use of volunteers need to be addressed and where necessary overcome.[2]

What are the key challenges of using volunteers?

In archives the key issues that arise are:

- confidentiality; often due to restricted access or sensitivity of content
- security
- health and safety
- liability and insurance
- training and supervision – the impact on staff time
- changing groups of volunteers requiring regular training and updating sessions
- the rising cost of travel expenses (where these are paid by the volunteer).

However, a number of cultural organizations now work closely and very effectively with volunteer groups. For archives, this has been in parallel with the growth of community archives,[3] groups of individuals who collect and provide access to the archives of a specific community or locale. This material may often not be covered by, or accepted by, a local archive service. Consequently there is a growing group of people who want to help and assist with preservation and who may have more direct experience than in the past.

Volunteering: principles for success

- Schemes embedded in the organisation via induction, training and recognition of their value
- Evaluation and promotion of the scheme to sector and community
- Activities fulfil organisational aims
- Selection of suitable volunteers
- Effective training – for the volunteer and the supervisor
- Clear written instructions of tasks to be carried out
- Enough time given to ongoing supervision and 'chatting time'
- Well planned scheme of work
- Activities and volunteer well matched
- Appropriate resources – enough space, supervision time.

(Lindsay, 2011. © Archives and Records Association)

Using volunteers for preservation activities

An important development has been the publication of a best practice guide by the Archives and Records Association UK and Ireland, compiled by Helen

Lindsay in 2011. The report that accompanies the guide effectively highlights the range of views and issues and offers analysis via case studies, which set out the range of benefits to the organization.[4]

UCL Special Collections and Archives: preparation for move of all collections November 2010–August 2011

During the period of the move the University College London (UCL) Preservation Librarian oversaw the deployment of over 300 volunteers. This group was primarily managed by eight professional conservators (who also undertook mould removal), and was split into four teams. The teams concentrated on the packaging of the individual books and archive collections to a set standard specification. This included attaching archive-quality identification labels to each item, box or group of items and cross-checking the barcodes generated by the moving contractors.

Additionally, two specialist collection move consultants were employed to provide expert guidance and to assist with the project management.

The volunteer corpus consisted of:

- UCL staff and students (approximately 250 persons)
- volunteers from the National Association of Design and Fine Art Societies (NADFAS)
- University of the Arts London, Camberwell College of Art conservation students
- staff from other institutions.

The total collections moved amounted to 7,000 linear metres. The total time taken to prepare for the move was 24 months, and the total time to move the collections to The National Archives (including barcoding) was 10 months.

The importance of documentation

As in so many other aspects of preservation management it is vital to get the documentation right and for it to be clear and approachable. The starting point is the compilation of a volunteer policy (see Appendix 4) that sets out why and how the organization will manage a volunteer programme. This document must address the process and include all the risks identified earlier. 'With even the most basic work it should be clear *how* it benefits the organization as a whole and *what* the volunteer is getting out of it' (Lindsay, 2011). Alongside this policy there needs to be the sub-policy documents that will include a formal agreement between each volunteer and the organization, and a handbook to address day-to-day functional, practical arrangements.

These formal documents will underpin and support the organization's inclusion of volunteers to assist with meeting corporate preservation objectives. There are many time-consuming tasks within preservation on which volunteers can make a significant impression; however, the tasks must not only be the repetitive tasks that no one else wants to do. This is a vital part of the planning that must be addressed by the preservation manager or volunteer co-ordinator. The task may be a general cleaning or packaging project, or it may be a more specialized or specific activity that requires a particular set of skills. It is therefore very important that a thorough description of the task be compiled so that the volunteer is clear about what is expected of them. Often individuals who wish to volunteer come with a set agenda – what they want to get out of the experience and within this there are elements of expectation. A well constructed procedure with clear objectives results in a shared success and will not undermine the overall objectives.

Volunteering: the most common activities

- repackaging
- numbering and stamping
- surveying
- surface cleaning books and documents
- flattening and re-folding documents
- box making
- documenting and making inventories
- scanning.

(Lindsay, 2011. © Archives and Records Association)

To assist with this part of the process the organization will need to assess the candidates via a semi-formal interview. This enables the co-ordinator to select the best people for the proposed project. The promotion and advertising of the project is key, and the wording (and placement) of the advertisement is vital in attracting likely volunteers and managing expectation. A further aim should be the opportunity to broaden the diversity of the volunteers and so reach specific community groups or those who can assist with particular collections that require knowledge of a different culture or language.

Volunteers and the interface with conservation

Volunteers also have a potentially useful role to play in supporting conservation programmes. Suitable volunteers can be trained to undertake basic cleaning and flattening of documents, although a high degree of supervision is required. The development of such expertise may be viewed as a bonus for the conservator, who is thus freed to carry out more demanding professional work, although this needs very careful management and control. An added positive impact is the potential for groups of volunteers to work in a conservation department, and those who are more experienced can assist those who are inexperienced and so create a learning culture within the group. Initial training and supervision is vital and every effort should be made to ensure the availability of an inexhaustible supply of material on which to work. Some organizations have groups working in the stacks or the strongrooms; others that are fortunate enough to have the available space may accommodate volunteers in the conservation workshop.

The National Association of Design and Fine Art Societies (NADFAS)[5] has many local UK groups who are often enthusiastic about working in an archive. NADFAS has drawn up clear guidelines about what is expected of both the volunteers and the host organization. Training, health and safety compliance and understanding of the type of work that the volunteers can undertake are the major commitments for the archive. However, experienced or particularly skilful volunteers may present a professional conundrum − how far do you progress an individual before they start to undertake tasks that existing paid staff normally process? This issue is for each organization to

York Minster Library and Archives: NADFAS volunteers

The York Minster Library and Archives benefits from the work of a number of NADFAS volunteers who are trained by Caroline Bendix (Library Conservator and National Trust Advisor). A team of six volunteers contributes approximately 720 person hours per annum. The team has a separate room within the building but also carries out activities within the storage areas.

The team is well established and very competent and carries out specific tasks, including:

- cleaning of dusty books
- stabilising repairs to damaged covering materials
- application of consolidants and leather dressings (where appropriate)
- manufacture of tailor-made book shoes and phase-boxes
- tying up books with loose spines or detached boards using archival webbing tapes
- in situ tissue conservation repairs using archival adhesives (all training carried out by the Library Conservator, who also provides the materials and adhesives)
- collection of data on each item processed.

The 'NADFAS Volunteers Record Sheet' is a vital part of the programme of work carried out by the team and all the complete sheets are stored in hard copy within the NADFAS room. The sheet provides a useful (and not over-detailed) analysis of the preservation and conservation issues facing each of the items processed and the resultant treatment. Each item is considered on its merits, condition and needs.

address and there is no easy 'fit all' solution. In some cases, the NADFAS team are undertaking quite advanced tasks, such as:

- sticking in loose pages
- paper repair
- repair of books
- simple re-binds.

Summary

Training is all-important both for professionals and also for volunteers, who form a major resource for preservation activities. Professional training is available through the appropriate channels and should form part of the professional development of all those with a responsibility for preservation activities. Volunteers also need ongoing training and their activities must be monitored and evaluated in a similar way to permanent staff, not least to avoid overlap in responsibilities. Similarly those involved in moving records must be trained for special handling and packing expertise.

Note and references

1   The Preservation Advisory Centre provides a range of preservation training in the UK, www.bl.uk/blpac/events.html.
2   Wider and more complex issues to do with employment law, insurance and the liaison with Trades Unions in the UK are covered by the following sites:
     www.volunteering.org.uk/component/gpb/insurance
     www.tuc.org.uk/workplace/index.cfm?mins=349&minors=4&majorsubjectID=2.
3   The UK Community Archives and Heritage Group's Collection Care guidance, www.communityarchives.org.uk/category_id__59_path__0p4p.aspx.
4   The Archives and Records Association UK and Ireland's best practice guideline and report (Lindsay, 2011) underpins this section and provides very useful detail. Report:
     www.archives.org.uk/images/documents/VOLUNTEERING_in_
     COLLECTIONS_CARE_-_REPORT-2.pdf.
     Best Practice Guide:
     www.archives.org.uk/images/documents/VOLUNTEERING_in_
     COLLECTIONS_CARE_-_GUIDE-1.pdf.
5   NADFAS Heritage volunteering, www.nadfas.org.uk/default.asp?section=173.

14

Putting preservation into practice

Introduction

The previous chapters have covered many of the issues encountered by
archives when trying to preserve their holdings, often against a background
of increasingly tight budgets and the inexorable rise in expectations of public
services. Those who oversee preservation programmes have to ensure that all
the relevant issues over enhanced access are discussed, that the needs of the
documents, in whatever format, are considered and costed and that the effect
of improving services does not shackle future generations with mounting
preservation or storage costs. They have to present well argued choices for
preservation strategies, and they have to manage preservation in an
environment which may be financially stringent, politically pressured or is
developing strategically in other directions. How can it be done? This chapter
covers

- choices and weighing up the options
- responsibilities
- policies and strategies
- benchmarking and preservation assessment
- costs and funding
- planning a programme over time.

Choices and options

Choosing the right preservation tactics at the right time does much to ensure
success. Fortunately several options are available and no archive has to
undertake all of them all the time. The choice may appear bewildering to
those who are desperately trying to do anything but the trick lies in a
measured approach, often spread over several years, matching the activity to

the resources available at any one time. The result should be that the archive has a well embedded, coherent preservation programme which recognizes and mitigates risk while allowing as much access to the holdings as possible.

Details of how to develop such a strategy follow, but it is important to review the options available in particular circumstances. These have been discussed in previous chapters and may, or should, include in some cases:

- regular building maintenance
- dry, cool storage
- adequate storage space
- a boxing programme
- good security procedures
- conservation facilities, or a budget for conservation
- digital preservation arrangements
- a disaster control programme
- an integrated pest management programme
- a surrogacy programme
- document handling training for readers and staff.

Who is responsible?

None of the above can be undertaken without specific responsibility being allocated. In theory everyone in the organization plays a part but all too often that is not understood. Emphasizing the scope of preservation activities, from accurate cataloguing to time-limited display, sometimes brings surprised reactions and dismissive comments. Nevertheless it is inescapable that no section of an archive can ignore its preservation responsibilities, since it is only possible to give access to original archive materials in a stable condition. Responsibility must be recognized at all levels, from the parent organization to the more focused activity of individual members of staff.

Naming a member of staff is essential, despite the fact that overall responsibility will remain with the management board of the archive (or the parent organization). If responsibility is devolved entirely an archive will lose sight of its commitments, storing up problems for future access to its holdings. However, it is also important that the person designated is of sufficient seniority to enable him or her to wield influence at all levels within the organization; powerful interests in favour of other priorities can destabilize a preservation strategy which all too often must be fought for.

In a small archive it may be necessary to assign the role to an individual with other responsibilities, but it should be formally recognized and acknowledged in the job description. For obvious reasons it is preferable to appoint a knowledgeable candidate and at a senior level; if this is not possible training must be offered as part of continuing professional development. Much of the job will consist of risk management, leading initiatives to improve the preservation status of the holdings, giving appropriate advice to colleagues and readers and co-operating with staff in all sections of the organization to ensure good practice and adherence to standards.

What is a preservation policy?

The next step is to draw up a preservation policy (see also Appendix 3). This offers an archive, or its parent, the opportunity to explore and publicize its responsibilities. A policy 'should translate the organization's guiding purpose, values and mission into statements which lay out the rules on how the organization intends to behave in principle in most circumstances' (Keene, 1996, 182). A preservation policy:

- reminds both staff and public of their obligations
- sets such obligations out in a relationship that makes it clear that securing the survival of the archival material requires joint action
- ensures that staff at the highest and lowest levels are made aware of the importance attached to preservation issues
- publicizes that importance to the rest of the community
- offers transparency
- is a valuable document in the context of applications for funding, being evidence of responsible stewardship
- can be used to evaluate the effectiveness of the policy.

What should a policy contain?

The statement is intended to be a broad one; organizations vary in the amount of detail they commit to at this stage, and it is worth looking at a number (either in print or on the internet) before deciding on the correct format for any archive. Its purpose is publicity for the philosophy and concepts behind the decisions made by the archive and not, for example, a full explanation of the details of the behaviour required in the reading rooms. It must also be clear about, and have appropriate links to, the other high-level policies produced by the organization. It should refer to agreed standards wherever possible and cover the main areas of responsibility, including:

- any statutory or high-level statement of responsibility (e.g. the board of the British Library or the council of a local authority) – this adds authority to the document; this commitment is most effectively promoted via a mission statement to which the policy should refer

- the commitment to carry out the most cost-effective solutions for the preservation of material held by the archive for permanent access
- the provisions for access which demonstrate the commitment of the archive to the needs of the documents as well as those of the readers
- the commitment to providing appropriate storage and environmental conditions
- the commitment to ensuring adequate security to guarantee authenticated custody of the archival material
- the right to restrict access to material in poor condition where handling would further damage it
- the commitment to provide copying facilities for the public, but also the right to refuse copying orders using methods inappropriate for the archival material
- the commitment to provide resources for conservation by accredited conservators either on-site or elsewhere.

If the policy is outlined in this way, the broad scope of subsequent strategies should be clear. Drawing up such a document will provoke debate among staff, who should participate in preliminary discussions, but at the same time will raise awareness of what is expected of them. Once a policy is written in

Example of a simple preservation policy

Scott Trust Foundation (Guardian Media Group) Archive Preservation and Conservation Policy

The Scott Trust Foundation will strive to preserve accessioned material through:

- appropriate storage in a controlled and secure environment
- repackaging of material in acid-free folders and boxes removing any packing materials likely to have a long-term detrimental effect on the archival material
- the transfer of data onto media more likely to ensure its long-term preservation (i.e. recording mini-disc interviews onto CD)
- the production of surrogate copies where the original may be damaged due to over-use
- supervised access to the material for research in line with the reading room rules
- appropriate housing for any material displayed in exhibitions
- when material requires conservation work it will be sent to specialist conservators on the MLA's register of conservators.

Reproduced with kind permission of the Scott Trust Foundation.

this way, it is unlikely that it will be frequently or substantially altered, unless the overall policy and priorities of the archive change. It is more likely that the means by which the policy is carried out will alter – e.g. a contract copying service may be introduced to replace in-house facilities.

How can it be publicized?

Promulgation of the policy, both in some public document such as an annual report or some public forum like an advisory body, gives authority to the aims of the archive and provides a basis for defending decisions that may prove unpopular. Create it in leaflet form, put it on the website and have a copy on the wall in the reading room. Use it to demonstrate responsibility – e.g. if a reader challenges a decision by staff to restrict access to a document in poor condition.

What about strategies?

Preservation policies contain a commitment to ensuring the survival of the archival material. These translate into strategies – the 'how to' element that underpins the policy statement. To develop effective strategies it will be necessary to have as much background information on the following as possible:

- the physical condition of the documents
- the quality of current storage arrangements
- current and anticipated use
- the historic importance of particular documents, such as founding charters or seminal development reports
- the overall development plans of the archive
- the likely budgets over the next few years.

Evidence-based strategies are the most likely to succeed.

Few archives have this information in any detail, since the collection of data in the past has tended to be patchy and, without computers, difficult to manipulate. In recent years, however, more statistical information has been collected, particularly on usage and preservation needs. The two are inextricably linked, being needed for decisions on the future direction of archive services. Developments such as the provision of online catalogues or off-site storage involve considerable change within an organization and are expensive. The archive needs to be sure of its commitment, with a well documented supporting argument and cost-benefit analysis. Neither preservation nor access can be taken in isolation.

Collecting the information listed above will enable an archive to decide on the strategies and priority areas for preservation action. It is rarely possible to undertake all the necessary tasks at once, and any progress will be incremental. A logical plan should be mapped out, following the available budget and the business planning of the archive, or the organization, as a whole (see below). This plan may be for a one-year period but should also have the capacity to extend to three or even five years ahead. Within this period it will be possible to make substantial improvements in the quality of preservation care given to the archives, but it is essential to know what actions will have the most impact, which are the most cost-effective and in what order they should be carried out. The plan resulting from analysis of this information constitutes the preservation strategy of the archive. It should be publicized as part of the business plan and is a valuable supporting document for any funding application.

What should be done first?

Initially the current status of preservation within the archive needs to be assessed. This constitutes a baseline from which incremental improvements can be measured; this is important, in order to demonstrate that resources are being used effectively and are making a difference. Within the archive the decision to undertake any evaluation must be clearly explained, planned and resourced; staff at all levels must support the idea, like any other project.

One way to assess how well an archive is meeting preservation needs is by using the self-assessment checklist in *Benchmarks in Collection Care for Museums, Archives and Libraries* (MLA, 2011).[1] The Collections Trust now hosts the benchmarks methodology as a web-based resource, which not only includes the benchmarks document, but also a Microsoft Excel spreadsheet,[2] guidance and a glossary. All of the constituent parts are downloadable from the Collections Trust website. The authors drew on a wide range of standards, guidelines and benchmarks to make it possible to assess preservation needs and measure levels of collection care. 'A benchmark is an agreed level of performance by which something can be measured. In *Benchmarks in Collection Care* individual benchmarks are drawn from published sector standards and used to define, measure and compare different areas of collection care activity' (MLA, 2011, 1). A three-tier model of basic, good and best practice is suggested and there is a checklist of entries defining the different levels against which current practice can be assessed. It is intended that the organization should use the scoring process to develop a set of priorities for action and identify those which are most easily achieved in particular circumstances. This is essentially a toolkit for periodic evaluation, which should be undertaken regularly to record progress (see Appendix 5). Owing to the fact that these benchmarks are for use by museums as well as libraries and archives, this approach is necessarily rather broad in outlook; more detailed methods of assessment have been developed specifically for archives and libraries – commonly referred to as a survey. Traditionally surveys of archives have been developed for specific needs:

- to assess the condition of proposed acquisitions (often on-site with the depositor)
- to enable the development of a cataloguing plan or programme
- to gather data on condition needs as part of a grant application.

However, the issue with most collections is the number of items they contain and this presents logistical problems. To address this, statistically valid results are produced using random samples of items from a collection, however large or small. The results will direct decisions towards cost-effective preservation in each particular situation. The use of the same methodology by organizations, either nationally or internationally, allows comparisons to be made and demonstrates where the greatest gaps are in provision, thus controlling the extent and complexity of the data. In turn this enables funders to target their resources where the need is greatest.

In the UK a survey model has been developed by the British Library's Preservation Advisory Centre (BLPAC), which has been used extensively amongst museums, libraries and archives – the Preservation Assessment Survey. The BLPAC also offers the survey methodology for photographs, glass plates and slides, architectural drawings, flat art works and museum objects. By 2012, 326 surveys have been carried out since inception in 2001, 63% from archives and 37% from libraries (this is the breakdown of institutions, not sampled collections). The data from these surveys is used anonymously by the BLPAC to build a picture of national preservation needs.[3]

The following graph (Figure 14.1) presents the aggregated data over the period 2006–11 for libraries and archives in the UK and Ireland. This data comes from 86 completed surveys and contains 35,216 sampled records.

This level of data provides hard evidence to funders and government of the requirements of the sector to manage collections and provide future access.

Other types of media can also be assessed using a sampling methodology such as that devised for cellulose acetate film;[4] this is essentially the same system as that described above but slightly adapted.

Thus armed with some solid information about its current preservation status, an archive is in a good position to be confident about selecting options for improvement.

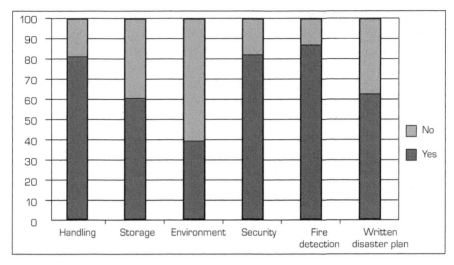

Figure 14.1 Graph illustrating the extent of deficiencies in basic preservation practice
Copyright © The British Library Board

Costs, funding and options

The archive with little or no money for preservation activities is not necessarily unable to achieve any changes.

Low-cost options include:

- regular inspection of premises to record maintenance needs
- backing up digital records, whether 'born digital' or digitized, off-site
- ensuring good security procedures to avoid loss
- boxing or wrapping material whenever possible; even non-archival boxes are better protection than nothing
- storing material on shelving and away from external walls; any shelving is better than none
- monitoring and recording environmental conditions
- developing the procedures to be carried out in an emergency
- introducing an integrated pest management scheme
- ensuring regular cleaning of the storage areas
- training staff and readers in good handling practice – tender loving care goes a long way towards retarding deterioration
- providing equipment in the reading rooms incrementally.

None of these options cost much more than the staff time taken to introduce better procedures; these should become normal practice and will go a long way towards improving preservation of the archives.

Medium-cost options include:

- regular building maintenance with associated costs – these will depend on the age of the building, the building materials used, previous maintenance history and level of repairs needed; once a full survey has been done the actions required can be costed, prioritized and spread over a period of time
- implementation of a digital preservation strategy
- insulation of the storage area or introduction of local controls to improve environmental conditions
- installation of blinds, neon light filters, and film on glass where appropriate to reduce visible and ultraviolet light
- installation of good-quality shelving, cabinets and plan chests
- boxing all material in archivally sound containers
- installation of a modern security system for storage areas
- conservation budget identified for employing external conservators.

Longer-term options include the following, but may not be appropriate for all archives:

- new storage accommodation, built to appropriate standards
- full-scale system for the migration or emulation of all digital records
- installation of an HVAC system
- installation of an air filtration system
- installation of an integrated security system throughout the building
- installation of a new conservation workshop
- employment of conservators by the archive.

Getting the resources needed

Identifying an annual preservation budget within the archive is important; many archives have little or no money allocated regularly for this purpose. Without a visible budget the preservation needs of the organization have little credence, even if the money is located in the budget of another department. A combination of sound planning and promotion of the preservation policy will ensure that money is available annually rather than as a need arises. To do this may mean producing a costed three-year strategy covering the priorities (as ascertained by benchmarking or preservation assessment) to demonstrate the need for ongoing resources.

Before starting, determine what such a budget should cover; preservation is a wide term and could encompass many of the items listed above, and it may not be desirable to take on responsibility for all these. Storage, for example, is often one of the highest costs for an organization, including rent, rates, HVAC and high maintenance. It might be preferable to concentrate on a budget to replace poor-quality shelving or to box material which has been unprotected in the past, leaving the higher costs to come under a building maintenance budget. Managing budgets takes time and in many cases it will be wiser to influence another budget holder to ensure preservation issues are covered than to create a new cost centre which carries with it additional responsibilities.

Outside funding is another option for obtaining the necessary resources for preservation, especially for particular projects. The Heritage Lottery Fund in the UK is one of the larger funding organizations but there are many others.[5]

The results of a benchmarking exercise or preservation assessment will be essential for making an application for outside funding, demonstrating that it is grounded on solid evidence of need. Additionally, the organization demonstrates to funders that it has considered the range of preservation issues important enough to apportion resources to collect effective data. Alternatively it may be necessary to provide a conservation statement or management plan. This is useful in cases where the funding body has no knowledge of the applicant or the circumstances, and may be particularly important when preservation is needed not only for the archive but also for the building in which it is housed. Historic building conservation is regulated in most countries and plans for improving the conditions of any archive within one will need to comply. Quite simply a conservation statement should contain:

- a statement about the significance of the archive
- a statement about the significance of the building (if applicable)
- the current condition of both
- the proposals for stabilizing and preserving both in a sustainable fashion.

It can be useful to prepare one of these statements for general purposes since the process is likely to clarify thoughts.

Staff and volunteers are part of the resources needed to carry out a preservation strategy; virtually all staff working in an archive are involved, and at the least should be alert to the preservation implications of other programmes. In many instances harnessing such awareness will be the only option for effecting change; few organizations, apart from national archives or libraries, can afford specialized staff apart from those involved in conservation or digital preservation. The skill of the preservation co-ordinator in these circumstances is to ensure that the development of the programme is understood and that both staff and volunteers are interested in being involved and committed. The use of volunteers and training issues are covered in Chapter 13.

How is a programme planned and put into action?

Planning a preservation programme in great detail too far in advance is a mistake. Circumstances and priorities may change, forcing a different direction; an incremental plan is often easier to manage than a large-scale attempt to sort out everything at the same time.

Armed with the information gained from a benchmarking exercise or a preservation assessment, as well as a rough idea of the finance and staff resources available, work out what it is possible to achieve. This must fit within the business plans of the archive or the parent organization for the next few years; if, for example, the overall plans are to increase access, the preservation programme might be geared towards ensuring that material is in a suitable condition to be microfilmed or digitized. Alternatively, if the emphasis will be on education, the preservation programme might concentrate on work on preparing documents for exhibitions. It may also be possible to carry out more than one defined preservation programme at the same time, perhaps by using volunteers to re-box poorly housed paper documents. The only financial outlay attached to this would be the purchasing of new boxes, the other resource required being staff time for training and supervision. The outcome? Archives stored in appropriate boxes and a new workforce with some experience of basic preservation.

For many archives use, or potential use, is the main criterion for consideration when deciding conservation priorities, to avoid wasting costly resources on material which is perhaps rarely consulted. Planning such conservation work can appear tricky, but most conservators are now trained to estimate how long a piece of work will take. However, they cannot work in isolation from the archivists, and must be involved in the planning of any programmes or projects to understand the level of conservation required. For example, the difference in the time required to carry out major conservation on a seriously damaged volume of iconic importance for exhibition, and the time required to make a volume fit to be microfilmed, is considerable. Equally, issues such as the final format of a volume of newspapers taken apart to enable copying must be discussed. Is the binding of real importance to the integrity of the volume? Is it contributing to the protection of the contents? Is the considerable cost of rebinding poor-quality paper justified when the information is available in another format? Many archives and libraries have concluded that such material may be preserved as well, if not better, and much more cheaply if left unbound but protected by good packaging and stored appropriately. If, however, a volume is part of a series on shelves in a historic setting, the answer may be different. It all depends on the circumstances. Asking such questions, and receiving the answers from different perspectives, will help to shape programmes and priorities.

Planning digital preservation is covered in Chapter 3, as it is closely connected with the creation of digital archives. Nevertheless, the programmes must be integrated into the working operations of the archive and become as much a part of the procedures accepted and adopted by all staff as other, more traditional, preservation activities.

Major preservation undertakings, such as building or refurbishing a storage area, will require long-term planning both for the project itself and the necessary finance. Developing such a project, however, can take place concurrently with putting other preservation programmes into practice, such as introducing an integrated pest management scheme into the existing facility. The outcome? Archival materials in better condition and known to be clear of infestation before they are moved into new or refurbished premises.

Working out a timetable is an important part of the planning; not only does it require thought to estimate the likely time required but it also introduces discipline. Good project planning involves setting target dates for incremental stages of completion and regular evaluation of progress. Preservation planning is no different. Not all preservation work will be project-based but milestones can be included in a programme to indicate progress. For example, an incremental programme for introducing training in handling archival materials might target users in the first phase, followed by different groups of staff in the following and any subsequent periods. The result? At the end of a three-year period all those who need training will have been offered an opportunity and it will be time to consider introducing refresher sessions. 'Preservation management is a continuum' (Peterson, 1997, 97); and experience suggests that it must be maintained at a high level to ensure that familiarity does not result in standards slipping. While the investment in new storage furniture and environmental control will have substantial impact, the maintenance of these improvements will be vital.

Once an archive, stimulated by an energetic leader to improve its preservation status, has begun to incorporate well thought-out preservation activities into its wider programmes, it becomes easier to develop preservation management as a norm. This has the advantage of raising general awareness and, although progress may seem slow, every time the issues surrounding preservation come up, the problems will be a little better understood. For this reason it is important that those with preservation responsibilities are members of management and project teams. The need to seek further and onward preservation improvements must be emphasized whenever possible.

And the results?

Preserving archives is a fascinating and demanding business. It has its problems, not least that it is an activity which has little apparent immediate result, apart from visible conservation. The benefits of a good approach are likely to be felt by subsequent generations, although the resources are required now. That in itself is not an easy argument to put over. A danger also exists in that it appears to be such common sense that it is taken for granted by many archivists. For that reason it is always important to ensure that preservation considerations are explicit, rather than implicit, in any statements or project documents put out by the archive. Not only is preservation integral but it must be evident (to greater and lesser degrees) at all levels of collection management. Others outside the profession may have different priorities or points of view and the importance of preservation will need to be made clear. For the preservation manager or co-ordinator, however, satisfaction comes from understanding, devising and executing an evidence-based programme, whether large or small. Incrementally this will add up to a level of preservation management which will assure future access to information. No archive can afford to ignore the preservation needs of the documents entrusted to its care, in whatever format, to ensure both current and future access.[6]

Notes and references

1   Now managed by the Collections Trust as an online resource, www.collectionslink.org.uk/programmes/benchmarks-for-collections-care.
2   www.collectionslink.org.uk/discover/site-information/410-benchmarks-in-collections-care-20.
3   The draft of the new Knowing the Need report was available as this book went to press, www.bl.uk/blpac/ktndraft.html.
4   See www.bl.uk/aboutus/stratpolprog/ccare/introduction/preservation/camf/CAMF.html.
5   www.dsc.org.uk/Publications/Fundraisingtechniques
    www.hlf.org.uk/HowToApply/furtherresources/Pages/furtherresources.aspx
    www.institute-of-fundraising.org.uk/home.
6   Compiling a preservation policy; an advisory template, www.bl.uk/blpac/pdf/safetemplate.pdf.

The National Archives Conditions for Loans policy

(www.nationalarchives.gov.uk/information-management/our-services/ conditions-for-loans.htm)

Identifying items

Discovery, The National Archives' new catalogue, provides information about our records. There are also many images of documents and parts of documents available online through the 'Image Viewer' on Discovery. When requesting a loan, the borrower must give details of the exact folio, or folios, to be displayed. If necessary, the borrower can make use of The National Archives' research service in order to identify a suitable folio.

Timescales

- We must receive your application for a loan not less than six months prior to the opening date of the exhibition. This is to allow sufficient time for the necessary condition checks, paperwork, conservation, photography and mounting to be carried out.
- We will normally acknowledge your application within ten working days.
- The normal loan period is three months.
- Irrespective of the terms of the loan, the borrowing authority must return any or all of the exhibits at the written request of The National Archives.
- The National Archives reserves the right, at any time, not to proceed with a loan.

Suitability

The suitability of a loan will normally be assessed by Collection Care staff at The National Archives. In cases where we are unable to lend a document due to its condition, size, format or similar reason, we will suggest a good quality facsimile as an alternative.

The documents will usually be accompanied to and from the exhibition by a designated member of The National Archives' conservation staff, who has absolute discretion to withdraw the documents on loan if dissatisfied with the conditions at the designated venue.

We do not usually lend more than ten documents to any one exhibition.

Costs

The borrower will be responsible for expenses incurred by The National Archives in making a loan, including:

- standard charges for staff time required for administration, conservation treatment, documentation, mounting, packing and couriering exhibition items as set out in the current Lord Chancellor's Statutory Instrument
- the cost of security negatives, microfilm, photographic or facsimile copies and insurance where required
- travel and accommodation for The National Archives' staff member who accompanies the item; for security purposes, air travel will usually be at business class rate
- subsistence expenses, which will be included in the invoice we send you, and must not be paid to The National Archives' staff member.

Once your loan has been assessed we will provide an estimate of costs.

If the loan is cancelled, for whatever reason, all reasonable costs incurred to that date will be borne by the borrower.

Care of the document

Documents are lent for the purpose of public exhibition only and may not be made available for study or other purposes outside their showcases without the written consent of The National Archives.

After they have been mounted in the showcase for exhibition, documents must be left undisturbed – except in the case of any emergency – until the exhibition is dismantled.

Documents are lent to a single institution. No application for a touring exhibition will be accepted.

No mark in pencil, ink, paint or any other material may be made on any document, nor may any such existing mark be obliterated. No adhesives of any kind may be applied to the documents. All materials used within the cases, with which the documents may come into contact, must be acid-free and free of any pollutants.

No conservation measures of any description may be carried out other than at The National Archives, or when The National Archives' staff are present.

Reproduction

Photography is only allowed with the written consent of The National Archives, or its accompanying member of staff who has discretion to decide on the appropriate level of lighting.

Security copies will be made of all items before they leave The National Archives. If appropriate, any prints required can be taken from them. Please order copies when you apply for a loan by contacting the Image library.

Captions and credits

Any caption or credit used for display purposes, and any description given in a catalogue, must state that the document is on loan from 'The National Archives, UK' and give The National Archives' reference, found in Discovery or The National Archives' catalogue.

One copy of the exhibition catalogue must be sent to The National Archives free of charge.

Exhibition premises

Exhibition premises must be safe and secure in all respects and adequate safeguards in place before any items are borrowed. The standards required are those of the National Security Advisor laid out in Appendices of the Government Indemnity Scheme (for non-nationals). These can be found on the Arts Council website.

First time applications for a loan may be subjected to an evaluation by the National Security Advisor. Borrowers may be asked to send Facilities and Security Reports for the exhibition venue.

Showcases

All documents must be displayed in locked showcases. Any other method of display, particularly wall mounts, must be discussed with the Collection Care

Department at The National Archives.

Documents must be placed in their showcases by the accompanying member of staff from The National Archives, or an authorized representative, who will supervise the locking of the case. After this time the exhibits and their mounts must remain undisturbed. An alarmed case may be specified by The National Archives.

Environment

Required environmental conditions will be declared prior to the loan agreement and will be dependent on the exhibits. We will require written assurance that the environmental conditions are suitable for the exhibits and will stipulate any necessary changes. Lighting requirements will take into account previous display exposure of the exhibit(s).

No food, drink or smoking can be allowed in the exhibition area.

Insurance against damage

The National Archives will determine the insurance value required in all cases.

UK government indemnity can be accepted from libraries, galleries and museums within the United Kingdom, but commercial insurance will be necessary where that facility is not available, and from foreign borrowers. Proof of insurance will be required before the loan is made.

Insurance arrangements must be made by, and at the expense of, the borrower.

Packing and display

The National Archives, or an authorized representative, will pack all items for transport to and from the exhibition.

Packaging must be stored safely by the borrower during the course of the exhibition, to enable it to be used for the return of the exhibits.

The National Archives will mount all exhibition items in consultation with the exhibition organisers. Wherever possible, the items will travel ready-mounted. If this is not possible, the display will be arranged by or under the supervision of the accompanying member of The National Archives' staff, or an authorized representative, in accordance with any previously agreed design. None of the mounts or cradles is to be removed or changed in any way during the exhibition.

A condition report will accompany each item on loan and must be agreed with the borrower before display. The report must be checked and agreed at the end of the exhibition.

Travel

Items should travel shortly before the exhibition opens to minimise risk and to avoid inconvenience to readers at The National Archives.

We will liaise with the borrower with regard to carrier, and transport and travel arrangements which will be organized by the borrower. For overseas loans, the borrower will be responsible for appointing a shipping agent, subject to approval by The National Archives; the shipping agent will handle customs formalities.

All items must travel under the constant personal supervision of the member of The National Archives' staff, or an authorized representative, even if that necessitates the purchase of extra aircraft or train seats. Cargo haulage will only be considered if the size restricts cabin transportation.

No loan is to be unpacked, other than by the member of The National Archives' staff, or an authorized representative, for examination at any point on either journey.

Borrowed documents must not be stored anywhere other than the stated place of exhibition, unless specifically agreed with The National Archives.

A conservation workshop

Establishing an in-house conservation workshop is a choice to be made by each archive, weighing up the advantages and disadvantages of outsourcing the work against the capital cost, employment costs and ongoing commitment of an in-house resource. Either way it will be a senior management decision, with the appropriate need for support. Quantifying the need for conservation work, following an appraisal of the general condition of the material (see Chapter 14) is essential before making any decisions.

If the decision is to establish a new workshop in-house an expert will be required to install and manage it. This is likely to be a senior conservator and appointing someone initially with the appropriate accreditation and skills will have major benefits for the project; planning a building programme and a conservation programme will be part of the job specification. Additional staff will be needed but the number will depend on the amount of work to be undertaken and the skills required; resources to meet these needs may only be possible when specified as part of an externally funded project. Conservators will contribute to preservation activities such as monitoring the conditions in the strongrooms and assisting with disaster control and can also run volunteer programmes for basic preservation work such as cleaning and dusting volumes or flattening large documents for protective boxing. Administrative assistance will be needed in large workshops as treatment records (including digital photographs) need to be kept; documents need to be checked in and out of the workshop and materials and equipment ordered and maintained. In smaller workshops, conservation staff will undertake these tasks.

Planning

Planning the installation project is a shared activity between the archivist, the conservator, the architect and the engineer; clearly it must fit within the overall business plan of the archive and adequate time must be allowed to plan the project properly. Visits to other institutions to view any new, or benchmark facilities are vital. Robust specifications, rigorously drawn up, tested and scrutinized are the basis of a successful project. The location of the workshop will depend on whether the facility is to be part of a new build for the whole organization or is to be an adaptation of a part of an existing building. Either way it is important to note that neither basements nor attics are suitable, owing to the danger of flooding in the former and the build-up of heat in the latter. Two main considerations must be taken into account:

- the health, comfort and safety of the staff
- the security and wellbeing of the documents.

If possible the room(s) should face away from the sun with plenty of natural light and on the ground floor to facilitate the delivery of documents and conservation equipment and supplies. Load-bearing considerations must also be taken into account, as some of the equipment is extremely heavy. When planning the workshop the following requirements should be borne in mind:

- space for conservation benches and equipment; as a guide 18–20 sq. metres should be allowed for each conservator to allow adequate circulation space and provision for standing equipment
- dedicated electrical and cabling supplies
- wet area water supply and drainage
- an administrative office or area to include professional research resources
- a secure area for storing archival material with space for trolleys holding current work overnight; this area should conform to the same specifications for fire and security as other storage areas in the archive
- a racked storeroom for conservation materials and small equipment
- lockable cupboards for small equipment and for personal possessions
- a machine room for noisy or dusty work, particularly if many exhibitions are planned
- a chemical cupboard compliant with current health and safety (and COSHH) requirements.

Layout and fitting out

A flow chart devised to make the movement of documents and staff in the conservation area as logical and smooth as possible is a valuable tool in deciding on the layout of the space, remembering that conservators working on different types of material have very varying requirements.

Fire and security protection must be factored into the design.

If air conditioning is installed it must be kept on permanently, as constant variation in temperature and relative humidity is detrimental to archival materials.

A conservation workshop will require a high level of general ambient lighting – a background level of between 500–600 lux. The ceiling units can be fluorescent and with modern diffusers this should provide a flicker-free and shadow-free level of lighting. It is important that there is a consistency of colour-rendering between the ambient and the task lighting. The equipment needs to be flexible and track lighting can be helpful, either on a single directional track or preferably manoeuvrable through 360 degrees. Workbenches should be equipped with individual task lights as well as overhead provision.

Window orientation should face away from the sun to ensure the best quality of light and ideally the windows should be all down one side.

Sinks should be close to the bench area as well as in any space devoted to wet processes such as leaf casting. Analysis of the quality of the water will dictate whether it is necessary to provide purification. De-ionization equipment can be installed, with carbon and particulate pre-filters and a reverse osmosis membrane for the removal of dissolved ions and organics.

Safe chemical disposal is now frequently carried out by local authorities or private contractors, who should be contacted for advice. Fume extraction units will be required when using chemicals – especially organic solvents or any spray procedures. The height of the extraction chimney above roof level, the volume of air needing extraction and precautions against accidental spillage or gaseous escape will need careful planning. Ventilation engineers can advise on the best methods, including the option of using localized exhaust ventilation to remove all vapours and dust at source; that solution will affect the volume of air in the whole room, which must therefore be factored into the calculations.

Equipment

The equipment and furniture should be designed to ensure the safety of the archival material and the health and safety of the conservators at all times. The furniture should consider both a modular and mobile format to ensure that the workshop space can be used effectively and to enable different configurations. The height of such equipment is extremely important, as conservators spend much time leaning over benches and tables and lifting fragile materials. As a rough guide a height of 1050 mm is the norm, but adjustable legs will ensure that furniture is comfortable for all. Mobile units facilitate the sharing of equipment such light boxes, vacuum suction tables or fume cupboards. Other shared equipment, such as power guillotines, presses or large board choppers will necessarily be static.

Workbenches should have adequate space to spread out individual and associated documents; the surface area should be approximately 15 sq. metres with comfortable leg room underneath. Sufficient power sockets for using additional electrical equipment and computers should be located conveniently near the front of the bench. Adjustable comfortable stools or chairs should be provided. For modular and mobile units access to power can be from floor sockets or from overhead-suspended power sources.

Large surfaces for working on maps and plans may be either horizontal or vertical, in the form of wall boards or the modular/mobile units mentioned earlier. All such surfaces should be made of smooth non-reflective material, wherever possible in a single sheet. It should be washable and hard-wearing, similar to the surface materials used in laboratories. If the surface is horizontal the height will need to be adjustable to ensure that the centre can be reached; if the surface is vertical an appropriate ladder, with lockable wheels and a large standing platform, will be required to reach the top edge.

Flat storage drawers or plan chests are used to keep paper and thin board flat and clean. The drawers should be shallow to avoid too much being forced into them.

Trolleys are necessary to move fragile or heavy archival material or bulky rolls of material around. The trolleys need to be flat; book trolleys are not appropriate.

Tabletop trimmers are used to cut single sheets of paper, as are tabletop guillotines, though bench-end guillotines or free-standing paper or board choppers are better options. These usually incorporate safety guards on the blades and some have foot pedals to operate a clamp that allows the conservator to use both hands to position the paper and move the blade. All such equipment must be sharpened and serviced regularly. Electric guillotines are used by book conservators to cut through substantial piles of paper very accurately. They are probably the largest pieces of equipment found in a workshop and necessarily incorporate safety guards; due to their size they will need good circulation space round them. All staff should receive appropriate safety training before use.

Various types of presses will be needed. Nipping presses (with a vertical screw which bears down on two horizontal plates) are made of iron and should be securely bolted down. Both paper conservators and book conservators will need regular access to these. Standing presses are larger and require considerable floor space. Lying presses are used to hold volumes securely while cutting edges with a plough, backing or edge gilding. They can be situated at the end of a work bench on a sturdy wooden tub. A finishing press (used for the final work on a volume) is smaller and can be moved as appropriate, as can a blocking press, used to letter and decorate spines.

Vacuum and suction tables are used for spot cleaning, safe washing of dirty materials, the removal of old adhesives or localized stains (with both water and organic solvents) or the filling of small areas with considerable accuracy and speed. A variety of equipment is available, ranging from full scale mobile vacuum and suction tables to hand-held devices; the choice depends on the identified applications.

Mobile and tabletop fume cupboards incorporate carbon or High Efficiency Particulate Absorbing (HEPA) filters, brushless electric motors and fans. A horizontal and down-flow draught work together to remove all incoming and contaminated air away from the operator.

Leafcasting machines for infilling missing parts of paper with new paper pulp consist of a casting tank and a holding tank for water. They need to be plumbed into the water supply, have good drainage and a single phase electricity supply. This operation also requires adequate table space for preparation and wire mesh drying racks (which will be needed for other processes as well). Small leaf casting machines, to infill gaps in the gutters of double leaves which require re-sewing into a binding are much smaller. A pulp mixer, typically a strong commercial liquidizer or blender, will be necessary and, optionally, a computerized imaging system to calculate exact quantities of pulp (Mowery, 1991).

Encapsulating machines (polyester welders), to construct protective sleeves or covers for large or fragile material, use ultrasonic sealing to weld the polyester film together. Large ones will require space in which to move documents around.

Mobile cleaning machines incorporate a work surface, from which air is extracted via low-level gullies as well as suction walls. Hand-held vacuum cleaners with adjustable suction levels are used in a number of conservation processes.

Other equipment may include a refrigerator – this is used to store film, if used by the conservators, or made up solutions including adhesives – and drying racks for flat sheet material.

Small tools and equipment for conservators should include:

- awls or bodkins
- balances (electronic) for weighing small quantities
- bone folders used for smoothing and folding (traditionally made from animal bone but synthetic alternatives are available)
- bowls, beakers, dishes and trays of stainless steel, heavy duty plastic or glass

- brushes of different sizes and qualities
- cotton gloves for handling photographic material; Nitrile gloves for handling other material and for handling chemicals
- cutting mats which reseal themselves
- fibre-optic sheets for examining damage to individual sheets
- mobile light boxes
- needles, especially for book conservation
- scalpels
- scissors and shears
- set squares, steel rules and straight edges
- sponges
- tacking irons (for localized repairs utilizing heat-set adhesive tissues)
- weights.

Basic materials for conservation

In all cases, the emphasis must be on the use of high-quality (and if possible archival) materials. Papers need to be tested for permanence and for materials used in the manufacture. The pH is important since acidic (and/or poor-quality) paper is not suitable to be used either for conservation itself or for wrapping archival materials. Conservators will require a variety of papers depending on the requirements of the processes they are using. A review of the range and standard of papers supplied by conservation suppliers is vital. Special prepared cloths are used for book conservation and box covering. Leathers will be needed for any conservation workshop which handles old volumes; several thicknesses and colours will be required, especially those tawed with a solution of alum and salt for durability. Board is used for bookbinding processes, and for creating tailor-made phase boxes and other protective formats. Archival polyester film is available in a variety of coatings and finishes but those used in conjunction with archival material must contain no plasticisers or surface coatings and be resistant to chemicals or moisture. Tape or thread: conservators use several varieties including cotton or linen tape, unbleached, sewing thread and webbing and tape for tying-up folders and other packaging formats. Adhesives are used according to their properties, the degree of flexibility required and the speed with which the material is required to dry. The main ones are:

- polyvinyl acetate; an archival standard commercially available preparation
- wheat or rice starch paste used on paper; this has to be specially prepared and has a long drying time due to the high water content
- glue made by boiling organic gelatine with glycerine.

Compiling a Preservation Policy:
an advisory template

Produced as one of the outputs of the joint-funded RLUK and British Library Preservation Advisory Centre preservation learning programme 2009-2012 (www.rluk.ac.uk/node/575; www.bl.uk/blpac/rluk.html).

Introduction

This template has been designed to support staff preparing a Preservation Policy for their own organization. Preservation Policies vary between different organizations depending on specific needs. Staff preparing policies may also wish to refer to the Preservation Advisory Centre booklet *Building Blocks for a Preservation Policy* and examples from other organizations when considering what to include.

1. Setting the scene

The Preservation Policy is a high level document whose key objective is the long-term preservation of, and provision of access to, collections. The process of collections care is an ongoing (and never-ending) commitment and responsibility for each heritage organization to ensure that the information contained on and within the range of collection media is accessible both now and into the future.

The baseline responsibility of any organization involved in the management of heritage collections is to ensure that all risks to the materials are assessed and, where possible, removed. To achieve this, organizations need to develop appropriate collection care methodologies with reference to national and professional standards. However, before this stage, and acknowledging the growing and oncoming challenges of digital media and the management of digital data, the organization will need to set out clearly what it is trying to achieve by managing its collection materials.

The Preservation Policy is an important document and needs to address all those who come into contact with, and have aspirations for, the collections.

A policy is a *'plan of action and should address the questions of **what** needs to be preserved, **why**, for **what purpose** and for **how long**'* .[1]

2. Legislative framework?

This document must reference the key national and local policy documents that underpin the responsibility for collections care. Such documents are at the highest level of national governmental policy for the sector and firmly set in context the core responsibilities of the heritage organization. Additionally, these documents identify the expectations of users, stakeholders and funding bodies. These may include, or be supplemented by, national standards specifically addressing the needs of archive and library collections, local corporate or advisory professional guidance.

3. Definition of terms

It is vital to ensure that all those that read the Policy, those that represent its objectives, and those that apply those objectives, understand the terminology used throughout the document. A misunderstanding of terminology, and the resultant weakness of poor definition when taken out of context or viewed outside of professional circles, can seriously undermine the messages within the policy document. It must speak equally to:

- politicians
- stakeholders
- users
- staff.

This section does not need to be lengthy; it may be useful for the authors to reduce the number of profession-specific terms used throughout the document.

4. The Mission Statement

Each organization needs to set out in simple and direct terms what are its key objectives and in effect its reasons for being. If the purpose of a heritage organization is to provide access to the collections and the information they contain, then preservation must always be included as an integral part of the mission.

It is useful at this point to be clear that the objectives of preservation and access are equal and parallel in this mission.

This can best be illustrated via the organization's published Mission Statement and this serves to define the objectives, and to identify the organization's main aims. The preservation of library collections requires a long-term and consistent commitment of resources from the parent organization – not only to enable the interpretation of the information contained in the collections to enable access, but also to ensure that that information survives into the future.

5. Commitment and responsibility

This section needs to set out the key elements that define the organization's ability to be able to meet the demands of the Mission Statement. It must be clear that the objective of long-term preservation brings a key responsibility to address risk to the collections at all levels. It therefore follows that the organization must compile policy, strategic and advisory documents to guide all those who come to use the collections, and thus ensure a consistency of standard approaches.

A co-ordinated multidisciplinary approach to developing policies relating to the care of collections is encouraged to ensure consistency throughout all levels of an organization. All those who come into contact with collection material must acknowledge and appreciate the duty of care.

6. The key policy principles

Collections management is a complex activity which not only recognizes the enduring value of the intellectual content, but also needs to be underpinned by guidance (both to staff and users) on how best to use and at the same time protect the carriers of the information – the formats themselves, including documents, books, maps, photographs and modern media. This guidance is best expressed via a collection of policies, which sit below this over-arching Preservation Policy, and consequently address the risks to the collections at all levels of their management and use. The links between both high level and sub-policies must be very clear to anyone using them, and therefore promote transparency and corporate priorities.

The production of these sub-policies (see section 9) will not only reflect the purpose of the organization, as defined in the Preservation Policy, but also the use and development of the collection material in its care.

This section will reflect the core approach of the organization and define the principles that support this, for example:

'The xxxx recognises that the nature and diversity of its collections are a significant strength and that the use of the collections can result in damage. To ensure the highest quality of conservation for the collections xxxx will only use accredited conservators.'

7. The use of standards and benchmarking

The document must be clear about the standards that underpin the principles outlined in the Preservation Policy, drawing attention to those that are more specialized, and therefore reflect the range and complexities of collection management, and those that are specific to collection care. The standards will cover all levels; national, professional, local and organization specific.

A clear distinction will need to be made between the use of standards that set out a specific approach and level of activity, and benchmarking, which is primarily a management and self-assessment tool. The Benchmarks in Collection Care have been developed to aid the collection manager in assessing current levels of provision, to identify areas of weakness, and provides a methodology to compile priorities, develop timescales and the opportunity to evaluate and update as an ongoing process.

The key opportunity presented by the use of standards is to underline the fact that heritage institutions work to common and comparable levels. The benchmarks enable those levels to be appropriately highlighted and analysed; this process has the added value of requiring input from management, from those responsible for budgets and most importantly, from those directly involved with the maintenance and management of the building.

8. Risk assessment and management

One of the key principles of preservation management is the assessment of risk for all activities pertaining to the management of collections. The organization needs to describe the methods used to assess risk, the procedures in place to address identified risks and the process of monitoring and evaluation. It must be made clear that this is an integral part of the process that informs the Preservation Policy, and is a core representation of the organization's duty of care.

Once the analysis of risk has been completed, each organization will need to decide the priority of each individual risk, and this will build into the strategy (outlined in section 13). It is important to acknowledge that this process will be both assisted and hampered by factors specific to each organization. These factors could include:

• listed building status

- funding body criteria
- shared accommodation (different priorities of multiple occupants)
- resources.

9. Safeguarding physical collections

This section needs to set out the challenges inherent in the long-term preservation of the different collection formats. The needs of the various formats must be set out to ensure that it is quite clear exactly what the challenges are, for example:

- photographic material consisting of mixed media and requiring specific environmental storage requirements and specialized packaging
- maps and plans presenting access issues due to their size and orientation (rolled or flat)
- modern media requiring specific environmental storage levels and presenting access challenges.

This specific emphasis will therefore require a linked set of sub-policies; each organization will need to decide how strong this emphasis, and the extent of the detail, should be within the policy document.

This is an opportunity to celebrate and promote the organization's commitment of resources and maintenance of standards, and will include outline information on:

- storage
- security
- environmental monitoring and control
- use of surrogacy (providing an alternative to the original)
- the role of remedial conservation
- disaster planning.

10. Digital preservation

This section will be vital to ensure that the organization, senior managers, trustees, council members, general stakeholders and staff all appreciate and acknowledge that the process of capturing digital images and maintaining the data requires significant investment and complex management.

At this time, the core commitment of the organization to a digital preservation strategy can be outlined:

'The Library has a business interest in and commitment to preservation and has been

active in developing infrastructure to collect, manage, preserve and keep our digital collections available. This is recognized as ongoing core business for the Library and critical to its future relevance.

The National Library defines digital preservation as the process of maintaining, and if necessary, recovering accessibility to digital information resources.' [2]

11. Providing access to the collection

This section will outline the various ways that the organization makes the information that it is preserving accessible to all those who wish to use it. It is important here that all methods of access are outlined and that the benefits to the users and any added value is promoted and celebrated. This section could include an overall, policy statement from the organization, for example:

'The xxxx acknowledges the key objective for preserving its collections is to enable access to the important information that they contain. The xxxx will ensure that users are provided with effective and technologically advanced opportunities for access to its collections.'

At this point, clear links to other policies that enable access will need to be included, such as:

- loans
- exhibitions
- website
- social media
- publicity.

12. Establishing priorities

This section must acknowledge that while all organizations will need to prioritise their preservation activities, these activities will be influenced by many and varied factors – particularly those that are specific (and local) to the organization, including:

- overall objectives of the organization
- existing and likely (future) resources
- funding – both internal and external; in both cases there may be criteria and controls over the use of those resources
- management commitment
- user needs
- existing and/or developing partnerships
- an effective knowledge of the collections across the organization and collection strengths.

However, while this sets out the objectives, it will be the strategic document (outlined in section 13) that provides the detail of how these objectives will be met and all links to associated documents will need to be clearly accentuated.

13. The Preservation Strategy timetable

It is important that the methodology for addressing the objectives set out in the Preservation Policy is clearly expressed and that the links to other (existing) management policies within the organization are coherent and logical (i.e. budgetary, facilities, access, collections development etc.). This process will inevitably lead to the 'how to' document, the Preservation Strategy. The timetable will obviously be an evolving and changing document that is not included in the Preservation Policy, however, access to this information can be provided via the organization's website links.

The timetable will need to include:

- a decision on the timescale or likely cycle of activities
- clear verification that the preservation elements are interactive with and responsive to other collection and service objectives
- responsive activities to specific timescales and the target dates required by funding bodies
- apportionment of responsibilities and identification of all training implications
- the option to commission external expertise? e.g. a specialist conservator or project manager

A very important element of the strategy process (often overlooked) is to ask the hard questions about the weaknesses (and in some cases, failures) of a chosen course of action after implementation. To address this, the process needs to include:

- a structured programme of assessment at each project deliverable; both quantity and quality
- the provision for freezing a project element for more detailed analysis
- an assessment of value for money
- an analysis of original projections against actual
- an honest assessment at the completion of the project of the success impacts and the failures/shortcomings

14. Implementation

This section will verify the timescale for the Preservation Policy and how it will be enacted, and additionally identify a date for a review. This is also the place to underline (again) the commitment of the organization to the policy and its objectives.

This is the point for the authors to identify the key success factors that will gauge and illustrate the successful implementation of the Preservation Policy, such as:

- senior management buy-in and the apportionment of resources
- an acknowledged understanding of the policy by all staff
- appreciation of the objectives and rationale by users and stakeholders
- a clear linkage to other core policies within the organization (this acts as final check that there are no inconsistencies).

15. Evaluation and updating

This final section will outline the method (and stress its transparency), effectively evaluating the policy and setting out a clear process to enable the organization to update and change the content of the document. The opportunity for change is becoming increasingly important in an unpredictable economic environment. Additionally, there may also be local, political and corporate changes that will need to be accommodated. The policy must be flexible enough to move with the times.

Notes

1   Foot, Dr. M., *Building Blocks for a Preservation Policy*, Preservation Advisory Centre (2001).

2   The National Library of Australia, *Digital Preservation Policy*, 3rd edn, 2008 (section 2), www.nla.gov.au/policy-and-planning/digital-preservation-policy.

UCL Library Services: Volunteer Agreement

Reproduction of the UCL Volunteer Agreement, and information about UCL Library Services Volunteering activities, is reproduced here with kind permission from UCL.

I .... (name of volunteer) agree to work as a volunteer for UCL Library Services and I freely commit myself to a placement / project and to

- give active support to the objectives of UCL Library Services and to perform the voluntary duties which I have freely accepted to the best of my ability.
- read and accept the UCL Library Services Volunteer Policy, plus all the institution's regulations and instructions on security, health and safety, fire and other emergency procedures and confidentiality of information.
- take part in the UCL Library Services induction procedures (where appropriate) and accept training for the role where necessary.
- agree to abide by the Library Regulations and the rules governing access to the Library's manuscript collections and College Archives held in the Library, including photographs, films, tapes or machine-readable records. I undertake to indemnify the College and also the owners of any such papers, where applicable, against all claims and actions on the part of other persons arising out of the inclusion in any manuscript of mine, or the disclosure of publication by me in any other way, of any matter taken from the papers consulted which constitutes or may constitute a libel upon any person, an infringement of copyright, or breach of confidence.
- inform the person to whom I report as soon as possible if I am unable to meet my voluntary obligation to UCL Library Service.

In the event that we no longer require your voluntary services we will advise you in accordance with UCL Library Services Volunteer Policy. Should you wish to discontinue your voluntary work with us, please inform us as soon as possible in accordance with UCL Library Services Volunteer Policy. This agreement is not a legal document or intended to create the relationship/ responsibilities of employer/ employee.

Volunteer's Name ....

Signature...**Date:**....................

Please state if you are UCL STAFF

YES ❑   **NO** ❑

If a Student please state the College are you studying with and the subject
....

Contact Details:
Address:
....

E-mail:...

Tele: ....

Mobile:...

Supervising Manager's Name ....

Signature:...   **Date:**....................

Benchmarking entries: MLA

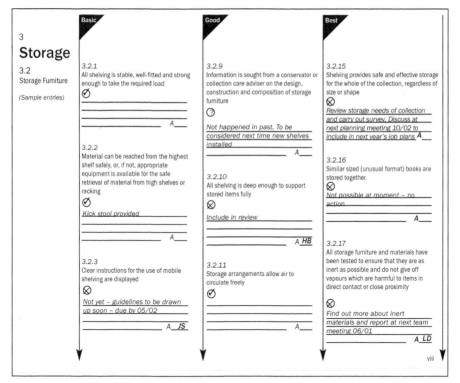

Basic	Good	Best

3

Storage

3.2
Storage Furniture

(Sample entries)

3.2.1
All shelving is stable, well-fitted and strong enough to take the required load
⊘
_____
_____
_____ A___

3.2.2
Material can be reached from the highest shelf safely, or, if not, appropriate equipment is available for the safe retrieval of material from high shelves or racking
⊘
Kick stool provided
_____
_____ A___

3.2.3
Clear instructions for the use of mobile shelving are displayed
⊗
Not yet – guidelines to be drawn up soon – due by 05/02
_____ A_*JS*

3.2.9
Information is sought from a conservator or collection care adviser on the design, construction and composition of storage furniture
⊙
Not happened in past. To be considered next time new shelves installed
_____ A___

3.2.10
All shelving is deep enough to support stored items fully
⊗
Include in review
_____ A_*HB*

3.2.11
Storage arrangements allow air to circulate freely
⊘
_____
_____
_____ A___

3.2.15
Shelving provides safe and effective storage for the whole of the collection, regardless of size or shape
⊗
Review storage needs of collection and carry out survey. Discuss at next planning meeting 10/02 to include in next year's job plans A___

3.2.16
Similar sized (unusual format) books are stored together.
⊗
Not possible at moment – no action
_____ A___

3.2.17
All storage furniture and materials have been tested to ensure that they are as inert as possible and do not give off vapours which are harmful to items in direct contact or close proximity
⊗
Find out more about inert materials and report at next team meeting 06/01
_____ A_*LD*

viii

Figure A5.1 Sample page from *Benchmarks in Collection Care for Museums, Archives and Libraries* [Re:source, 2002]. Reproduced with kind permission from the Museums, Libraries and Archives Council.

Bibliography

To aid the reader (when using this bibliography) in understanding the complexities of core bodies with a responsibility for preservation in the UK, the changes have been as follows:

Museums, Libraries and Archives grew out of the Museums and Galleries Commission (MGC), which was established in September 1981. In April 2000, the MGC and the Library and Information Commission were combined into Re:source which was later renamed the MLA Council. After the abolition of the MLA in 2011/2012 a range of the previous MLA responsibilities were taken over by Arts Council England (ACE).

Texts within the bibliography will therefore be referenced to different bodies by their dates, but will most likely be held under the auspices of the Collections Trust, within Collections Link (under 'Caring for Collections'). Additionally, this bibliography does not include URLs because of the speed at which internet resources become out-of-date. Readers are advised to use internet search engines to identify existing digital articles.

Adcock, E. (1998) *IFLA Principles for the Care and Handling of Library Materials*, International Preservation Issues 1, International Federation of Library Associations and Institutions.

Albrecht-Kunszeri, G. and Loescher, M. H. (2001) Moving Archives: guidelines for preservation, *Comma*, **3/4**, 259–87.

ARLIS/UK and Ireland Visual Archives Committee (2004) *First Steps in Archives*.

Ashley-Smith, J. (1999) *Risk Assessment for Object Conservation*, Butterworth-Heinemann.

Baker, C. A. and Silverman, R. (2005) Misperceptions about White Gloves, *International Preservation News*, **37**, 4–9.

Baker, N. (2001) *Double Fold: libraries and the assault on paper*, Random House.

Bellinger, M. (2003) *On Technical and Logistic Aspects of Preservation Microfilming and Digitisation*, Liber.

Bendix, C. (2010) *Damaged Books*, Preservation Advisory Centre, guidance leaflet.

Bendix, C. (2011) *Cleaning Books and Documents*, Preservation Advisory Centre, guidance leaflet.

Bendix, C. (2012) *Packing and Moving Library and Archive Collections*, Preservation Advisory Centre, guidance leaflet.

Blades, N., Oreszcyn, T., Bordass, B. and Cassar, M. (2000) *Guidelines on Pollution Control in Museum Buildings*, Museums Association.

Bradley, K. (ed.) (2004) *Guidelines on the Production and Preservation of Digital Audio Objects*, IASA TC 04.

British Library (2004) *Future Life of Collections*.

Brown, A. (2008) Care, Handling and Storage of Removable Media, *Digital Preservation Guidance Note* 3, Issue 2 (August), Research Document Reference DPGN-03.

Brown, A. (2013) *Practical Digital Preservation: a how-to guide for organizations of any size*, Facet Publishing.

Buchmann, W. (1986) Planning an Archive Building: the co-operation between architect and archivist. In *Archive Buildings and the Conservation of Archival Material*, Mitteilungen des Österreichischen Staatsarchivs, **39**, 202–17.

Bülow, A. E. and Ahmon, J. (2010) *Preparing Collections for Digitization*, Facet Publishing.

Byers, F. B. (2003) *Care and Handling of CDs and DVDs: a guide for librarians and archivists*, National Institute of Standards and Technology/Council on Library and Information Resources (NIST/CLIR).

Callister, T. and Blake, R. (2009) *Identifying and Specifying Requirements for Offsite Storage of Physical Records*, The National Archives.

Canadian Conservation Institute (2009) *Mould Outbreak: an immediate response*.

Casey, M. (2008) *The field audio collection evaluation tool*, Indiana University Digital Library Programme.

Cassar, M. (1995) *Environmental Management: guidelines for museums and galleries*, Routledge.

Cassar, M. (2009) *Environmental Management Performance Standards: guidelines for historic buildings*, English Heritage.

Chapman, S. (2003) Counting the Costs of Digital Preservation: is repository storage affordable? *Journal of Digital Information*, **4** (2), No. 178.

Child, R. E. (2011) *The Prevention and Treatment of Mould Outbreaks in Collections*, Preservation Advisory Centre, guidance leaflet.

Clark, S. (2009) *Preservation of Photographic Material*, Preservation Advisory Centre, guidance leaflet.

Coleman, D. C. (1958) *The British Paper Industry, 1495–1860, a Study in Industrial Growth*, Clarendon Press.

Council on Library and Information Resources (CLIR) (2006) *Capturing Analog Sound for Digital Preservation*, CLIR and Library of Congress.

Craig, R., Selzer, C. T. and Seymour, J. (2006) *There is Disaster Planning and There is Reality: the Cayman Islands National Archive (CINA) experience with Hurricane Ivan 1*,

Journal of the Society of Archivists, **27** (2), 187–99.

Dadson, E. (2012) *Emergency Planning and Response for Libraries, Archives and Museums*, Facet Publishing.

Darlington, J., Finney, A. and Pearce, A. (2003) Domesday Redux: the rescue of the BBC Domesday Project videodiscs, *Ariadne*, **36**.

Dawson, A. (ed.) (2011) *Benchmarks in Collections Care for Museums, Archives and Libraries*, Museums, Libraries and Archives.

Deegan, M. and Tanner, S. (2006) *Digital Preservation: strategies for the information age*, Facet Publishing.

Digital Preservation Coalition (2006) *Decision Tree for Selection of Digital Materials for Long-term Retention*.

Duchein, M. (1966) *Les Bâtiments d'Archives: construction et équipements*, Archives Nationales.

Dumbleton, N. (2005) CASS: exploring the benefits of joint storage in Scotland. In Webster, J. (ed.), *Where Shall We Put It? Spotlight on collection storage issues*, National Preservation Office, 51–7.

Dunn, F. I. (1994) *Security: a guide for use in appraising and implementing security systems and procedures in archive operations, covering buildings, staff, the public, and repository management*, Best practice guideline 2, Society of Archivists.

Elliott, P. (2002) *Standards in Action: managing archive collections in museums*, Museum Documentation Association (MDA).

English Heritage (2008) *Climate Change and the Historic Environment*.

Feather, J. P. (2004) Introduction: principles and policies. In Feather, J. P. (ed.) *Managing Preservation for Libraries and Archives: current practice and future developments*, Ashgate.

Finch, L. and Webster, J. (2008) *Caring for CDs and DVDs*, Preservation Advisory Centre, guidance leaflet.

Foot, M. (2000) Moving the British National Collections, *Liber Quarterly*, **10** (3), 387–92.

Foot, M. (2001) *Building Blocks for a Preservation Policy,* Preservation Advisory Centre, guidance leaflet.

Forbes, H. (2003) Preparation, Prevention and Practice: attempting to avoid disasters at Canterbury Cathedral Archives, *Journal of the Society of Archivists*, **24** (2), 189–97.

Forde, H. (1996) Strategies for Survival, *Archivum*, **42**, 345–59.

Forde, H. (1997) Preservation Policies – who needs them? *Journal of the Society of Archivists*, **18** (2), 165–73.

Fortriede, S. (2010) *Moving Your Library: getting the collection from here to there*, Chicago: American Library Association.

Gollins, T. (2009) *Parsimonious Preservation: preventing pointless processes! (The small simple steps that take digital preservation a long way forward)*, The National Archives.

Gorman, G. E. and Shep, S. (2006) *Preservation Management for Libraries, Archives and Museums*, Facet Publishing.

Haines, B. (1994) Materials Analysis: the physical and chemical characteristics of parchment, casings, goldbeater's skin and gelatine. In Woods, C. S. (ed.), *Conservation for the Future*, Society of Archivists.

Hallam Smith, E. M. (1986) *Domesday Book through Nine Centuries*, Thames and Hudson.

Hendley, T. (1998) *Comparison of Methods and Costs of Digital Preservation*, British Library Research and Innovation Report 67.

Hibbert, C. (ed.) (1984) *Queen Victoria in her Letters and Journals*, John Murray.

Hillhouse, S. (2008) *Collections Management: a practical guide*, Collections Trust.

Hills, R.L. (1988) *Papermaking in Britain 1488–1988*, Athlone Press.

Holden, P. (2004) 'Heaven Helps Those Who Help Themselves': the realities of disaster planning, *Journal of the Society of Archivists*, **25** (1), 27–32.

Hollaender, A. E. J. (ed.) (1962) *Essays in Memory of Sir Hilary Jenkinson*, Society of Archivists.

Hughes, I. (2004) *Digitizing Collections: strategic issues for the information manager*, Facet Publishing.

Hughes, S. (2002) *Managing the Preservation of Library and Archival Collections in Historic Buildings*, Preservation Advisory Centre, guidance leaflet.

Henderson, J. (December 2010) *Managing the Library and Archive Environment*, Preservation Advisory Centre, guidance leaflet.

IFLA PAC (2008a) *Library and Archives Facing the Challenges of Sustainable Development*, International Preservation News, No. 44.

IFLA PAC (2008b) *The Collections Security: access versus protection*, International Preservation News, No. 45.

IFLA PAC (2008c) *Preservation of Audiovisual Collections: still images and sound*, International Preservation News, No. 46.

Image Permanence Institute (2004) *IPI Media Storage Quick Reference*.

Image Permanence Institute (2010a) *A Consumer Guide to Materials for Preservation Framing and the Display of Photographic Images*.

Image Permanence Institute (2010b) *Knowing and Protecting Motion Picture Film*, (poster).

International Council on Archives (2003) *Bibliography of Books, Journal Articles, Conference Papers and Other Printed Sources Relating to Archival Buildings and Equipment*, Committee on Archival Buildings in Temperate Climates.

Jefcoate, G. (2003) *Preservation or Access? Developing strategies for microfilming and digitisation*.

Jones, M. and Beagrie, N. (2001) *Preservation Management of Digital Materials: a handbook*, British Library.

Kahn, M. B. (2004) *Protecting your Library's Digital Sources*, American Library Association.

Keene, S. (1996) *Managing Conservation in Museums*, Butterworth-Heinemann.

Kejser, U. B, Nielsen, A. B. and Thirifays, A. (2011) Cost Model for Digital Preservation: cost of digital migration, *International Journal of Digital Creation*, **6** (1), 255–67.

Kennedy, J. (1995) Norfolk Record Office Fire: an initial report, *Journal of the Society of*

Archivists, **16** (1), 3–6.

Kingsley, H., Pinniger, D., Xavier-Rowe, A. and Winsor, P. (2001) *Integrated Pest Management for Collections Proceedings of 2001: a pest odyssey*, English Heritage.

Kitching, C. J. (1993) *Archive Buildings in the United Kingdom 1977–1992*, HMSO.

Kitching, C. J. (2007) *Archive Buildings in the United Kingdom 1993–2005*, Phillimore.

Knight, B. (2008) Assessing New Developments in Collection Security, *LIBER Quarterly*, **18** (2).

Lavedrine, B. (2003) *A Guide to the Preventive Conservation of Photograph Collections*, Getty Conservation Institute, Los Angeles, CA.

Lee, D. M. (2001) *Film and Sound Archives in Non-specialist Repositories*, Society of Archivists.

Lindsay, H. (2011) *Volunteering in Collections Care: best practice guide*, Archives and Records Association UK and Ireland.

Ling, T. (1998) *Solid, Safe, Secure*, National Archives of Australia.

Ling, T. (2000) Shifting the Sands of Time: moving an archive, *Journal of the Society of Archivists*, **21** (2), 169–81.

Lusenet, de Y. (2003) Microfilm and Digitization as Choices in Preservation, *LIBER*.

MacKenzie, G. (1995) Layout and Equipment in Conservation Areas, *Janus*, 1995 (2), 101–6.

Matthews, G. (2005) Disaster Management: sharing experience, working together across the sector, *Journal of Librarianship and Information Science*, **37** (2), 63–74.

Matthews, G. and Feather, J. P. (eds) (2003) *Disaster Management for Libraries and Archives*, Ashgate.

Matthews, G., Smith, Y. and Knowles, G. (2009) *Disaster Management in Archives, Libraries and Museums*, Ashgate.

McCormick-Goodhart, M. H. (1996) The Allowable Temperature and Relative Humidity Range for the Safe Use and Storage of Photographic Materials, *Journal of the Society of Archivists*, **17** (1), 7–21.

McIlwaine, J. (2005) *First Do No Harm – a register of standards, codes of practice, guidelines recommendations and similar works relating to preservation and conservation in libraries and archives*, IFLA, Preservation and Conservation Section.

Moss, M. and Currall, J. (2004) Digitisation: taking stock, *Journal of the Society of Archivists*, **25** (2), 123–37.

Mowery, J. F. (1991) A Stand-alone Imaging System to Assist in Leafcasting, Developed at the Folger Shakespeare Library, Washington, DC, *Restaurator*, **12** (2), 110–15.

Mumford, J., Pearson, D. and Walker, A. (2010) *Understanding and Caring for Bookbindings*, Preservation Advisory Centre, guidance leaflet.

Munoz-Vinas, S. (2004) *Contemporary Theory of Conservation*, Butterworth-Heinemann.

Museums Documentation Association Collections Link website.

The National Archives (2003) *Digital Preservation Guidance Note 3*.

The National Archives (2004) *Standard for Record Repositories*, 1st edn.

The National Archives (2010) *Digital Preservation FAQs*.

The National Archives (2011a) *Risk Assessment Handbook*, Version 1.2.

The National Archives (2011b) *Digital Preservation Policies: guidance notes*.

National Library of Australia (2013) *National Preservation Policy*, 4th edn.

National Preservation Office (1992) *Mellon Microfilming Manual*, British Library.

National Preservation Office (2000) *Guide to Preservation Microfilming*, British Library.

National Preservation Office and Library Association (1995) *From Rags to Ruin*.

National Trust (2005) *National Trust Manual of Housekeeping: The care of collections in historic houses open to the public*, Butterworth-Heinemann.

Newman, J. and Jones, W. (2002) *Moving Archives: the experience of eleven archivists*, Scarecrow Press, Oxford.

Olney, D. (2005) A UK First: an automated, high density solution for the British Library. In Webster, J. (ed.), *Where Shall We Put It? Spotlight on collection storage issues*, National Preservation Office.

Pacifico, M. and Wilsted, T. (2009) *Archival and Special Collections Facilities: guidelines for archivists, librarians, architects, and engineers*, American Library Association.

Padfield, T. and Aasbjerg Jensen, L. (2011) Humidity Buffering of Building Interiors By Absorbent Materials. In *Proceedings of the 9th Nordic Symposium on Building Physics, Tampere, Finland May (2011)*.

Palm, J. (2006) *The Digital Black Hole*, Training for Audiovisual Preservation in Europe.

Parliamentary Archives (2009) *A Digital Preservation Policy for Parliament*.

Peraudeau, M. A. and Maget, E. (1973) *Le Moulin à Papier Richard de Bas*, P. Gaudin.

Peterson, T. H. (1997) Putting Records First to Make Them Last. In de Lusenet, Y. (ed.), *Choosing to Preserve Amsterdam*, European Commission on Preservation and Access.

Pinniger, D. (2008) *Pest Management: A practical guide*, Collections Trust.

Pinniger, D. and Winsor, P. (2004) *Integrated Pest Management: a guide for museums, libraries and archives*, Museums, Libraries and Archives Council.

Preservation Advisory Centre (2006) *Preservation Assessment Survey for Libraries and Archives: users guide*, British Library, PAC.

Preservation Advisory Centre (2013) *Knowing the Need and Optimising the Preservation of Library and Archive Collections*, Preservation Advisory Centre.

Preservation Advisory Centre and British Library (2011) *Using Collections*, Preservation Advisory Centre, guidance leaflet.

Re:source (2002) *Benchmarks in Collection Care for Museums, Archives and Libraries*.

Re:source (2003) *Security in Museums, Archives and Libraries*.

Reed, R. (1972) *Ancient Skins, Parchments and Leathers*, Seminar Press.

Rhys-Lewis, J. (2012) *Specifying Library and Archive Storage*, Preservation Advisory Centre, guidance leaflet.

Ritzenthaler, M. L. (2010) *Preserving Archives and Manuscripts*, 2nd edn, Society of American Archivists, Archival Fundamentals Series.

Roosa, M. (2003) *Care, Handling and Storage of Photographs*, IFLA PAC, International Preservation issues, No. 5.

Ryan, R. (2005) Shelving Systems for Libraries, *SCONUL Focus*, **35**, Summer/Autumn, 51–2.

Ryhl-Svendsen, M. (1999) Pollution in the Photographic Archive: a practical approach to the problem. In Mogens, S. K. and Palm, J. (eds), *IADA Congress 1999 Preprints*, Copenhagen, The Royal Academy of Fine Arts.

Shenton, H. (2006) Rotating the Treasures on Display in the British Library, *Icon News*, Issue 5, 28–30.

South-East Asia Pacific AudioVisual Archive Association (n.d.) *Preserving Film*, SEAPAVAA.

Stagnitto, J. (1992) *The Shrink Wrapping Project at Rutgers University Library and Archives*, American Institute for Conservation of Historic and Artistic Works.

Standing Conference on Archives and Museums (2002) *A Code of Practice on Archives for Museums and Galleries in the United Kingdom*, 3rd edn.

Szczepanowska, H. and Wilson, W. (2000) Permanency of Reprographic Images on Polyester Film, *Journal of the American Institute for Conservation*, **39** (3), Article 5.

Teygeler, R. (2001) *Preservation of Archives in Tropical Climates; an annotated bibliography*, International Council on Archives.

Thickett, D., Rhee, S. and Lambarth, S. (2007) *Libraries and Archives in Historic Buildings*, Museum Microclimates.

Thompson, B., Manning, A. and Townsend, J. (eds) (2006) *Conference Proceedings: Third International Conference on Preservation and Conservation Issues Related to Digital Printing and Digital Photography*, Institute of Physics, London.

Thomson, G. (1977) Stabilization of RH in Exhibition Cases: hygrometric half-time. In Mills, J. S. (ed.), *Studies in Conservation*, International Institute for Conservation of Historic and Artistic Works, 22 (2).

Thomson, G. (1986) *The Museum Environment*, 2nd edn, Butterworth.

Van der Doe, E. (ed.) (2010) *Archives Damage Atlas: a tool for assessing damage*, The Hague, Metamorfoze project.

Walker, A. (2010) *Basic Preservation Guidelines for Library and Archive Collections*, Preservation Advisory Centre, guidance leaflet.

Waller, M. and Sharpe, R. (2006) *Mind the Gap: assessing digital preservation needs in the UK*, Digital Preservation Coalition.

Webb, C. (2001) Disaster Recovery in the York Flood of 2000, *Journal of the Society of Archivists*, **22** (2), 247–52.

Webster, J. (ed.) (2005) *Where Shall We Put It? Spotlight on collection storage issues*, National Preservation Office.

Wellheiser, J. and Scott, J. (2002) *An Ounce of Prevention*, 2nd edn, Scarecrow Press/Canadian Archives Foundation.

Wilstead, T. (2007) *Planning New and Remodelled Archival Facilities*, Society of American

Archivists.

Woods, C. (1992) Designing a Conservation Room: an example from Dorset, *Journal of the Society of Archivists*, **13** (2), 132–5.

Woods, C. (2002) Meeting the Montreal Protocol, *Journal of the Society of Archivists*, **23** (2), 179–86.

Wythe, D. (ed.) (2004) *Museum Archives: an introduction*, Society of American Archivists.

British and international standards relating to archive preservation

British details are available on the website: www.bsigroup.co.uk/en/standards-and-publications.

Sometimes the BS title will be accompanied by the letters EN and/or ISO. These mean that the standard was developed as a European (EN) or International (ISO) standard and then adopted by the UK as a British Standard. The European standards will gradually replace the national British standards.

American standards are available on www.ansi.org, and Australian ones on www.standards.org.au.

BS 476 (all parts and amendments 1993-2011). *Fire tests on building materials and structures.*

BS 1153: 1992. *Recommendations for the processing and storage of silver-gelatine type microfilm.*

BS 1449-1.1: 1991. *Specifications for steel plate, sheet and strip. Carbon and carbon-manganese plate, sheet and strip.*

BS 3484: Record Inks Part 1: 1991. *Specifications for blue-black record inks.* Record Inks Part 2: 1994. *Specification for permanent inks.*

BS 3621: 2007 + Amendment 2: 2012. *Thief resistant lock assemblies. Key egress.*

BS 4783: 1998 (parts 1-4), *Storage, transportation and maintenance of media for use in data processing and information storage.*

BS 4971: 2002. *Recommendation for repair and allied processes for the conservation of documents.*

BS 5306-0: 2011. *Fire protection installations and equipment on premises – Part 0: Guide for selection of installed systems and other fire equipment.*

BS 5306-8: 2000. *Fire extinguishing installations and equipment on premises – Part 8: Selection and installation of portable fire extinguishers – Code of practice.*

BS 5498: 1977. *Specification for the safety of hand operated paper cutting machines.*

BS ISO 3897: 1992. *Photography. Processed photographic plates. Storage practices.*

BS 5699. *Processed photographic film for archival records.* Part 1:1979. *Specification for silver gelatine type on cellulose ester base (ISO 4331: 1977).* Part 2:1979. *Specifications for silver gelatine type on polyethylene terephthalate base (ISO 4332: 1977).*

BS 5839-1: 2002 + Amendment 2: 2008. *Fire detection and fire alarm systems for buildings. Code of practice for system design, installation, commissioning and maintenance.*

BS 6660-1: 2005. *Guide to setting up and maintaining micrographic and digital imaging units.*

BS 7273-1: 2006. *Code of practice for the operation of fire protection measures – Part 1: Electrical actuation of gaseous total flooding extinguishing systems.*

BS 7273-3: 2008. *Code of practice for the operation of fire protection measures – Part 3: Electrical actuation of pre-action watermist and sprinkler systems.*

BS 7451: 1991. *Specification of archival quality bookbinding leather.*

BS 8418: 2010. *Installation and remote monitoring of detector-activated CCTV systems – Code of practice.*

BS 8533: 2011. *Assessing and managing flood risk in development – Code of practice* BS EN 2, *Classification of fires.*

BS EN 54-20: 2006. *Fire detection and fire alarm systems – Part 20: Aspirating smoke detectors.*

BS EN 779: 2012. *Particulate air filter for general ventilation. Determination of the filtration performance.*

BS EN 12101-6: 2005. *Smoke control and heat systems. Specification. Kits.*

BS EN 12845: 2004 + Amendment 2: 2009. *Fixed firefighting systems – Automatic sprinkler systems – Design, installation and maintenance.*

BS EN 15004: 2008 (parts 1-4). *Fixed firefighting systems – Gas extinguishing systems.*

BS EN 15635: 2008. *Steel static storage systems – Application and maintenance of storage equipment.*

BS EN 15878: 2010. *Steel static storage systems – Terms and definitions.*

BS EN 50131-1: 1997. *Alarm systems. Intrusion systems. General requirements.*

BS EN 50133-2-1: 2000. *Alarm systems. Access control systems for use in security applications. General requirements for components.*

BS EN ISO 3696: 1995. *Water for Analytical Laboratory Use – Specification and test methods.*

BS EN ISO 11844-1. *Corrosion of metals and alloys – Classification of low corrosivity of indoor atmospheres – Part 1: Determination and estimation of indoor corrosivity.*

BS EN ISO 14001: 2004. *Environmental management systems. Requirement with guidance and use.*

BS ISO 4087: 2005. *Micrographics. Microfilming of newspapers for archival purposes on 35 mm microfilm.*

BS ISO 6199: 2005. *Micrographics: microfilming of documents on 16mm and 35mm silver-gelatine type microfilm. Operating procedures.*

BS ISO 15489-1: 2001. *Information and documentation – Records management – Part 1: General.*

BS ISO 15686-1: 2011. *Buildings and constructed assets – Service life planning – Part 1: General principles and framework.*

BS ISO 18934: 2011. *Imaging materials – Multiple media archives – Storage environment.*

BS ISO 31000: 2009. *Risk management – Principles and guidelines.*

BS ISO 80000-7: 2008. *Quantities and units – Part 7: Light.*

DD 8489-1:2011. *Fixed fire protection systems – Industrial and commercial watermist systems – Part 1: Code of practice for design and installation.*

ISO 9706: 2000. *Information and documentation – paper for documents – requirements for permanence.*

PAS 197: 2009. *Code of practice for cultural collections management.*

PD 5454: 2012. *Guide for the storage and exhibition of archival materials.*

PD 6662: 2010. *Scheme for the application of European Standards for intrusion and hold-up alarm systems.*

The development of European Standards

Across Europe conservators, scientists, architects and registrars continue to be engaged in the formulation of conservation standards. The key committee concentrating on this objective is formally titled CEN/TC 346 Conservation of Cultural Property. The standards cover both the moveable and the built cultural heritage, and the project is proving especially successful in bringing together practitioners from these two specific areas. Each participating European country has its own Mirror Committee, which in the UK is the British Standards Institution's Committee, B/560 Conservation of Tangible Cultural Heritage.

Examples of current standards completed as of March 2013	
BS EN Number and Date	**Standard Title**
BS EN 15757: 2010	**Conservation of cultural property:** Specifications for temperature and relative humidity to limit climate-induced mechanical damage in organic hygroscopic materials
BS EN 15758: 2010	**Conservation of cultural property:** Procedures and instruments for measuring temperatures of the air and the surfaces of objects
BS EN 15759-1: 2011	**Conservation of cultural property:** Indoor climate. Guidelines for heating churches, chapels and other places of worship
BS EN 15801: 2009	**Conservation of cultural property:** Test methods. Determination of water absorption by capillarity
BS EN 15802: 2009	**Conservation of cultural property:** Test methods. Determination of static contact angle
BS EN 15803: 2009	**Conservation of cultural property:** Test methods. Determination of water vapour permeability
BS EN 15886: 2010	**Conservation of cultural property:** Test methods. Colour measurement of surfaces
BS EN 15898: 2011	**Conservation of cultural property:** Main general terms and definitions
BS EN 15946: 2011	**Conservation of cultural property:** Packing principles for transport

Index